John A. Williams
Muzaffer Uysal
Editors

Current Issues
and Development
in Hospitality and Tourism
Satisfaction

Current Issues and Development in Hospitality and Tourism Satisfaction has been co-published simultaneously as *Journal of Quality Assurance in Hospitality & Tourism*, Volume 4, Numbers 3/4 2003.

*Pre-publication
REVIEWS,
COMMENTARIES,
EVALUATIONS . . .*

More pre-publication
REVIEWS, COMMENTARIES, EVALUATIONS . . .

"INVALUABLE FOR STUDENTS, INSTRUCTORS, RESEARCHERS, AND INDUSTRY PRACTITIONERS . . . Addresses issues at the conceptual level as well as offering new, effective approaches for the provision of quality service. ESSENTIAL READING for all who wish to better understand the complex challenges involved in understanding the nature of service satisfaction and implementation of strategies to achieve this."

Larry Dwyer, PhD
Qantas Professor
of Travel and Tourism Economics
University of New South Wales

"AN IMPORTANT BOOK . . . VALUABLE . . . Presents a good mix of theory and practice, making it suitable for the novice reader as well as those with a stronger background in this area. The book CAN BE USED AS A STAND-ALONE TEXT OR AS A SUPPLEMENTARY READER, offering students a set of case studies for further evaluation. Both undergraduate and postgraduate students will find this book of value. The organization and structure are reader friendly . . . The book is cohesive, which is often not the case with edited works."

Dr. Bob McKercher, PhD
Associate Professor
School of Hotel
and Tourism Management
The Hong Kong Polytechnic University

"TIMELY AND IMPORTANT TO OUR INDUSTRY . . . Includes recent advances and current issues in hospitality and tourism satisfaction research . . . OFFERS NEW AND POTENTIALLY VERY USEFUL NEW APPROACHES to understanding guest satisfaction and positively impact profit. The book also looks at various cultural groups in terms of satisfaction as well as unique tourism venues . . . Theme parks, cultural heritage sites, and satisfaction among different demographic sectors are addressed. This book provides you with current service answers for delivering guest hospitality and tourism satisfaction."

Frederick J. DeMicco, PhD, RD FMP
Professor and ARAMARK Chair
Hotel, Restaurant
and Institutional Management
University of Delaware, Newark

Current Issues
and Development
in Hospitality and Tourism
Satisfaction

Current Issues and Development in Hospitality and Tourism Satisfaction has been co-published simultaneously as *Journal of Quality Assurance in Hospitality & Tourism,* Volume 4, Numbers 3/4 2003.

The *Journal of Quality Assurance in Hospitality & Tourism*™ Monographic "Separates"

Executive Editor: Sungsoo Pyo

Below is a list of "separates," which in serials librarianship means a special issue simultaneously published as a special journal issue or double-issue *and* as a "separate" hardbound monograph. (This is a format which we also call a "DocuSerial.")

"Separates" are published because specialized libraries or professionals may wish to purchase a specific thematic issue by itself in a format which can be separately cataloged and shelved, as opposed to purchasing the journal on an on-going basis. Faculty members may also more easily consider a "separate" for classroom adoption.

"Separates" are carefully classified separately with the major book jobbers so that the journal tie-in can be noted on new book order slips to avoid duplicate purchasing.

You may wish to visit Haworth's website at . . .

http://www.HaworthPress.com

. . . to search our online catalog for complete tables of contents of these separates and related publications.

You may also call 1-800-HAWORTH (outside US/Canada: 607-722-5857), or Fax 1-800-895-0582 (outside US/Canada: 607-771-0012), or e-mail at:

docdelivery@haworthpress.com

Current Issues and Development in Hospitality and Tourism Satisfaction, edited by John A. Williams and Muzaffer Uysal (Vol. 4, No. 3/4 2003). *Focuses on emerging approaches that measure customer satisfaction and how to apply them to improve hospitality and tourism businesses.*

Knowledge Management in Hospitality and Tourism, edited by Ricarda B. Bouncken and Sungsoo Pyo (Vol. 3, No. 3/4, 2002). *"Of great value. . . Introduces the concepts associated with knowledge management and provides examples of these concepts through case studies and unique real-world applications. . . . A lot of great information on a fascinating topic. . . ." (Cary C. Countryman, PhD, CHE, CHTP, Director, Technology Research and Education Center, Conrad N. Hilton College of Hotel and Restaurant Management)*

Benchmarks in Hospitality and Tourism, edited by Sungsoo Pyo (Vol. 2, No. 3/4, 2001). *"A handy single volume that clearly explains the principles and current thinking about benchmarking, plus useful insights on how the techniques can be converted into profitable business operations. Includes conceptual, practical, and operational (or 'how-it-is-done') chapters." (Chris Ryan, PhD, MEd, MPhil, BSc (Econ) Hons, Professor of Tourism, The University of Waikato, Hamilton, New Zealand)*

Current Issues
and Development
in Hospitality
and Tourism
Satisfaction

John A. Williams
Muzaffer Uysal
Editors

Current Issues and Development in Hospitality and Tourism Satisfaction has been co-published simultaneously as *Journal of Quality Assurance in Hospitality & Tourism,* Volume 4, Numbers 3/4 2003.

The Haworth Hospitality Press®
An Imprint of The Haworth Press, Inc.

New York • London • Victoria (AU)
www.HaworthPress.com

Published by

The Haworth Hospitality Press®, 10 Alice Street, Binghamton, NY 13904-1580 USA

The Haworth Hospitality Press® is an imprint of The Haworth Press, Inc., 10 Alice Street, Binghamton, NY 13904-1580 USA.

Current Issues and Development in Hospitality and Tourism Satisfaction has been co-published simultaneously as *Journal of Quality Assurance in Hospitality & Tourism,* Volume 4, Numbers 3/4 2003.

The development, preparation, and publication of this work has been undertaken with great care. However, the publisher, employees, editors, and agents of The Haworth Press and all imprints of The Haworth Press, Inc., including The Haworth Medical Press® and Pharmaceutical Products Press®, are not responsible for any errors contained herein or for consequences that may ensue from use of materials or information contained in this work. Opinions expressed by the author(s) are not necessarily those of The Haworth Press, Inc. With regard to case studies, identities and circumstances of individuals discussed herein have been changed to protect confidentiality. Any resemblance to actual persons, living or dead, is entirely coincidental.

Cover design by Marylouise Doyle

Library of Congress Cataloging-in-Publication Data

Current issues and development in hospitality and tourism satisfaction / John A. Williams, Muzaffer Uysal, editors.
    p. cm.
"Co-published simultaneously as Journal of Quality Assurance in Hospitality & Tourism, Volume 4, Numbers 3/4 2003." Includes bibliographical references and index.
     ISBN 0-7890-2433-0 (alk. paper) – ISBN 0-7890-2434-9 (pbk. : alk. paper)
1. Hospitality industry. I. Williams, John A. (John Alan) II. Uysal, Muzaffer. III. Journal of quality assurance in hospitality & tourism.
TX911.C83 2004
647.94–dc22

2003023286

Indexing, Abstracting & Website/Internet Coverage

This section provides you with a list of major indexing & abstracting services. That is to say, each service began covering this periodical during the year noted in the right column. Most Websites which are listed below have indicated that they will either post, disseminate, compile, archive, cite or alert their own Website users with research-based content from this work. (This list is as current as the copyright date of this publication.)

Abstracting, Website/Indexing Coverage . . . . Year When Coverage Began

- *CIRET (Centre International de Recherches et d'Etudes Touristiques). Computerized Touristique & General Bibliography <http://www.ciret-tourism.com>* **2000**

- *CNPIEC Reference Guide: Chinese National Directory of Foreign Periodicals* **2000**

- *HTI Database (Hospitality, Tourism Index); EBSCO Publishing* **2003**

- *Injury Prevention Web <http://www.injurypreventionweb.org>* . . . . . *****

- *INSPEC <http://www.iee.org.uk/publish/>* **2000**

- *Leisure, Recreation & Tourism Abstracts (c/o CAB Intl/CAB ACCESS) <http://www.cabi.org>* **2000**

- *Management & Marketing Abstracts <http://www.pira.co.uk>* . . **2000**

- *New Zealand Bibliographic Database <http://www.mngt.waikato.ac.nz>* **2003**

(continued)

*Exact start date to come.

Special Bibliographic Notes related to special journal issues (separates) and indexing/abstracting:

- indexing/abstracting services in this list will also cover material in any "separate" that is co-published simultaneously with Haworth's special thematic journal issue or DocuSerial. Indexing/abstracting usually covers material at the article/chapter level.
- monographic co-editions are intended for either non-subscribers or libraries which intend to purchase a second copy for their circulating collections.
- monographic co-editions are reported to all jobbers/wholesalers/approval plans. The source journal is listed as the "series" to assist the prevention of duplicate purchasing in the same manner utilized for books-in-series.
- to facilitate user/access services all indexing/abstracting services are encouraged to utilize the co-indexing entry note indicated at the bottom of the first page of each article/chapter/contribution.
- this is intended to assist a library user of any reference tool (whether print, electronic, online, or CD-ROM) to locate the monographic version if the library has purchased this version but not a subscription to the source journal.
- individual articles/chapters in any Haworth publication are also available through the Haworth Document Delivery Service (HDDS).

Current Issues
and Development
in Hospitality and Tourism
Satisfaction

CONTENTS

ABOUT THE EDITORS

John A. Williams, PhD, is Department Head of Hotel, Restaurant, and Institution Management & Dietetics at Kansas State University. He is also Director of the Graduate Program of HRIMD. In that role, he oversees both masters and doctoral education. Previous to joining Kansas State University in 2002, he was a member of the faculty at Virginia Tech in the Department of Hospitality and Tourism Management and served as Coordinator of the Undergraduate Program and Chair of the Undergraduate Committee. Dr. Williams' research interests are human resource management, service quality and customer satisfaction, and managed services. He has conducted research for restaurants, hotels, and managed service companies.

Muzaffer Uysal, PhD, is Professor in the Department of Hospitality and Tourism Management at Virginia Polytechnic Institute & State University. Dr. Uysal has extensive experience in the travel and tourism field, authoring or co-authoring a significant number of articles proceedings, book chapters, and monographs. He also has conducted workshops and seminars on similar topics and field research in several countries. Dr. Uysal is a member of the International Academy for the Study of Tourism and serves as co-editor of *Tourism Analysis: An Interdisciplinary Journal*. In addition, he sits on the editorial boards of eight journals–including *Journal of Travel Research*–and is resource editor of the *Annals of Tourism Research*. His current interests center on tourism demand/supply interaction, tourism development and marketing, and international tourism.

Introduction

John A. Williams
Muzaffer Uysal

SUMMARY. This paper concentrates on the importance of customer satisfaction in today's business environment. It emphasizes the fact that customer satisfaction strategies must have both long-term and immediate results. It further focuses on the individual papers included in the volume and how they address new and effective approaches for understanding customer satisfaction and providing quality service at all levels of the hospitality and tourism industry. *[Article copies available for a fee from The Haworth Document Delivery Service: 1-800-HAWORTH. E-mail address: <docdelivery@haworthpress.com> Website: <http://www.HaworthPress. com> © 2003 by The Haworth Press, Inc. All rights reserved.]*

KEYWORDS. Quality service, customer satisfaction, competition

John A. Williams is Department Head, Associate Professor, and Director of the Graduate Program, Hotel, Restaurant, Institution Management and Dietetics, Kansas State University, 103 Justin Hall, Manhattan, KS 66506 (E-mail: williams@humec. ksu.edu).

Muzaffer Uysal is Professor, Virginia Polytechnic Institute and State University, Department of Hospitality & Tourism Management, 355 Wallace Hall, Blacksburg, VA 24061-0429 (E-mail: samil@vt.edu).

[Haworth co-indexing entry note]: "Introduction." Williams, John A., and Muzaffer Uysal. Co-published simultaneously in *Journal of Quality Assurance in Hospitality & Tourism* (The Haworth Hospitality Press, an imprint of The Haworth Press, Inc.) Vol. 4, No. 3/4, 2003, pp. 1-5; and: *Current Issues and Development in Hospitality and Tourism Satisfaction* (ed: John A. Williams and Muzaffer Uysal) The Haworth Hospitality Press, an imprint of The Haworth Press, Inc., 2003, pp. 1-5. Single or multiple copies of this article are available for a fee from The Haworth Document Delivery Service [1-800-HAWORTH, 9:00 a.m. - 5:00 p.m. (EST). E-mail address: docdelivery@ haworthpress.com].

http://www.haworthpress.com/web/JQAHT
© 2003 by The Haworth Press, Inc. All rights reserved.
Digital Object Identifier: 10.1300/J162v04n03_01

Consumer satisfaction research started as early as the 1960's (Cardozo, 1965). During the 1980's, customer satisfaction increased in popularity as an important topic. Since then, the dynamics of the consumer marketplace have changed substantially. The aggressive business environment has made it mandatory to value the customer and ensure their satisfaction.

With our technologically, advanced global economy, competing organization's can rapidly duplicate another organization's price and product. This process is now accelerated by the Internet and e-mail and can be achieved in much less time than was possible a few years ago. Organizations are also dealing with a more highly-educated customer that is aware of the varied services and levels of quality that are available. There has been a virtual explosion of options for the consumer. However, competitors cannot duplicate another organization's customer relationships. The ability to satisfy customers, therefore, becomes the key ingredient of continued success.

The importance of customer satisfaction has become an essential business issue as organizations have realized the significant outcomes achieved when providing effective customer service. For hospitality and tourism, satisfaction has always been important, but there is a growing awareness that it can make the difference between a company's survival and failure.

As businesses know, it has been shown over and over again that reselling to an existing customer costs far less than gaining a new one. Subsequently, customer satisfaction strategies are looking for long-term as well as immediate results. Research by PricewaterhouseCoopers (2002) shows that firms are aware that customer satisfaction and quality can be more important than current financial results in creating long-term shareholder value. Successful leaders, either in small business or larger organizations, are continually concentrating on their customers and how they can please them better than their competitors.

This volume includes recent advances and timely issues in hospitality and tourism satisfaction research and offers new, and potentially effective, approaches for understanding customer satisfaction and providing quality service at all levels of the hospitality and tourism industry. Eleven original papers are included in this volume.

The first paper by Noe and Uysal examines social interaction linkages in the service satisfaction model. The starting premise of the paper is that the locus of satisfaction resides between the service provider and customer. The approach taken is largely qualitative because of its theoretical nature. It draws from the fields of social psychology, leisure-tourism, sociology, and business and offers insight into how best to handle and manage such social interactions. It is proposed that this intrinsic interaction model is key to unlocking the complex exchange mechanisms between the service provider and the tourist customer.

The second paper by Knutson and Beck is also a conceptual one in nature and proposes a holistic, three phase model structured to incorporate the major components of the experience construct. It is articulated that the complex relationship among value, service quality, satisfaction, and experience is in its infancy. Before this relationship can be fully examined, dimensions of these four critical components need to be incorporated into a unified, holistic model that includes the three primary constructs of Service Quality, Value, and Satisfaction.

Kozak, Bigné, and Andreu examine one of the areas of satisfaction–cultural differences in tourist satisfaction–that has received little attention in the past. While providing discussion on equivalence issues regarding the measurement of tourist satisfaction, the authors (1) emphasize the significance of exploring cross-cultural differences in measuring customer satisfaction in tourism, (2) recommend alternative research methodology to analyse cross-cultural tourist satisfaction, and also (3) point out limitations of conducting cross-cultural research in tourist satisfaction from both the theoretical and practical point of view.

Ekinci's paper provides empirical research that is designed to examine whether consumers use single or multiple comparison standards for the evaluation of service quality and when determining their satisfaction, in the context of the hospitality industry. The findings indicate that consumers use multiple comparison standards for the evaluation of service quality and satisfaction. Predictive expectations, deserved expectation, desire congruence and experience-based norm are considered very important constructs in measuring satisfaction.

The fifth paper by Fallon and Schofield also compares the predictive validity of six models used in the measurement of satisfaction; it is concerned with their application at destination level, with particular reference to Orlando, Florida. From tourists' 'performance' ratings, five 'dimensions' of Orlando's tourism offering were identified: 'primary,' 'secondary' and 'tertiary' attractions, 'facilitators' and 'transport plus.' Orlando's reputation as the world's theme park capital, 'secondary' attractions (such as shopping and dining opportunities) and 'facilitators' (such as accommodation and customer service) were identified as having the most influence on overall tourist satisfaction with Orlando.

Knutson, Singh, Yen and Bryant's paper focuses on guest satisfaction in the U.S. lodging industry using the American Consumer Satisfaction Index (ACSI) Model as a service scoreboard. The authors analyzed guest scores for three important standards: overall satisfaction, expectancy-disconfirmation, and customer experience compared to an ideal product. Their findings indicate that the lodging industry scores slightly better than the entire service sector and about the same as the national score.

The seventh paper by Shanka and Taylor examines the perceived importance of the service and facility attributes to hotel satisfaction in Perth, Western Australia. The three delineated factor groupings of "physical facilities," "service experienced" and "services provision" of the service and facility scale were found to significantly contribute to the overall importance rating of the hotel attributes. Statistically significant differences were also noted for age and residence on the physical facilities and services provided components.

The eighth paper by Clemenz, Weaver, Han, and McCleary focuses on trainees' expectations in the development of training programs. Utilizing a factor analytic procedure, the authors identified five dimensions of trainees' expectations: courtesy, entertainment, climate, tangibles, and relevance. These expectations of training dimensions are then used to cluster analyze trainees into three groups: "the good-timers," "the high hopes," and "the serious students." It is implied that understanding trainees' expectation dimensions may be of help in improving morale and satisfaction level of employees, thus better satisfied customers in the end.

The paper by Baloglu, Pekcan, Chen, and Santos focuses on the relationship between destination performance, overall satisfaction, and behavioral intention for segment types. It is argued that destination performance, visitor satisfaction, and favorable future behavior of visitors are key determinants of destination competitiveness. Most empirical work, assuming that overall tourist population is homogenous, investigates the relationships among product performance, satisfaction, and/or behavioral intentions in an aggregated manner. The authors conclude that the segment-based approach is more pragmatic because it provides segment-specific implications for destination management and marketing.

Neal's study tests empirically the effects the number of nights spent on a vacation have on the levels of satisfaction recent travelers report for three service aspects of the travel destination: perceived satisfaction with tourism service providers; perceived "freedom from defects" of tourism services; and perceived reasonableness of the cost of tourism services. Differentiation in satisfaction scores between "short-term visitors" and "long-term visitors" were examined. Her study revealed that significant differences between the two groups of visitors were present for (1) perceived satisfaction with industry professionals delivering the service experience at the travel destination, (2) perceived satisfaction with "freedom from defects" of the actual services at the destination, and (3) perceived reasonableness of the cost of services at the travel destination.

The last paper by Huh and Uysal attempts to investigate the relationship between cultural/heritage destination attributes and overall satisfaction, and to identify the difference in the overall satisfaction of tourists in terms of selected demographic and travel behavior characteristics. The findings indicate that there is a relationship between destination attributes and overall satisfaction with cultural/heritage experience. The authors also found that overall satisfaction may show variation by gender, length of stay, and decision horizon.

It is an enormous challenge for businesses to successfully attain customer satisfaction in hospitality and tourism services. The customer is the most important person in a business. It is essential to systematically provide current research as service expectations continue to rise. Customer satisfaction programs should envision the process of looking at new insights as a perpetual process. To remain current, it is necessary to look beyond the scope of your own business situation and examine how others operate in similar markets. It is our hope that a variety of topics covered in this volume would be of help to both academicians and practitioners currently and for further research in the area and provide a better understanding of the salient dimensions of satisfaction and its variants.

Finally, we wish to acknowledge the *Journal of Quality Assurance in Hospitality & Tourism* Editor, Professor Sungsoo Pyo, for his support in developing this volume. We owe a great debt to all authors for their diligent work on the papers and prompt revisions.

REFERENCES

Cardozo, R.N. (August, 1965). An Experimental Study of Customer Effort, Expectation, and Satisfaction, *Journal of Marketing Research*, 2, 244-249.
PricewaterhouseCoopers, Management Barometer, April, 22, 2002.

ARTICLES

Social Interaction Linkages in the Service Satisfaction Model

Francis P. Noe
Muzaffer Uysal

SUMMARY. Many of the articles in this special issue on customer satisfaction are dealing with very specific concerns associated with explaining tourist and customer satisfaction. This article is more generic in nature and reaches down to a more fundamental level of recognizing that the locus of satisfaction resides between the service provider and cus-

Francis P. Noe is Retired Researcher, U.S. National Park Service and Adjunct Professor in Hospitality and Tourism Management, Virginia Polytechnic Institute and State University.

Muzaffer Uysal is Professor in Hospitality and Tourism Management, Virginia Polytechnic Institute and State University, Department of Hospitality & Tourism Management, 355 Wallace Hall, Blacksburg, VA 24061-0429 (E-mail: samil@vt.edu).

Address correspondence to Muzaffer Uysal at the above address.

[Haworth co-indexing entry note]: "Social Interaction Linkages in the Service Satisfaction Model." Noe, Francis P., and Muzaffer Uysal. Co-published simultaneously in *Journal of Quality Assurance in Hospitality & Tourism* (The Haworth Hospitality Press, an imprint of The Haworth Press, Inc.) Vol. 4, No. 3/4, 2003, pp. 7-22; and: *Current Issues and Development in Hospitality and Tourism Satisfaction* (ed: John A. Williams and Muzaffer Uysal) The Haworth Hospitality Press, an imprint of The Haworth Press, Inc., 2003, pp. 7-22. Single or multiple copies of this article are available for a fee from The Haworth Document Delivery Service [1-800-HAWORTH, 9:00 a.m. - 5:00 p.m. (EST). E-mail address: docdelivery@haworthpress.com].

tomer. It is the interaction process that transpires between these roles that creates a dissatisfied or satisfied, and in some cases a delighted tourist. The approach taken is largely qualitative because of its theoretical nature. It draws from the fields of social psychology, leisure-tourism, sociology, and business that offer insight into how best to handle and manage such social interactions. It is proposed that this intrinsic interaction model is key to unlocking the complex exchange mechanisms between the service provider and the tourist customer. This article is an initial step in examining the positive interaction process that leads to reinforcing satisfactory experiences in a tourist situation, thereby broadening our understanding of service satisfaction. *[Article copies available for a fee from The Haworth Document Delivery Service: 1-800-HAWORTH. E-mail address: <docdelivery@haworthpress.com> Website: <http://www.HaworthPress.com>*

KEYWORDS. Social interaction, service satisfaction, satisfactory experiences

INTRODUCTION

A major focus in any hospitality and tourism service model should be the personal linkage between the service provider and customer. But for the most part, employees in direct contact with the customer, the service provider on the front-line has received far too little attention, "one marketing relationship which has a direct affect on customers, and which has received too little attention, is the one involving the company's personnel" (Liljander, 2000, pp. 162, 171). In essence, we wholeheartedly concur with this observation and judgment that in any service industry, the service role is basic and essential to performance. The institutions supporting tourist service include: transportation systems, hotels, resorts, restaurants, shopping establishments, historic-natural parks, and entertainment in the arts such as in music and the theater. The systems and human infrastructure supporting them are even more specific including artisans of all manner, the social events and physical places, including beaches, wilderness areas, theme parks, resorts, festivals, fairs, and seasonal recreation and sporting venues as prescribed in various cultures throughout the world.

The social processes bonding these systems together are service providers. They encompass the desk clerks, waiters, park rangers, door and bell men, maids, and stewards on the front-line interacting with the customer. Contact personnel at frontdesks are a standard in the service industry. These people often set the tone for a customer's ensuing perceptions of satisfaction. There are also behind the scene personnel whose contributions are significant but not necessarily recognized by the customer as an essential part of the service team. The behind the scene area also functions as an oasis and regrouping area for the front-line staff to retreat to for needed rest, recovery, and consultation.

Organizations requiring enduring periods of emotional labor along the front- line must recognize that service employees need to step 'out of character' to relax and regain composure, off from the front-stage of customer interaction (Ashforth and Humphrey, 1993, p.105). These same organizations need to go a step further by offering a balance of work with free time and a life away from the job. Burnout is cited as a negative factor affecting service performers through emotional exhaustion, a depersonalized self-image of being talked down to by customers, and feelings of lack of work accomplishment. Such negative self-feeling by service providers is a result of far too many interpersonal contacts, the frequency, duration and length of work without adequate relief and time off (Ford, 1998, pp. 130-1). In addition, withdrawal from the situation and perceptions of self-conflict may also be a result of stressful work interaction situations with too few providers and resources to meet the customers' expectations. Controlling the above negative impacts on the service worker makes work-life more enjoyable.

This introductory article begins to evaluate the role of the service provider in offering direct satisfactory service and what needs to be done in the tourist interaction setting. None of us as customers expect to be dissatisfied or disappointed by our service. We expect satisfaction at least and delight at best, rarely hanging in a neutral position. In our large impersonal urban world, where a sense of community is missing, the individual may disappear into loneliness and become nothing more then a credit card number. All service organizations must recognize that the individuals they deal with possess feelings and judgments. The service personnel representing that organization have the responsibility of recognizing their customer as a responsible human being. Liljander (2000, p. 171) cites studies that show that "every employee who is in contact with external customers affects customer satisfaction and knowing what the customer wants and being able to deliver it gives the employee a feeling of accomplishment and satisfaction." This interactive work process is itself a rewarding experience, as are often the more tangible benefits as well. Employee happiness, economic benefits, family care, and job security serve to maintain and promote employee loyalty and a spirit of well being (Liljander 2000, pp. 176-800). Unhappy employees compromise the service act and then take their frustration out on the customer. In the end, all parties lose and satisfaction's alter-ego, dissatisfaction or noncommittal neutrality, reigns over the service act.

The service act in a tourist situation has to be built on a solid formulation since the service situation is not always acted out between familiar participants.

When a customer has frequent contacts with a service provider, they become part of a relationship though a history of transactions, get to know personal things about each other, develop expectations for one another, and anticipate future interaction. However, service encounters are usually a single interaction, or repeated with different providers who are strangers to the customer (Ford, 1998, p. 82). This is especially true in a tourist situation, complicating the exchange process. As a start in managing this process, Day (1999, p. 62) indicates that the Marriott Hotel corporation has a "fanatical eye for detail." 'This begins with the hiring process that systematically recruits, screens, and selects from as many as 40 applicants for each position . . . " Matching the correct employee with the customer is a first step in the satisfaction process. An enduring mutually-reinforcing relationship between a satisfied employee and customer produces what Heskett, Sasser, and Schlesinger (1997) call the "satisfaction mirror." The result produces employees who become more satisfied by dealing with satisfied customers, and customers in turn become more satisfied by dealing with satisfied employees. This reinforcing social effect was found in each of the service organizations for which data were available. Building that cycle of capability for the satisfaction mirror, two companies in the travel sector each oriented their hiring practices primarily for attitude and secondly for skills. Rosenbluth International and Southwest Airlines hire "nice or people with good attitudes" that enjoyed serving people. But the goal of achieving satisfaction does not stop with hiring. It continues with monitoring. Keeping the customer-employee interaction connected requires constant listening to their changing needs. Companies most cited by Heskett et al. (1997) are Disney, Club Med, American Express, Southwest Airlines, British Airways, Fairfield Inns, and the Ritz-Carlton hotels which have direct interests in the tourist marketplace. You have to be mindful of the way in which these companies engage in various customer informational and data gathering efforts that determines how well or poorly they are doing in fulfilling customer expectations. Employee attitudes, personality dispositions, skills, and monitoring needs are just a part of comprehending how to control the service act. It also necessitates knowing how the principle actors engage in the service process to achieve satisfactory outcomes, which means understanding what is being acted out on the service stage.

ACTING ON THE STAGE OF SERVICE

Service "Should be part of everyone's job description," not just the responsibility of the guest services department (Tschohl, 1991, p. 74). So everyone, not just the doorman or desk clerk, but even the CEO who walks through one of their corporate social situations has to be conscious that they are on a service stage. In an excellent summary of Erving Goffman's work relating to interactive expression, Morisaki and Gudykunst (1994, pp. 52, 59) agree that communicating expressions is not intrinsically lodged in the face or body, but rather in the interaction and encounter-taking place in an exchange. Goffman sees humans playing theatrical roles as if on a stage, the ultimate social analogy. But the drama is played out in real-life experiences. The social interaction of the players actually plays a major role in generating meaning. It is not just a static view of the face that communicates. Most Western researchers interpret face as an "independent construal of the self." This is defined as the individual being a unique and independent entity. It's how you use it in the exchange process that takes on meaning. It is the looks, smiles, nods, and shifts of the head that project what we are trying to convey. Humans ultimately use verbal communication in which messages are conveyed through language. These verbal and non-verbal mediums transmit the intended message. "It is through *interacting* with others that we acquire narrative skills, not through being acted upon." For example, 'a stability narrative' may be part of a person suggesting honesty or a 'progressive narrative' suggesting success. 'The important point here is that these implications are realized in action' and they become subject to social appraisal. 'Others may find the actions and outcomes implied by these narratives (according to current conventions) coherent with or contradictory to the telling(s)' (Gergen, 1994, pp. 188, 207). This interactive process is judgmental and service providers are very much being judged by their performances. First, the words and stories being told in the interaction process are the realities that the service provider and customer wish to convey to each other. "Information is conveyed in a social context, its interpretation may be guided in part, by the recipients' perceptions of why the information is being transmitted as well as its literal meaning. Consequently, the recipient actively attempts to interpret messages in a way that makes them informative." The motivation and meaning in a communication act are reinforced by a second and third process in an interactive exchange constituting 'accuracy' in a conveyed message, and also 'politeness' stating that communications should not offend the listener (Wyer et al., 1995, pp. 16-18). In transmitting messages in these social contexts or situations, Wyer et al. (1995, p. 25) refer to the research of others who see that stories are a fundamental way of individuals to identify with one another in a social situation. "We typically respond to descriptions of another's personal experience by recounting an experience of our own that has similar features, and use this story to understand the experiences the other has had" at that time. Such stories are often used to bridge the gap between the service provider and customer to ease an initial uneasy stranger exchange. Altogether the gestures, looks, posture, and words lead to an end result. The communication mediums through which the service provider works attempts to meet the customer's expectations.

In mastering the act of communication, the Disney Corporation finds no role is really small or menial. "All employees are taught to be enthusiastic members of the cast" (Liswood, 1990, p. 52). The Disney Corporation has long recognized that a happy employee does not leave the company but works to satisfy a customer. For example, projective techniques are used to sharpen employee-cast member skills. In one case, "elderly guests with a small child with tears in his eyes standing in the rain at Disney World" is shown for reactions. Cast members are then given an opportunity to suggest what might be done to help their guests feel better (Heskett et al., 1990, p. 217). The situation places a service act in a different context, where the service provider, which should lead to smiles, suggests steps. The service provider must always be sensitive, alert, and open to the customer. Tourist plays are not random acts between players. Indicators exist for the service provider in dealing with a social situation even though the actors change.

A social situation helps define the service play and stage that the service provider and tourist customer use to formulate a meaningful act. Remember that social situational definitions are comprised of at least four sets of factors that the interactive participants attend to when exchanging information (Sherif and Sherif 1969, pp. 12, 124). First, they include the characteristics of the individual: sex, approximate age, social class, and social relationships, such as patrons or customers in a service context. A second set of factors includes the activities, problems or tasks to be accomplished or resolved. Dealing with the requests and needs of the customers is one such set of goals. A third set pertains to the location such as a recreational place in a tourist setting. And finally, the individual's relationship to the above three sets of factors and the role performance they are exhibiting, i.e., stressed, at ease, relaxed, involved, bored etc., that may characterize either the service provider or customer acting in that situation. " As the factors in a social situation function *interdependently*, it follows that neglect of any one set will lead to conclusions that are in error or lack validity . . . It becomes particularly crucial when we consider how we appraise other people, for other people are sized-up in terms of how they are related to us." The end outcome is judgmental, resulting in the service situation as either being dissatisfying, satisfying, neutral, and, in some cases, delightful. It is always hoped that the participants act out a satisfied theme or story within a service situation.

The interactive process is at its most fundamental between a single service provider and a customer. "When two actors have reciprocally acknowledged each other's attention, any action taken by either actor can be seen by the other as being related to one's activity. This is why the first action that occurs in the context of RAA (Reciprocally Acknowledged Attention) must offer some explanation for the actor's allocation of attention and some indication of the actor's availability for continuing interaction" (Hintz and Miller, 1995, pp. 360-5). The authors note that social encounters are hierarchical, beginning with the simple and advancing to the complex. A hierarchical building process exists in which social accomplishments are contingent on the successful construction and maintenance of the more basic levels of meaning. Also, part of the interactive process involves mutual responsiveness that is interrelated to attending to another person's actions. "A person cannot respond to another's behavior without first attending to it. In fact, attending and responding are simultaneous in most situations," save where one of the actors deliberately ignores the other, perhaps serving to offend.

But the service interaction process does not just happen. Service can offend where a hierarchical management style puts front-line employees at the lower end of the corporate ladder and then ignores them. An organization style insuring positive contacts with the customer is premised and based upon employee and management mutual interpersonal respect. In communicating with customers, Desatnick (1987, pp. 20-26) sets out five steps where lack of respect for service employees is demonstrated by thoughtless supervisors and managers. Very simply, employee respect leads to customer respect in reverse order (1) When "there is an acute awareness that if management solves employee problems, employees solve customers' problems. It is as simple as that." Employees ask how they may be of assistance. (2) Management needs to spell-out service guidelines for employees. "All the things employees want and need to know are ensuring that their customers will get the proper service." Employees can then demonstrate that they know what kind of service is offered and are not left guessing. (3) Management "rewards customer-related actions beyond the call of duty and publicly praises those who set examples of personal accountability." Employees who exercise personal responsibility and are empowered to do so are recognized for their positive contributions for the benefit of customers. (4) "Companies develop profound problems in employee morale through the overt lack of respect for individual employees demonstrated by the thoughtless supervisors and managers." Such thoughtlessness destroys spirit that is witnessed by the customers (5) "All of us can think of times in our careers when we have had a non-supportive boss, someone who inevitably passed the buck on to us for whatever went wrong, and worse still, took personal credit for our contributions." Employees who can count on management not to pass the buck and reward them will have customers looking to them with the same kind of acceptance.

Though there is a social interactive set of communicative actions to achieve the needs of customers following upon a hierarchical process, it is built upon a supportive organizational context between the service employee and management mutually respecting and reinforcing each other. Service is part of everyone's explicit or implicit performance descriptive in order to keep the tourist customer in focus as being the paramount goal to satisfy.

GETTING THE SERVICE ROLE RIGHT

Customer service begins with employee satisfaction and well being according to Gitomer (2000, p. 3B). In summarizing much of the above service conditions, an excellent service organization begins by hiring: "happy people," providing a supportive work environment, evaluating performance rather than reprimanding, even rewarding mistakes to reduce fear of employees hiding in a service shell. Also, employee performance is further increased by listening to the employee, offering low cost benefits, making service providers feel valuable and promoting self worth, and finally encouraging a fun atmosphere in the work place. This may sound very obvious but it is most often overlooked for time and cost reasons. To reiterate, a company in building a service-minded organization must "(1) hire the right people, (2) develop people to deliver service quality, (3) provide the needed support systems, and (4) retain the best people" (Zeithlaml and Bitner, 2000, pp. 293, 297). Certainly outgoing and caring people come to light in a service situation, and the research shows that those individuals who are helpful, thoughtful, sociable, and are also socially adjusted, likable, have social skills and are willing to follow guidelines make good service employees. As already indicated, Southwest Airlines, a leader in customer service "looks for people who are compassionate and who have common sense, a sense of humor, a 'can do' attitude, and an egalitarian sense of themselves (They think in terms of 'we' rather than 'me')" (Zeithlaml and Bitner, 2000, pp. 293, 297).

In their study employing various qualitative techniques, Panter and Martin (1991) identified six frontline employee roles for managing customer behavior. The roles that may be needed in a tourist situation are the "Matchmaker," whose function is to group different and incompatible income, sex, or age generation groups to avoid self-encroachment. The "Teacher" who is used to socialize individuals to where functional areas are located and what is appropriate behavior. The "Santa Claus" role rewards the customer for cooperating with the organization for their congenial behavior. The "Police Officer" who enforces the rules that will not disrupt the service process. The "Cheerleader" who acts as a host or hostess by bringing people together. And finally, the "Detective" who investigates what satisfies and what is dissatisfying to customers on a routine basis to keep the organization on guard for change. These roles are held in such high regard that the recruitment process is on the same level of importance as targeting the customer segment. Others too have suggested the requirement for fitting organizational roles containing a similar continuity in function. In that respect, Baldasare and Mittal (1997) identify four service roles that need serious thought when implementing a service process. The first is that of the "Coach" who essentially teaches or guides the user into the service provided. Second is the "Facilitator" who informs the customer about how your company conducts itself, its general culture, modus operandi, and general philosophy. Third, the "Integrator" who teaches the customer about the services offered and what departments to tap into for obtaining a particular service. And finally, there is the "Student" role, where you put yourself at the disposal of the customer to learn where your weaknesses and strengths are within the service process to create improvements.

Very particular role functions that specialize in the scope of employee limits do not transcend more encompassing requirements. The organization has to set limits on how far an employee is allowed to function and interact with the customer. But these processes cannot be smothering to the front-line initiative of those employees. For example, Furlong (1993, pp. 192-7) specifies more general employee norms about implementing role behavior with customers that increases customer retention by placing limits on the interaction process.

1. "Let employees know they can't pass the buck."
2. "Don't let your people get hung up on job descriptions."
3. "Spell it out in dollars and cents" that the value of satisfying customers is paramount."
4. "And don't let them believe (the employee) that money solves everything."
5. "Remind employers that they have a better finger on the customer pulse."
6. "Spread the responsibility," especially across the front-line personnel.

Such "explicit service standards clarify the service task and provide benchmark norms against which employees can judge their own performance and managers can judge the employees . . . performance" (Berry, 1995, pp. 72-3). The Ritz-Carlton's basic list of twenty principles offers ways of dealing with the customer and representing the company. For example, "any employee who receives a customer complaint owns the complaint." The development of performance standards cannot remain solely at the level of mid or upper management. The service employee must also be involved and free to operate within their situation.

Employees "must have the authority to do what's necessary to achieve customer satisfaction. They must be *empowered* and should help develop specifications for their own performance" on the front-line (Tschohl, 1991, p. 72).

But role-taking is only one part of interaction theory. There is also role-making where persons "create their own version of their role performance over time." Modifications exist because there is "considerable leeway" (Albrecht et al., 1987, p. 156) between a person's performance and the role expectations chosen for action, and creating one's own personal style. The institutions, culture, and social situations are dependent upon how tightly they are defined normatively will either be more open or more closely restricted to role variations and personal styles. One of the most difficult norms for a service organization is to allow their front-line staff to personalize and make decisions relative to the customer. However, hotels such as the Ritz-Carlton have succeeded through employee trust. In that regard, Heil et al. (1997, p. 147-162) clearly specify that those in a serving capacity should be ready, willing, and able to serve. But the employer must grant the employee the authority, empower them, trust them; and concomitantly, the employee must possess a spirit and enthusiasm about what they are doing. When the service provider "demonstrate a love and interest for their work their spirit is infectious." It draws the customer into the service process, and provides emotional warmth that sometimes can be just as important as the service sought. Then, the freedom of authority, empowerment, and trust given the employee helps build that foundation for superior service. We have been fortunate to see it happen, and witness the beneficial outcome to the customer and service provider alike.

SERVICE INTERACTION ROLE PERFORMANCES

Which types of service roles perform the most satisfactory in the customer and service provider situation? Following the symbolic interactional–dramaturgical approach to hiring employees as cast members, Bell and Zemke (1992, pp. 5-6) identify three universal role requirements. First, "great service performers must be able to create a relationship with the audience" the customer. Second, "great service performers must be able to handle pressure" and control themselves. Third, "great service performers must be able to learn new scripts" and implement them because expectations and situations are constantly changing. Based on these performance assumptions, the service provider has to be careful to implement measures to enhance the tourist customer's experience. The following list of actions on the part of the service provider is expected to produce positive reactions in the customer leading to a satisfactory judgment about the tourist experience (Figure 1). This is far from a complete list, but an initial working list. It is based largely on qualitative evidence but it is a start in examining the interaction process. Also, the description of each of these actions is only briefly described herein, and is part of a larger text in progress.

FIGURE 1. Service Provider Action and Expected Customer Reaction

1. When You Personalize, You Increase Self-Worth

In this highly impersonal world, where many of us are mere numbers, we are delighted and highly satisfied when someone takes a personal interest in our tourist experience. To illustrate this point, Club Med, requires "providers that are able to interact with guests" to be responsive and organize activities that also involve the guest (Heskett et al., 1990, pp. 67, 101). To illustrate, a charter flight from New York to the Cancun Airport arrived ten hours late. For their time 2 A.M. arrival time, the management and staff organized and prepared a "lavish welcoming banquet, complete with a mariachi band and champagne." That party lasted to dawn with guests "commenting that it was the most fun they had since college." This kind of personalized service and attention avoided irate feelings and helped the guests recover their positive expectations for the remaining days of their stay. The positive self-worth of the guests was directly affected by such a pre-emptive action.

2. When You Know, You Clarify Expectations

In determining the competence of an employee, it is crucial to know the "expectations" of the customers, and then match those skills of the employee to meet those customer expectations (Healy, 1996). More then likely there will be very specific informational requirements, and most likely whatever the setting, accurate communication will be a necessity for satisfying the customer. The Holiday Crowne Hotels, as an upscale chain, has launched an approach to attract and built a following of loyal guests through its "Get to know us, we'll get to know you," advertising campaign. They can track customer preferences for such things as pillows, snacks, and types of service preferences to meet those specific tastes (Rauscher, 1997a, p. 78).

3. When You are Friendly, You Become Close

"Hire people who want to be friendly and helpful" (Tschohl, 1991, p. 109). The Marriott Corporation's focus in its Fairfield Inn's division is clean rooms, a friendly atmosphere, and budget prices. It then focuses on the roles of the housekeeping and front desk staff (Berry, 1995, p. 166). Providing a social welcoming situation sets a most positive tone for the services offered. This is obviously a very basic service performance norm, probably learned from those who first cared for us.

4. When You Surprise, You Bring Joy

Wonder is a part of leisure and tourist experiences that are created through social interaction with the customer. It is the perceived freedom, intrinsic satisfaction and positive reinforcement that result from being surprised in a free-time situation (Labone, 1996). Disney Corporation makes wonder intrinsic to its theme parks. Epcot schedules unannounced performances including parades and appearances by Disney characters that result in the customer feeling fortunate that they were at the right place and time to receive this extra value for their tourist dollar.

5. When You Promise, You Commit

What can I expect and how I will be treated, as a customer is essential to the interaction experience. "A customer-contact role carries certain normative expectations, including display rules" (Ashforth and Humphrey, 1993, pp. 99-104). These rules identify with the positive impact of fulfilling the expectations of the customer through positive interaction. For example, Ashforth and Humphrey (1993, pp. 99-104) cite one organization that had its service providers pin a dollar to their uniforms and customers were entitled to it if they did not receive "a friendly greeting or a sincere thank you." In a tourist situation, we would think friendly would be basic, and being sensitive to all reasonable requirements is a guarantee. In fact, this relates to all transactions and no matter how minimal grows with use; for example, there is the "role of a skier who makes use of the many services of a ski lodge" not just the slopes (Deighton, 1994, p. 135).

6. When You Listen, You Learn

Service providers on the team who can listen are essential to knowing the customer. "We hope you've hired people who are customer-focused, who can listen, understand, communicate with, and relate to customers as well as demonstrate . . . knowledge" (Connellan an Zemke, 1993, p. 89). "Truly service-driven companies . . . listen and they respond" to the customer. "They hold hands" with their customer and adjust, improve, mend, abandon, and make right at every step in the service process. They strive to be characterized as "dependable" by their customer (Tschohl and Franzmeier, 1991, pp. 195-6). Most of us can recall those in the tourist sector who listened to our requests, questions, and tales of woe with compassion.

7. When You Reward, You Positively Reinforce

Rewarding the loyal customer is top priority. For example, "The pricing strategies of many, if not most, companies shortchange loyal customers and reward the most disloyal ones. So Southwest (Airlines) has one price for advance purchase and one for unrestricted purchase. Customers know that they are getting a fair deal" (Reichheld, 2001, pp. 142, 144). As an important point of reference for the customer, this kind of pricing strategy should be clearly linked to the benefits program. A more basic reward is making the customer a part of the corporate family. Zeithaml et al. (1990, p. 109) argue that treating customers as partial employees facilitates role clarity and more effectively produces quality service. In such situations, "providing customers with realistic service previews, training customers how to perform, providing visible rewards such as upgrading a customer to a first class seat" are excellent ways of creating stronger customer reinforcement. To illustrate, on a crowded flight, a stewardess sympathetically told two of their rushed passengers boarding last to stay in first class status rather than struggle to the back. They relaxed, the plane was not delayed, and the customers were delighted

8. When You Recognize Needs, You Acknowledge Importance

Social competence is "absolutely necessary" in face-to-face service contact, and customers must be made to "feel welcome and comfortable" because the service provider knows their needs and expectations (Petite, 1989, p. 111). It is in this way that "appreciation means actively acknowledging the value of a customer by recognizing his existence and by establishing a knowledge of his particular needs and desires" (Vavra, 1992, p. 37). That action is central to the interaction process between the service provider and customer. Knowing that clean, quiet, and comfortable is not just a slogan for a room in the hospitality industry, but a reality, makes the tourist feel their needs are important.

9. When You Solve a Problem, You Become Special

The service providers on the front-line know where problems arise. According to Furlong (1993, p. 115) "studies by a U.S. research organization prove that front-liners can predict almost 90 percent of cases where customers will have complaints." Given the front-liners' knowledge of problems, they have to be able to break-down the interpersonal barriers that customers construct to protect themselves in problem service situations. They "should therefore be sensitive to critical contact situations; they should be able to quickly recognize the potential for escalation and then be able to reduce this potential by applying their finely honed communication and conflict solving skills" (Jeschke et al., 2000, p. 207). The service provider gives a personal commitment upon which the customer may directly rely for solution to a service problem. At a well-known hotel, an employee dropped a guest's computer but immediately replaced it with a new one to avoid an even greater problem.

10. When You Are Leisure-Hearted, You Bring a Smile

A positive outlook toward life insures life satisfaction. Such a disposition is reinforced by the psychological and social interactions of the individuals that lead to personal happiness and contentment. It is the opposite of worry, depression and sadness. Such employees do not hide in a social vacuum but reach out to the guests around them. They joke, smile, and laugh and it shows in their sincerity. If any service sector requires such an action, it is the tourist and leisure business, where a recreational seeker is expecting a little time off from the serious chores of work life and expects the service providers to respond in kind. As an illustration, Zeithaml and Bitner (2000, p. 76) report that the positive and negative emotions of river guides "had a strong effect on their customers . . . overall satisfaction." However, the overall positive emotions by the guides produced a stronger effect than negative ones.

The goal in acting out the above interactions between the service provider and customer is to go beyond just satisfying the customer. The next step is to bring "delight" to the customer and create loyalty in the interaction process. We have only touched on some of the interaction processes that affect satisfaction.

In closing, while we have laid emphasis on the positive, it is always necessary to remember the negative part of human interaction. When the rendered service cannot fulfill the tourists' expectations and the service provider is rude in their interaction, "you add to the fire" of insult, emotional pain (Gitomer, 2002, p. 28). Such action could adversely affect the chances of future contacts and many more patrons through word-of-mouth communication. Keeping the front-line service employees interacting positively with the customer lies at the heart of ensuring satisfaction in a tourist situation.

REFERENCES

Albrecht, S.L., Chadwick, B.A., and Jacobson, C.K. (1987). Social Psychology. Englewood Cliffs, NJ: Prentice-Hall.

Ashforth, B.E., and Humphrey, R.H. (1993). Emotional Labor in Service Roles: The Influence Identity. *Academy of Management Review*, 18(1, Jan), 88-115.

Baldasare, P.M.,and Mittal,V. (1997). Strategies to Manage Customer Relationships. *Marketing News*, 31(11, May) 6.

Bell, C.R.,and Zemke, R. (1992). *Managing Knock your Socks Off Service*. New York, NY: Amacom.

Berry, L.L. (1995). *On Great Service*. New York, NY: The Free Press.

Connellan, T.K.,and Zemke,R. (1993). *Sustaining Knock Your Socks Off Service*. New York, NY: AMACOM.

Day,G.S.(1999). *The Market Driven Organization*. New York, NY: The Free Press.

Deighton, J. (1994). Managing Services when the Service Is a Performance. In R.T. Rust and R.L.Oliver (Eds). *Service Quality*. Thousand Oaks, CA: Sage Publications.

Desatnick, R.L. (1987). *Managing to Keep the Customer*. San Francisco, CA: Jossey-Bassey Pub.

Ford, W.S.Z. (1998). *Communicating with Customers*. Cresskill, NJ: Hampton Press, Inc.

Furlong, C.B. (1993). *Marketing for Keeps*. New York, NY: John Wiley & Sons, Inc.

Geddes, L.(1993). *Through the Customers' Eyes*. New York, NY: AMACOM.

Gergen, K.J.(1994). *Realities and Relationships*. Cambridge, MA: Harvard University Press.

Gitomer, J. (2000). Great Customer Service Begins with Employees. *Atlanta Business Chronicle* (April 21-27),3B.

Gitomer, J. (2002). What's Wrong with (Your) Customer Service? *Atlanta Business Chronicle* (Oct 4-10), 2B.

Healy,M. (1996). Max Weber's Comeback: Wearing Tropical Hats. *People Management*, (Jan 11), 17.

Heil, G., Parker, T., and Stephens, D.C. (1997). *One Size Fits One*. New York, NY: Van Nostrand Reinhold.

Heskett, J.L., Sasser, E.W., and Schlesinger, L.A. (1997). *The Service Profit Chain*. New York, NY: The Free Press.

Hintz, R.A., and Miller, D.E. (1995). Openings Revisited: The Foundations of Social Interaction. *Symbolic Interaction*, 18(3), 355-369.

Jeschke, K., Schulze, H.S, and Bauersachs, J. (2000). Internal Marketing and Its Consequences for Complaint Handling Effectiveness. In T. Hennig-Thurau and U.Hansen (Eds), *Relationship Marketing*. New York, NY: Springer.

Labone,M. (1996). The Roaring Silence in the Sociology of Leisure. *Social Alternatives*, 15(2), 30-32.

Liljander,V. (2000). The Importance of Internal Relationship Marketing for External Relationship Success. In T. Hennig-thurau and U. Hansen (Eds), *Relationship Marketing*. New York, N.Y.: Springer.

Liswood, L.A. (1990). *Serving Them Right*. New York, NY: Harper Business.

Morisaki, S.,and Gudykunst, W.D. (1994). Face in Japan and the United States. In Ting-Toomey, S (Ed.), *The Challenge of Facework*. Albany, NY: State University of New York Press.

Panter, C.A., and Martin, C.L. (1991). Compatibility Management: Roles in Service Performers. *Journal of Services Marketing* 5(2), 43-53.

Petite, A. (1989). *The Manager's Guide To Service Excellence*. Toronto, Canada: Summerhill Press.

Raucher, S.V. (1997a). Crowne Plaza Hotel Chain to Unveil New TV Ads. *The Atlanta Journal Constitution*. (Jan, 26), H8.

Reichheld, F.F. (2001). *Loyalty Rules*. Boston, MA. Harvard Business School Press.

Sherif, M., and Sherif, C.W. (1969). *Social Psychology*. New York, NY: Harper & Row, Publishers.

Tschohl, J. with Franzmeier, S. (1991). *Achieving Excellence Through Customer Service*. Englewood Cliffs,NJ: Prentice Hall.

Vavra, T.G. (1992). *AFTERMARKETING*. Homewood, IL: Business One Irwin.

Wyer, R.S., and Gruenfeld, D.H. (1995). Information processing in interpersonal communication. In D.E. Hewes (ed.), *The Cognitive Bases of Interpersonal Communication*. Hillsdale, NJ: Lawrence Erlbaum Associates, Publishers.

Zeithaml, V.A., Parasuraman, A. and Berry, L.L. (1990). Delivering Quality Service. New York, NY: The Free Press.

Zeithaml, V.A., and Bitner, M.J. (2000). *Services Marketing*. Boston, MA: Irwin McGraw-Hill.

Identifying the Dimensions
of the Experience Construct:
Development of the Model

Bonnie J. Knutson
Jeffrey A. Beck

SUMMARY. This article proposes a holistic, three phase model structured to incorporate the major components of the Experience construct. While speculation about what constitutes an experience abound, the complex relationship among value, service quality, satisfaction, and experience is in its infancy. Before this relationship can be fully examined, dimensions of these four critical components need to be incorporated into a unified, holistic model that includes the three primary constructs of Service Quality, Value, and Satisfaction. This article focuses on the first challenge by developing a model and offering some propositions to encourage future research about the experience construct in hospitality. *[Article copies available for a fee from The Haworth Document Delivery Service: 1-800-HAWORTH. E-mail address: <docdelivery@haworthpress.com> Website: <http://www.HaworthPress.com> © 2003 by The Haworth Press, Inc. All rights reserved.]*

Bonnie J. Knutson (E-mail: drbonnie@msu.edu) and Jeffrey A. Beck (E-mail: beck@bus.msu.edu) are affiliated with The School of Hospitality Business, Eli Broad College of Business, Michigan State University, East Lansing, MI 48824.

[Haworth co-indexing entry note]: "Identifying the Dimensions of the Experience Construct: Development of the Model." Knutson, Bonnie J., and Jeffrey A. Beck. Co-published simultaneously in *Journal of Quality Assurance in Hospitality & Tourism* (The Haworth Hospitality Press, an imprint of The Haworth Press, Inc.) Vol. 4, No. 3/4, 2003, pp. 23-35; and: *Current Issues and Development in Hospitality and Tourism Satisfaction* (ed: John A. Williams and Muzaffer Uysal) The Haworth Hospitality Press, an imprint of The Haworth Press, Inc., 2003, pp. 23-35. Single or multiple copies of this article are available for a fee from The Haworth Document Delivery Service [1-800-HAWORTH, 9:00 a.m. - 5:00 p.m. (EST). E-mail address: docdelivery@haworthpress.com].

KEYWORDS. Experience, model development, satisfaction, value, axiology, service quality

INTRODUCTION

In 1970, futurist Alvin Toffler (1970) pointed to a paradigm shift that would deeply affect goods and services in the future and would lead to the next forward movement of the economy. Calling it a strange new sector, he named it the experience industries. Three decades later, Pine and Gilmore (1999) echoed his belief by arguing that we have moved out of the service economy and into what they identified as the *experience* economy. Further, they propose that engaging the customer through experiences, rather than just servicing him, is necessary to create value in an increasingly competitive business environment.

Assuming that experience industries will provide the economic momentum for the future, our study takes the first step in identifying and measuring the dimensions of the experience construct. It proposed a model, structured to incorporate the four major components of the consumer's buying process: (1) expectations and perceptions of *Service Quality*, (2) the Customer's *Experience* with the organization, (3) *Value*, and (4) *Satisfaction*.

FOUNDATION FOR THE DEVELOPMENT
OF THE EXPERIENCE MODEL

Experiences. As with the concept of services quality, experience is an elusive and indistinct notion. It is a difficult construct to define, let alone measure, because of its multiple elements and individualized, personal nature. People don't even agree on the definition of the term. For example, the website *Dictionary.com* (2003) defines experience as "the apprehension of an object, thought, or emotion through the senses or mind . . . active participation in events of activities, leading to the accumulation of knowledge or skill . . . an event or a series of events participated in or lived through . . . the totality of such events" (*www.dictionary.com*). Webster (1983), on the other hand, defines it as "an actual living through an event . . . anything observed or lived through . . . all that has happened to one" (p. 644). Putting it into a business context, "experiences occur whenever a company intentionally uses services as the stage and goods as props to engage an individual" (Pine & Gilmore, 1999, p 11). Thus, experience can be infused into a product, used to enhance a service, or created as an entity unto itself. However different these perspectives are, however, there are two common threads that run throughout: First, experiences require involvement or participation by a person. A prospective guest cannot truly experience the breath-taking awe of the Hawaiian shore by sitting in his or her living room looking at a video or a brochure. How often have we tried to describe our rock climbing adventure, the smile on our children's faces when they first saw Mickey Mouse at Disneyland, or the exquisite service given us at a the Waldorf-Astoria? No matter how we try to visualize our experience for others, we end up by saying, "You should have been there." Second, experiences are internal in nature, and therefore individualized. This is what makes experience marketing and management so difficult. Think about the last time you went to a movie with someone. You both sat in the same theater, ate the same popcorn, and saw the same film, yet you each walked out with a totally different experience. This is because each of us–each consumer–is unique. We each bring a different background, values, attitudes and beliefs to the situation; we "experience" it through our individualized "rose colored glasses."

The notion of the experience economy has developed with the convergence of three major forces: (1) new technology to fuel innovative experiences, (2) a more sophisticated, affluent, and demanding consumer base, and (3) escalating competitive intensity. Is it any wonder, then, that experience venues such as Las Vegas theme hotels, eatertainment restaurants like Rain Forest Café, or spas like Canyon Ranch, increasingly populate the hospitality landscape? We even look for experiences in drinking more festive types of coffee.

Experiences are a distinct economic offering, but one that has until recently gone largely unrecognized and unstudied. Pine and Gilmore (1999) point out that there are clear economic distinctions between experiences, and commodities, goods (products), and services. Commodities are fungible materials extracted from nature. As such, they are only differentiated by price, as determined by supply and demand. Businesses use commodities to make and inventory goods, thus adding the ability to differentiate products, and in turn add value. The 1980s was the era of the product or goods economy. The mantra was on customer satisfaction, with zero-defects, quality initiatives, and product innovation at the forefront of business strategy to achieve a competitive advantage (Bell, 2002).

The bar was raised in the 1990s and the focus switched from goods to services. Services are intangible activities customized for individual consumers (Pine and Gilmore, 1999). Providers began wrapping services around their core products, launching the decade of personalized service, customized services, or "customerization" (Bell, 2002). Organizations began using technology to data mart and data mine large amounts of information about the customer–demographics, psychographics, and behavior patterns. And service quality replaced product quality as the strategy for differentiation.

In this first decade of the 21st century, goods and services have moved from being satisfiers to being dissatisfiers. That is, offering quality products and service is no longer enough to establish a competitive advantage. They are expected; they are the price of entry into any market segment. Thus, with the three converging factors previously mentioned in place–technology, more demanding consumers, and increasing competition–we enter the era of the experience economy. "While commodities are fungible, goods tangible, and services intangible, experiences are *memorable*" (Pine & Gilmore, 1999 p. 12). "Companies stage an experience whenever they engage customers, connecting with them in a personal memorable way" (Pine & Gilmore, 1999, p. 3).

Components of Experience. The parameters of an Experience have three stages, encompassing the "events or feelings that occur prior, during, and after participation" (O'Sullivan & Spangler, 1998, p. 23); these stages have been characterized as:

- Pre-experience–The first stage refers to anything and everything involved prior to the actual participation in the experience itself.
- Participation–The second stage refers to the actual involvement in the experience.
- Post-experience–The final stage of an experience is the aftermath of the participation; in other words, "it's not over when it's over" (O'Sullivan & Spangler, 1998, p. 28).

The concept of experiences in consumer activities has been studied, primarily in the retail literature, with most research attention going towards the tangible aspects of the shopping environment (Machleit & Eroglu, 2000; Underhill, 1999; Wakefield, & Blodgett, 1999). In one study, Wirtz and Bateson (1999) see experiences as having two dimensions–pleasure and arousal. In another, Mathwick, Malhotra and Rigdon (2001) develop an experiential value scale that reflects the aspects of playfulness, aesthetics, customer return on investment, and service excellence in the shopping experience. Yet another turns its attention to how well the emotion measures most frequently used in marketing relate to the shoppers' experience (Machleit & Eroglu, 2000).

O'Sullivan and Spangler (1998) have a more complex view of experiences. They see the construct as having multiple facets, which can be measured along a continuum. These facets include real to virtual, novelty or communality, degree of mass-production or customization, and level of interaction with other people. These elements, they claim, provide marketers with a host of options and opportunities.

In recent years, managers have become more aware of the need to create value for their customers in the form of experiences. "Unfortunately, they have often proceeded as if managing experiences simply meant providing entertainment or being engagingly creative" (Berry & Haeckel, 2002, p. 85). Walking through a lobby in a Las Vegas hotel and you can "experience" the ancient Roman forum, the canals of Venice, or the streets of Paris. But an experience is vastly more complex than architecture, décor and costumed employees. Businesses can't rely on these facets alone to provide a compelling guest experience. They must make them a part of a focused comprehensive strategy that manages the guests' journey–"from the expectations they have before the experience occurs to the assessments they are likely to make when it's over" (Berry & Haechel, 2002, p. 85). To manage the journey, an organization must recognize what Berry and Haechel (2002) call "clues," which they define as anything that the customer perceives or senses or recognizes by its absence.

They posit two categories of clues. The first relates to the actual functioning of the good or service and are processed by the logical side of the brain. Did the housekeeper clean the room thoroughly? Was my wake-up call on time? Is my bill correct? When these parts of a hotel stay are working the way they are supposed to, they provide a clue that other aspects of functionality will also be in good working order. As the president of one airline supposedly quipped: If there are coffee rings left on the drop down tray table in the cabin, it tells the passenger that the mechanics are not keeping the engines in good order.

The second category is comprised of emotional clues, which are those emitted by things or people in the environment and are perceived by the senses. The music played in the hotel elevator, the softness of the sheets on the bed, the aroma of freshly-brewed flavored coffee, the color of the marble floor in the lobby, the smile of the front desk staff, and the taste of the grilled steak are examples.

Another study approaches experience components from a different perspective. Mathwick, Malhotra and Rigdon (2001) reason that the value in a consumption experience is derived by interaction involving goods and services. In this vein, they believe that experiential value offers both extrinsic and intrinsic benefits. Whereas extrinsic benefit is usually derived from buying experiences that are utilitarian in nature (such as an errand), intrinsic value is derived from the appreciation of the experience itself (such as a theatrical performance).

Holbrook (1994) adds an activity dimension to the experience concept. He notes that, in a consumption experience, the customer can either be active or passive. The more active or participative the consumer is, the higher the collaboration between the consumer and the marketing entity. This proposition suggests that the typology of experiential value can be divided into four quadrants that are built on two axes: Intrinsic/extrinsic on one axis and active/reactive on the other (Mathwick et al, 2001).

Proposition 1: The environment in which the product or service is delivered will have an effect on value, level of engagement, emotional bond, degree of participation, and amount of stimulation of an experience.

While the physical surroundings and other sensory stimulations are certainly part of the environment, we would argue that behavior by both the consumer and the supplier are likewise part of the sensory environment. In fact, their interaction can set the tone for the environment. For example, if you're having a business dinner meeting in a fine dining restaurant, the tone of the physical environment, as well as your interaction with the serving staff, would be different than if you were having a romantic anniversary dinner with your spouse at the same table. We would identify this interaction component as a kinesthetic clue. Thus, the total environment in which the product or service is delivered will have an effect on value, level of engagement, emotional bond, degree of participation, and amount of stimulation of an experience.

The literature points to the fact that retailers are redefining themselves as a source of memories, rather than a product or service provider. The brick-and-mortar segment is being transformed into "retail interactive theater," with Nike Town, the American Girl (Chicago), and the Geek Squad (Minneapolis) serving as examples. As businesses grapple with the complex demands of staging experiential shopping environments, they need to remember that the buying experience must also deliver value if it is to turn a one-time shopper into a loyal customer. Thus, the full range of components that defined experience-based value should be identified and measured and the relationship between service quality and experience requires attention (Cronin & Taylor, 1992).

Proposition 2: The degree of complexity in interacting with the product or service will have an effect on the value of an experience.

Providing the "right" number of choices of a product or service, balanced by the "right" variety of choices adds value to the experience. For instance, the Cheesecake Factory provides a large menu of cheesecakes, yet the variety offered makes the mere selection off the menu part of the experience of visiting a Cheesecake Factory. Complexity does not imply that simple is better, however. A product or service may be quite complex, but as long as it does not add stress to the experience, value is still perceived.

Axiology as the Foundation. Customer value has long been seen as a foundation of marketing. To better understand the relationship between the two, researchers often turn to the Value Theory, or axiology. Axiology is the study of preferential behavior (Morris, 1964).[1] In consumption, value is "an interactive relativistic preference experience . . . [in which the] value attaches to an *experience* and pertains not to the acquisition of an object but rather to the consumption of its *services*. (i.e., its usage or appreciation)" (Holbrook, 1994, pp. 27-28).

This supports Pine and Gilmore's (1999) notion that experiences are internal while commodities, goods, and services are external to the consumer. They also contend that businesses need to engage the customer through experiences in order to create value. This engagement aspect corresponds to Holbrook's (1994) point about active or passive participation by the consumer.

Proposition 3: The degree of personalization that the product or service delivers to the consumer will have an effect on the intrinsic value of an experience.

Personalization in this case does not necessarily mean using the customer's name (which certainly is important), but is an authentic service offering that matches what the customer needs at that moment. Personalization also may allow the customer more control over the service interaction. Service that reflects the personality of the consumer adds to the intrinsic value of the experience.

Table 1 summarizes the components of the consumption experience as outlined in the previous section.

PROPOSED MODEL

While speculation about what constitutes an experience abounds, the complex relationship among value, service quality, satisfaction, and experience is in its infancy (Cronin & Taylor, 1992). Before this relationship can be fully examined, however, dimensions of these four critical components need to be (1) incorporated into a unified, holistic model that envelopes the three primary constructs of Service Quality, Value, and Satisfaction, and (2) identified and measured. This article focuses on the first challenge.

TABLE 1. Summary of Components of the Experience Consumption

Authors	Year	Components
Berry & Haeckel	2002	Functional–Emotional
Mathwick, Malhotra & Rigdon	2001	Extrinsic–Intrinsic
Wirtz & Bateson	1999	Pleasure–Arousal
Pine & Gilmore	1999	Absorption–Immersion
O'Sullivan & Spangler	1998	Real–Virtual Novelty–Communality Mass-produced–Customized Interaction with others–Alone
Holbrook	1994	Active–Passive

After reviewing nearly 600 articles looking for connections, correlations, or relationships among the four constructs listed in the previous paragraph, we have developed the proposed Experience Model shown in Figure 1.

Following the lead of O'Sullivan and Spangler (1999), our model has three distinct parts.

Part 1. The first can be considered the "pre-experience" stage of the consumption process and encompasses the expectations established by brand position, promotional activities of the organization, word of mouth (radial) advertising, and personal memories that have been "banked" from previous experience. Using Zeithaml, Parasuraman and Berry's (1990) archetype, expectations set the foundation for this pre-experience stage. Expectations are also the underpinning of the service quality construct. In developing SERVQUAL, Zeithaml et al. (1990) found that service quality is composed of five dimensions: Reliability, Assurance, Responsiveness, Tangibles, and Empathy and can be reliably measured via a pair of 22-item surveys–one for expectations, and one for perceptions. While some researchers have questioned the "gap theory" used to build SERVQUAL, it stands as a widely-used hallmark of service quality. With its pre- post-concept, this measure is a fitting element in our proposed model. The expectations that the consumer has about the product or service will have an effect on the value, level of engagement, emotional bond, degree of participation, and amount of stimulation of an experience.

Proposition 4: The expectations that the consumer has about the product or service will have an effect on the value, level of engagement, emotional bond, degree of participation, and amount of stimulation of an experience.

Part 2. The second part is the heart of the model; it is also the focus of our study. It represents the guest's actual real-time experience and includes *all* encounters throughout the journey with the organization. In the case of a hotel, this would include everything from booking the reservation (online, directly with the hotel's reservation staff, or through a central reservation system), through the actual stay, to the billing. The model illustrates the directional relationship between the various sets of experience characteristics suggested in the literature and listed in Table 1. On a secondary input level, it also includes service quality since this construct has been defined as having five components with a directional relationship to the overall experience.

Proposition 5: The degree of accessibility with the product or service will have an effect on the value of an experience.

Accessibility in the context of an experience relates to the cost, delivery, and availability of the product or service at the moment the customer wishes to purchase. It includes the speed at which the delivery takes place, the timeliness of the delivery, and the location of delivery. While complexity of the experi-

FIGURE 1

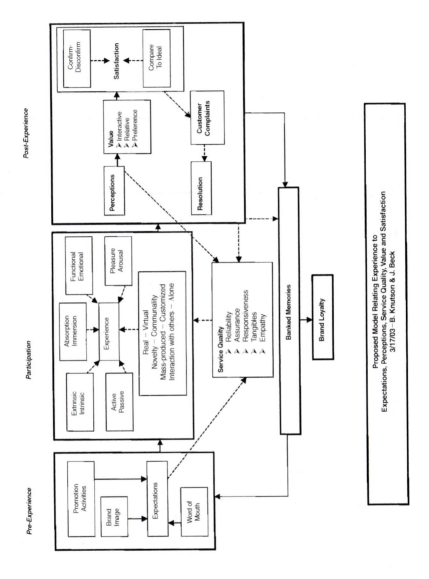

Proposed Model Relating Experience to
Expectations, Perceptions, Service Quality, Value and Satisfaction
3/17/03 – B. Knutson & J. Beck

ence focuses on the product or service offering, accessibility connotes the amount of hassle involved in acquiring the product or service.

Part 3. The third part of the model represents the "post-experience" or evaluative portion. It includes the guests' personal perceptions (second half of the service quality construct) of the experience, the value they place on the experience and their satisfaction with the experience. Value has been defined by relative preferences and can be measured by degree of preference (Holbrook, 1994). While researchers have developed a myriad of satisfaction measures, we find that the American Customer Satisfaction Index (ACSI) best fits our proposed model. The ACSI is a valid national economic indicator of customer evaluations of the quality of goods and services in the US and fits well into this model.[2] It is a weighted index of three imbedded components: (1) Overall Satisfaction, (2) Expectancy-Disconfirmation, which measures the degree to which the guest's expectation fell short or exceeded his or her expectations, and (3) Comparison to an Ideal, which measures how close the experienced product compares with the ideal product.

On a secondary level, the third part of the model also takes in customer complaints and their resolution on a feedback loop to the entire experience encounter.

Proposition 6: The utility of the product or service will have an effect on value and emotional bond of the experience.

At this point, the product or service must fit the purpose for which it was designed and for which it was purchased by the consumer. Product and service performance, capabilities, and esthetics are part of the utility experience. Going to the local 'hole in the wall' diner is likely to create an emotional bond in the context of the service performance and interactive nature of the environment.

Feedback Loop. As with most interactive models, the Experience Model we are proposing contains a feedback loop from Satisfaction (in Part 3 of the model) to Expectations (in Part 1 of the model). This mechanism we call Banked Memories. Service encounters have been likened to deposits and withdrawal for a bank account. If the encounter is positive, a "deposit" is made into the memory bank; if the encounter is negative, a "withdrawal" is made. The balance is what is left as a banked memory, which then affects expectations.

RESEARCH OPPORTUNITY

There is a business axiom that says: "You cannot manage what you cannot measure." Assuming this to be true, and accepting the notion that the Experience Economy is the future of the hospitality industry, we have to have a valid, reliable method for measuring what is meant by an *Experience*. Given the pace at which themed venues–ranging from restaurants like Rainforest Café to exotic hotels like the Venetian in Las Vegas–are opening, such a measure becomes increasingly critical. Before that can happen, however, researchers must reach two milestones. First, they must develop an Experience model that encompasses the major components of the Experience construct. Second, they must identify the dimensions (factors) that are embedded in this construct.

In this article, we take an initial step in reaching these goals. We offer an interactive model of the Experience Construct that incorporates three key elements: (1) Service Quality, (2) Value, and (3) Satisfaction. Each of these elements has been the subject of extensive research designed to uncover their underlying dimensions, as shown in Table 2, as well as illustrated in the model.

By extracting the embedded factors, researchers have given us tools by which each of these three constructs can be and have been measured. Thus, they can be managed. To date, however, the dimensions of the experience construct have not been extracted–only assumed. This model is designed to take the first step in rectifying this situation. While the literature suggests various sets of "clues" (refer to Table 1) for an experience, these clues have not been subjected to empirical research. Only through rigorous study can they be validated, refuted, or modified as dimensions of the experience construct. We hope this model is the impetus for such research.

If the experience factors can be extracted, identified and measured, much like Zeithaml et al. (1990) were able to do for service quality, the fourth piece of the holistic model will be in place and we will be able to calculate the relationship among these various components. This will give us a clearer understanding of guests' decision-making process relative to their hospitality purchases. It will

TABLE 2. Summary of Dimensions of the Three Primary Constructs Included in the Experience Model

Construct	Dimensions
Service Quality (Zeithmal et al., 1990)	Reliability Assurance Responsiveness Tangibles Empathy
Value (Holbrook, 1994)	Relativity Preference
Satisfaction (Fornell et al., 1998)	Overall Satisfaction Confirm-Disconfirm Comparison to Ideal

likewise provide management with additional direction for managing the guest's experience.

DIRECTIONS FOR FUTURE RESEARCH

The proposed experience model is a conceptual framework advanced from over 600 articles, a nomothetic approach to marketing theory development. We believe this model offers an ample agenda for further research.

- For example, a pilot study should be conducted to further develop and/or refine the experience model and begin to identify constructs appropriate to hospitality service experiences. This research will help to test those relationships proposed in the holistic model as well as uncover additional differences based on the type of experience.
- The experience model has its foundations in the theory of axiology, therefore we must, as Holbrook (1994) put it, concentrate on the value of the experience based on the macro service delivery system. The challenge will be to devise methods for measuring experiences in a standardized fashion. The experience model offers some potential relationships between value and experience.
- Another task for researchers is to identify the link between service quality and experience as well as between satisfaction and experience. In the experience model, we acknowledge the contribution of SERVQUAL and the ACSI. But the degree to which service quality and/or satisfaction influence the experience has not been clearly established.
- The concept of 'banked memories' requires further exploration too. Research is needed to explore the links between memories of earlier service experiences and the current one.
- Finally, if we view this model holistically, it must eventually be tested holistically. The model we have offered incorporates several well-known and well-tested constructs with confirmed dimensions. We don't know, however, what happens with these constructs or with their dimensions when taken together. In other words, what is the effect of the interaction of each construct/factor on every other construct/factor? For example, will totally new dimensions be found? If so, of which items will each be comprised? What will be the relationship among them? These are just a few of the questions that will need to be answered before we can fully understand this thing called an "experience."

We invite hospitality researchers, both nationally and internationally, to join us in this quest.

NOTES

1. For a more in-depth discussion of Value Theory and Customer Value, see M. Holbrook, "The Nature of Customer Value" in *Service Quality: New Directions in Theory and Practice,"* R. Rust and R Oliver (Eds.) Sage, Thousand Oaks, CA. 1994.

2. For a more detailed description of the ACSI, see ACSI Methodology Report (Fornell, Bryant, Cha, Johnson, Anderson and Ettlie, 1998) or visit the ACSI website at *http://www.theacsi.org*

REFERENCES

Bell, Chip R. (2002) In pursuit of obnoxiously devoted customers. *Business Horizons,* March/April 45 (2), 13.

Berry, Leonard L. & Haeckel, Stephan H. (2002) Managing the Total Customer Experience. *MIT Sloan Management Review,* 43 (3), 85-89.

Cronin, J. Joseph, Jr. & Taylor, Steven A. (1992) Measuring service quality: A reexamination and extension. *Journal of Marketing,* 56 (3), 55-68 *www.Dictionary.com* (2003) 21 February 2003.

Holbrook, Morris B. (1994) The nature of customer value: An axiology of services in the consumption experience, in *Service Quality: How Consumers View Stores and Merchandise,* Jacob Jacoby and Jerry C. Olson (Eds). Lexington Books. Lexington, MA. Pp. 21-71.

Machleit, Karen A., Eroglu, Sevgin A. (2000) Describing and measuring emotional response to shopping experience. *Journal of Business Research,* 49 (2), 101-111.

Mathwick, Charla, Malhotra, Naresh & Rigdon, Edward. (2001) Experiential value: Conceptualization, measurement and application in the catalog and Internet shopping environment. *Journal of Retailing,* 77 (1), 3-56.

McKechnie, Jean L. (ed) (1983). *Webster's New Universal Unabridged Dictionary.* Simon & Schuster, New York.

Morris. C. (1964) *Signification and significance.* MIT Press. Cambridge, MA.

O'Sullivan, E.L. & Spangler, K.J. (1998). *Experience Marketing: Strategies for the New Millennium.* State College, PA: Venture Publishing.

Pine, Joseph II & Gilmore, James H. (1999) *The Experience Economy.* Harvard Business School Press. Boston, Massachusetts.

Toffler, Alvin. (1970) *Future Shock.* (1980) Random House. New York.

Underhill, Paco. (1999) *Why we buy: The science of shopping.* Simon & Schuster. New York.

Wakefield, Kirk L., Blodgett, Jeffrey G. (1999) Customer response to intangible and tangible service factors. *Psychology and Marketing,* 16 (1) 51-68.

Wirtz, Jochen & Bateson, John E.G. (1999) Customer satisfaction with services: Integrating the environment perspective in services marketing into the traditional disconfirmation paradigm. *Journal of Business Research,* 44 (1) 55-66.

Zeithaml, Valarie A., Parasuraman, A. & Berry, Leonard L. (1990) *Delivering Quality Service.* The Free Press. New York.

Limitations of Cross-Cultural Customer Satisfaction Research and Recommending Alternative Methods

Metin Kozak
Enrique Bigné
Luisa Andreu

SUMMARY. Cross-cultural research in tourism is receiving increasing attention from academics. Little, however, has been done with regard to the assessment of cultural differences in tourist satisfaction. Research in tourism marketing has recognized the need for further research in cross-cultural satisfaction research, and specifically, in equivalence issues regarding the measurement of tourist satisfaction. Consequently, the aim of this conceptual paper is to focus attention on the importance of exploring cross-cultural differences in customer satisfaction research. The principal contributions are three-fold: (1) to emphasize the significance of exploring cross-cultural differences while attempting to measure customer satisfac-

Metin Kozak is affiliated with Mugla University, School of Tourism and Hotel Management, 48000 Mugla, Turkey (E-mail: M.Kozak@superonline.com).

Enrique Bigné (E-mail: Enrique.Bigne@uv.es) and Luisa Andreu (E-mail: Luisa.Andreu@uv.es) are affiliated with the University of Valencia, Faculty of Business and Economy Studies, Department of Marketing, Avda. dels Tarongers s/n, 46022 Valencia, Spain.

Address correspondence to Metin Kozak at the above address.

[Haworth co-indexing entry note]: "Limitations of Cross-Cultural Customer Satisfaction Research and Recommending Alternative Methods." Kozak, Metin, Enrique Bigné, and Luisa Andreu. Co-published simultaneously in *Journal of Quality Assurance in Hospitality & Tourism* (The Haworth Hospitality Press, an imprint of The Haworth Press, Inc.) Vol. 4, No. 3/4, 2003, pp. 37-59; and: *Current Issues and Development in Hospitality and Tourism Satisfaction* (ed: John A. Williams and Muzaffer Uysal) The Haworth Hospitality Press, an imprint of The Haworth Press, Inc., 2003, pp. 37-59. Single or multiple copies of this article are available for a fee from The Haworth Document Delivery Service [1-800-HAWORTH, 9:00 a.m. - 5:00 p.m. (EST). E-mail address: docdelivery@haworthpress.com].

37

tion in tourism, (2) to recommend alternative research methodology to analyse cross-cultural tourist satisfaction, and also (3) to point out limitations of conducting cross-cultural research in tourist satisfaction from both the theoretical and practical point of view. *[Article copies available for a fee from The Haworth Document Delivery Service: 1-800-HAWORTH. E-mail address: <docdelivery@haworthpress.com> Website: <http://www.HaworthPress. com> © 2003 by The Haworth Press, Inc. All rights reserved.]*

KEYWORDS. Tourism marketing, cross-cultural research, tourist satisfaction, construct development, research methodology

INTRODUCTION

During the last few decades, measuring customer satisfaction (CS) has acquired a noticeable importance in academic marketing publications (e.g., Churchill and Surprenant 1982; Fornell 1992; Oliver 1980, 1981, 1993). But this interest is not exclusively academic, as many companies have begun to appreciate CS as a key variable for gaining a competitive advantage (Honomichl 1993). The importance of studying and understanding CS is principally based on the impact of this variable on brand loyalty (Cronin and Taylor 1992; Oliver 1999), and word-of-mouth communication (Oliver 1997). Monitoring tourist satisfaction (TS) can provide invaluable feedback for detecting problems that cause dissatisfaction with holidays and have negative impact on future visitation (Baker and Crompton 2000; Bigné, Font and Andreu 2000; Reisinger and Turner 2003).

Studying the topic of multicultural research in tourism is pertinent because it is an international industry characterised as unique in terms of the service delivery. Specifically, consumption is made in a foreign destination and different tourists are acting as consumers in the same destination and time. Based on the World Tourism Organization (WTO), tourism has emerged as one of the most relevant sectors on a world level, as it is the major source of wealth in a number of countries (WTO 1997). Statistics provided by the WTO emphasize the economic significance of tourism at the global level (WTO 2003). Furthermore, the necessity of studying cross-cultural research emerges from the notion that people in different cultures may develop different norms regarding various similar objects, e.g., hotels, tourist destinations, or subjects, e.g., beliefs, attitudes (Messick 1988). Therefore, a key challenge for tourism businesses and destinations is to effectively deal with the structure of heterogeneity in consumer needs and wants around the globe and to target segments of consumers in different countries. Destination authorities working with heterogeneous tourist markets really need to deal with cross-cultural research and consider its management and marketing implications.

Studying cross-cultural research in any field or discipline helps to assess the generalizability of empirical findings, assess if the findings differ from one cluster to another and understand the behaviour of people living in a different culture (Costa and Bamossy 1995). Cultural differences are especially relevant to the tourism industry (Reisinger and Turner 2003). In the tourism environment, cultural differences have been analysed, for instance, in the vacation travel preference (Richardson and Crompton 1988), destination image (Kozak, Bigné, González and Andreu 2003), vacation travel patterns (Sussman and Rashcovsky 1997), service quality (Weiermair 2000), information sources (Chen and Gursoy 2000), tourist motivations (Kozak 2002), and many others. Little, however, has been done with regard to the assessment of cultural differences in TS. Culture determines expectations and perceptions of service quality that, in turn, determine satisfaction with tourism services and tourism destinations (Reisinger and Turner 2003).

Research in tourism marketing has recognized the need for further research in cross-cultural satisfaction research, and specifically, in equivalence issues regarding the measurement of TS. The aim of this conceptual paper is to focus attention on the importance of exploring cross-cultural differences in CS research. Specifically, the objectives are three-fold: (1) emphasize the significance of exploring cross-cultural differences while attempting to measure CS in tourism, (2) suggest alternative methods for practical use in carrying-out a comparative study, and also (3) point out limitations of conducting cross-cultural research from both the theoretical and practical point of view. This study is based upon a conceptual discussion of recommending cross-cultural methodology on the basis of quantitative data to be obtained from structured interviews because this is the most frequently used and a useful method in undertaking cross-cultural research (Pareek and Rao 1980).

THEORETICAL BACKGROUND

As national culture–even though there is not only one–is expected to influence one's behaviour, attitudes, motivations, perceptions, needs, expectations, norms and beliefs, it becomes vital to investigate the possible existence of differences between subjects from different cultural backgrounds; and if any difference exists, then to segment them in terms of their culture represented in a community (Kim, Prideaux and Kim 2002). Cross-cultural research includes studies of subjects from various cultures who have different experiences and significant differences in behaviour. This brings about the importance of a search for cause (culture) and effect (behaviour) relationships. Berry (1980) reports that cross-cultural research finds its roots in the two special approaches in linguistics of *phonemics* and *phonetics*. The former examines movements only in one culture. The latter looks at many cultures and compares the results. The term 'cross-cultural' encompasses both approaches: 'cultural' is similar to the meaning of the phonemic and 'cross' is similar to that of the phonetic.

Cultural Differences

The analysis of cultural differences indicates that there are a very large number of dimensions that differ between cultural groups. Hofstede (1980, 1991) identifies notably three dimensions of national culture that can be related to consumer buying behavior: individualism-collectivism, uncertainty avoidance, and masculinity-femininity. These dimensions are widely accepted and are used by many marketing researchers to locate and compare countries (e.g., Lynn, Zinkhan, and Harris 1993; Dawar and Parker 1994; Roth 1995). Individualists and collectivists have been shown to differ significantly in self-expression and social relationships, and such differences influence the efficacy of marketing strategies (Han and Shavitt 1994). Individualism measures the degree to which people in a country prefer to act as individuals rather than as members of a group. People in individualistic societies place their personal goals, motivations, and desires ahead of those of the in-group (Kagitcibasi 1997). In collectivist countries, there is a close-knit social structure, in which people expect their group to care for them in exchange for unwavering loyalty. In general, collectivist cultures are mostly Eastern countries, and individualist cultures are mostly Western countries (Hofstede 1980). From other view, Lodge (1990) further classifies the US as an exemplar of the individualistic ideology, and Germany along with France as more collectivist countries.

In designing marketing research, nation and culture have been used as if they were synonymous, with national boundaries separating one culture group from another. In other words, the country is often used as a substitute for the culture, even though it is an imperfect one (Inkeles and Levinson 1969; Clark 1990; Nakata and Sivakumar 1996). Rarely have more specific definitions of culture been used, nor has domestic cultural heterogeneity been considered. In essence, such studies should be labelled cross-national rather than cross-cultural. The development of effective marketing strategies that are sensitive to cultural differences across countries is of considerable importance for success in the global world.

A cross-cultural analysis requires a systematic comparison of similarities and differences in values, ideas, attitudes, symbols and so on (Engel and Blackwell 1982). Thus, the possible differences could occur in subjective or qualitative measures (e.g., level of tourist satisfaction or tourist motivation) and objective or quantitative measures (e.g., tourist expenditure or length of stay). The proposition is consistent with the findings of previous research in the tourism and hospitality fields and a reflection of the lack of sufficient research considering cross-cultural differences among a particular organisation's customers and between those visiting other competitor organisations. Karlof and Ostblom (1993), in a benchmarking research project, draw attention to the attempts to distinguish different markets if the organisation (or destination) serves more than one market.

Cross-Cultural Research in Tourism

From an academic view, conducting cross-cultural studies in tourism has both its supporters and its critics. On the one hand, proponents like Pizam (1999) show that this type of research can be justified, as a great deal of evidence suggests that nationality influences tourist behaviour. Others like Plog (1990) have pointed to a dearth of research related to the cultural differences and similarities of tourists, and have suggested that the rapid globalisation of the tourist phenomenon and its international nature warrants a better understanding of the global tourist. Critics, on the other hand, like Dann (1993) highlight the limitations of using nationality and country of residence as segmentation variables in tourism research. They both suggest that tourism is now well and truly a global phenomenon and destination societies are not culturally uniform.

Despite the criticisms, it is clear from a literature review that cross-cultural research in tourism has recently received increasing attention from academics (Hudson and Ritchie 2001; McGuiggan and Foo 2002). After all, one of the purposes for doing cross-cultural research is to explore other cultures, learn about them, and to test cultural differences in tourism marketing contexts. In today's developing global management and marketing approach, what is happening in one culture may not be so important, without direct correspondence to other cultures. Additionally, it is well known that, based upon products offered, one particular destination may attract customers from different nationalities. The investigation of potential cross-cultural differences and similarities between various customer groups representing different cultures in tourism visiting a particular destination is important for destination management to learn the profile of its customers, their values, preferences and behaviour, and to implement effective positioning and market segmentation strategies which are appropriate for each market (Reisinger and Turner 2003). From the local residents' point of view, members of one community can learn from other cultures about what or how they are doing and can learn that culture may not be uniform when differences are observed.

A tourist destination attracts customers from different cultures and countries, so tourists might be more or less satisfied or might have different motivations or different expenditure patterns depending on the countries from which they originate (Reisinger and Turner 2003). The analysis of customer surveys sought to investigate whether any cross-cultural differences in tourists' perceived satisfaction levels with their holiday experiences at the same destination, their motivations and expenditure levels is important to the decision-making process of destination managers regarding the implementation of destination management and marketing strategies which are appropriate for each market, e.g., positioning and market segmentation (Ryan 1995). Those who come from other main generating countries therefore need to be included in comparison research. However, it is not clear what action to take when one group perceives a set of attributes to be better or has stronger motivations than another.

A number of empirical studies have sought to explore the similarities and differences between multiple groups in relation to several vacation travel patterns and attitudes towards the selected destinations (Richardson and Crompton 1988; Pizam and Sussmann 1995; Sussmann and Rashcovsky 1997). The findings of the past research confirmed that tourist perceptions of a destination or hospitality businesses or their satisfaction levels, motivations, demographic profiles and the activities in which they participated during their stay may vary according to countries of origin (Choi and Chu 2000; Mattila 2000; Kozak 2001, 2002). Despite this, past destination research in tourist satisfaction is limited to homogeneous sample populations and sample destinations. Sampling respondents represent only one country and those tourists visiting only one destination. The comparative analysis of tourist satisfaction measures may help to reinforce the validity and generalisation of the findings and may also assist destination authorities to establish the positioning strategies and explore their core competencies for each group.

In an effort to classify the methods used when carrying out cross-cultural research, Pizam and his colleagues categorize two types of studies: indirect and direct studies. The first, 'the indirect method,' refers to how 'outsiders' such as local residents, tour guides or entrepreneurs see tourists or, in other words, how they perceive differences in the behaviour of tourists across various nationalities. The other, 'the direct method,' aims at exploring whether any differences exist in the behaviour, values or satisfaction levels of tourists representing different nationalities and therefore reflects tourists' opinions about themselves or their experiences. In general, researchers have previously employed both methods.

On the one hand, a review of indirect studies supports the proposition that national cultures have a moderating effect on tourist behaviour, although the research is based on subjective perceptions. On the other hand, other research is developed by means of direct methods of cross-cultural comparison research. This type of research explores the similarities and differences between multiple groups in relation to several vacation travel patterns, tourist satisfaction, tourist motivation and image perceptions of the selected destinations. Overall, direct studies have tended to focus on information sources used by travellers, destination choice, tourist expectations, and benefits received. The resulting data from all these studies reveal cultural differences that provide theoretical support for expanded research in the area of cross-cultural behaviour in tourism.

Concerns on Undertaking Cross-Cultural Research

Cross-cultural comparison studies ensure that customers visiting different organisations or destinations are homogeneous in terms of their socio-demographic and socio-economic characteristics as well as in terms of motivations, purchasing behaviour and loyalty. However, this is unlikely, in other words, one customer group shopping from one organisation will not necessarily be in the same category as another shopping at a different organisation. This argument has been underestimated within the related literature. Using an example from a destination comparison study, it is not reasonable to expect that tourists visiting Italy are the same as those visiting Greece or that both destinations attract similar markets.

There are a limited number of studies focusing upon the topic of cross-cultural comparison research in tourism either from the theoretical or practical point of view (e.g., Dimanche 1994; Becker and Murrmann 2000; Kozak 2000). Of a few researchers, Becker and Murrmann (2000) drew attention to the limitations of carrying out such an empirical study: equivalence, instrument development, sampling, and data analysis. In an attempt to develop a tourism-benchmarking model using two sample destinations and two sample tourist populations, Kozak (2000) identified various differences in terms of such topics as motivations, satisfaction, and spending. He also emphasised the major points of comparison as well as cross-cultural studies. A brief review of selected issues that are often neglected in cross-cultural research is given below (see Table 1).

Attitude scales including satisfaction and image measurement among different tourists' origins cannot be evaluated by playing with the scores as numbers are just symbols indicating the direction of scales for each item (from negative to positive or vice versa). It may be impossible to reach a conclusion

TABLE 1. Issues in Cross-Cultural Research

Researchers	Issues
Pareek and Rao (1980)	Subjective values depending on tourists' values and perceptions
Czepiel, Rosenberg and Akerele (1974)	Satisfaction scales measure a static position ("temporal satisfaction"
Samovar and Porter (1991); Warwick and Osherson (1973)	Structure of language and the meaning of words
Samovar and Porter (1991)	Cultural, social interactions, legislative and geographical differences
Messick (1988)	Misleading to view cultural differences exclusively as differences between people rather than differences between the institutions, norms or expectations
Crompton and Love 1995; Westbrook and Newman 1978	Different holiday-taking behaviour

by multiplying or dividing scale values (Moser and Kalton 1971; Hair, Anderson, Tatham and Black 1995). The interpretation of the strength of a scale, for example 'good,' could vary from one tourist to another. One person's feeling could be weaker or stronger than another's (Pareek and Rao 1980). As tourist opinions are not fixed, changes in people's values and perceptions are evident over time (Mayo and Jarvis 1981). This is defined in the marketing literature as 'temporal satisfaction' (Czepiel, Rosenberg and Akerele 1974).

In a reference to the difficulty of comparison research, Deutscher (1973) claims that the structure of language and the meaning of words in two different cultures or nationalities can be different. Warwick and Osherson (1973) further suggest that what is important to one nationality may be less important to another or not important at all. Matsumoto, Grissom and Dinnel (2001: 478) note that "statistically significant differences in culture may or may not mean/ reflect the existence of practically important differences between people of different cultures." With reference to the above statement, there appears to be a problem in collecting the right kind of information upon which destination/s are to be compared, what dimensions/elements are to be taken into account and the difficulty of implementing findings because of the cultural, social interactions, legislative and geographical differences (Samovar and Porter 1991). Thus, results obtained and assessed by using methods such as gap analysis and using the same set of questions in the survey instrument could still be problematic and superficial in a comparative research activity.

The different holiday-taking behaviour of two nationalities could influence the findings of cross-cultural comparison surveys (Kozak 2001). In other words, measuring the extent of tourists' first-hand experiences with several facilities, activities and services is limited in a cross-cultural comparison study. One group stays in a hotel with full board while another stays in a self-catering apartment.

One has to use the hotel restaurant; another has to choose a restaurant outside or prepare something themselves. Or the two groups take holidays of different lengths. Or one group has more repeat visits than another. One might speculate that the level of TS may be coloured by their past experiences and, as a result, either higher or lower satisfaction scores might appear in comparison with those of first-time tourists (Westbrook and Newman 1978; Crompton and Love 1995). All these propositions may signal an imbalance or unequal distribution of tourist experiences or observations regarding where they stayed.

It is probably easier to record cross-cultural differences than it is to prove that this is because of cultural differences. It is not easy to define the term 'culture.' Is it something to define samples of subjects from different cultural categories of different countries/nations? It is evident to see differences among people even in the same nation or country. Messick (1988: 47) underlines that "it may be misleading to view cultural differences exclusively as differences between people rather than differences between the institutions, norms or expectations that elicit different behaviour patterns. The question of why different cultures have different norms and institutions is an interesting question, but is a question that falls more into the domain of history and anthropology than social psychology."

Despite the numerous number of studies attempting to empirically investigate if culture is really a predictor of possible differences between people from different nations or countries, a few concerns still exist. Although the results of past research are successful to identify differences between the two groups for various items, they fail (1) to justify whether such differences really exist as a result of culture or any other potential reasons might become a predictor of such differences; (2) to control the inclusion of statistical tests to check if the sample population is homogeneous in terms of the demographic characteristics; and (3) to follow a well-designed research methodology applicable for cross-cultural comparison studies.

UNDERTAKING CROSS-CULTURAL 'CS' RESEARCH

Cross-cultural research has paid much attention to comparability of data and results across cultures, nations, regions, sub-cultures, groups, time, language and other cultural dimensions. According to Bhalla and Lin (1987), in order to provide precise comparisons and strengthen research comparability, marketing researchers must establish equivalence of constructs and measures across cultures. Therefore, in a cross-cultural investigation, research equivalence is an important issue because it enables us to argue that differences and similarities in results are caused by actual differences in two cultures, and not disparity in used methods (Sekaran 1983; Hui and Triandis 1985; Craig and Douglas 2000).

The literature consistently suggests that, while carrying out a methodology of cross-cultural research, four kinds of equivalence need to be demonstrated in order to provide dimensional identity (Warwick and Osherson 1973; Singh 1995; Vanltemert, Baerweldt and Vermande 2001): functional, conceptual, construct, and measurement. The first three categories need to be established before the data are collected or in the stage of designing research, e.g., development of questions and scales. On the other hand, it is the feature of metric equivalence to be established once the data are collected and analysed (see Figure 1). In short, a valid comparison demands adopting universal concepts and methods from other disciplines or demonstrating the equivalence of concepts and data across groups. As a consequence, the theory of equivalencies in the context of quantitative research (e.g., Davis, Douglas and Silk 1981) offers important issues to consider in building a methodology of cross-cultural CS research.

Functional Equivalence

Cultural differences in needs and expectations may cause problems, generate misunderstanding, and affect perceptions, and post-purchase evaluation (Pizam and Ellis 1999). The provision of functional equivalence is regarded as an initial condition of cross-cultural comparison research. Cross-cultural research needs to prove clear evidence of functional equivalence, e.g., referring to the same meaning, using simple wording, and appropriate item contents. In other words, it is necessary to make crystal clear that the focal concept or construct serves the same function in different nations. Hui and Triandis (1985) distinguish functional equivalence from conceptual equivalence. For them functional equivalence means "similarity between the goals of the two behaviours." Cultural differences in needs and expectations may cause problems, generate misunderstanding, and affect perceptions, and post-purchase evaluation (Pizam and Ellis 1999).

Applied to the tourism context, there are many reasons, sometimes differing between nationalities, which affect what tourists want from a particular destination. Each group of customers might have a different set of expectations, needs and wants as a reflection of their culture (Dimanche 1994). There may be no major problem for measures such as the level of language communication or the availability of facilities; but there may be differences between how two different nationalities perceive the overall cleanliness and the level of prices. Therefore, based on the functional equivalence criteria, "overall cleanliness" and "the level of prices" need to be rewritten and be more precise in their wording. An alternative method for measuring those items is the use of

FIGURE 1. Equivalence Issues in Cross-Cultural Research

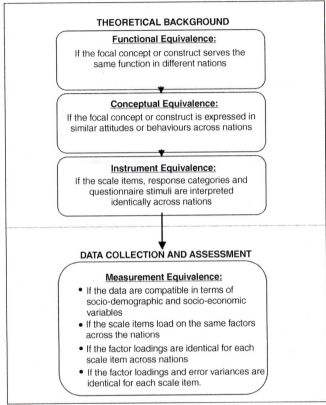

Source: Adapted from Singh 1994: 605.
Source: Own elaboration from the related literature.

scenarios or more detailed items and, therefore, going further into the interviewers' culture and evaluate the level of satisfaction in different situations. An additional method focuses on the comparison with the tourist country-of-origin or with reference to another visited tourist destination.

Conceptual Equivalence

The next issue in cross-cultural research is to determine whether the concepts used mean the same in different cultures. Conceptual equivalence means that concepts used in two different cultures can be meaningfully discussed in these cultures (Hui and Triandis 1985). Conceptual equivalence does not mean that concepts used in the study have exactly the same meaning in both cultures, but the same concept may have different aspects in different cultures, even if it serves the same purpose in several cultures (Brislin 1993). For example, the meaning of television is not alike in different cultures. In one culture, television is considered a means of information and entertainment, whereas in another it is a centre for social activities (Gould and Wong 2000). Applied to the tourism context, the tourist-host contact is perceived differently depending on cultural groups. In less developed countries where cultural differences between tourists and hosts are greater than in more developed countries, the negative effect of direct tourist-host contact is increased (Pearce 1982). Satisfaction with hosts is a critical component of TS (Turner, Reisinger and McQuilken 2001). Perceptions of the hosts as service providers, effect total holiday satisfaction and may influence the desire for repeat visitation. Therefore, the variability of situations between culture and tourist-host contact points to the need of being more precise in the items used for the quantitative research. A means-end analysis (Botschen, Thelen and Pieters 1999) could be useful to identify other factors that, in turn, determine the outcomes of the contact between tourist and hosts. Likewise, "satisfaction with hosts should be looked at in terms of the hosts' psychological and physical performance" (Turner, Reisinger and McQuilken 2001: 85).

Cross-cultural comparison research can be carried out when the common meaning among the sample groups is observed. This points out that there must be a consensus on how items will be generated and how their wording will be. As already mentioned earlier, concepts and methods developed in one culture/nation may hardly be relevant to be applied into others due to differences in feeling, understanding, lifestyle and so on. While studying cross-cultural research, there must be conceptual and linguistic equivalence in each language (Deutscher 1973). Translation equivalence, which is very closely related to conceptual equivalence, means equivalence in the translation of questionnaires in quantitative research (Secherest et al. 1972 in Usunier 1999). This can be divided into lexical, idiomatic, grammatical-syntactical and experiential equivalencies. Translation equivalence is crucial in survey research, particularly in mail surveys, since written meanings must be understood in a similar way by all respondents and this should be guaranteed a priori, because misunderstood or not understood meanings cannot be corrected or explained while the respondent fills-out the questionnaire.

Therefore, direct translation from the source language to the target language has several limitations. In this context, Erkut et al. (1999) recommend employing dual-focus approach and obtaining assistance from bilingual researchers who are familiar with the content area and who can speak both the source and the target languages in order to enhance conceptual and linguistic equivalence while generating the scale items or survey questions. Collaboration can be established with those who are familiar with the target culture or are indigenous researchers from the culture being studied. The authors believe that, as an alternative approach to the method of back-translation, this approach can minimize translation errors, save time and provide efficiency in wording. A question like 'how would you say X in language A and in language B?' would be helpful. This can make concepts to have cross-cultural validity. As in functional equivalence, conceptual equivalence is prerequisite for comparison research, too.

One obstacle of CS measurement is the development of the relative attributes that basically form the major part of the survey instrument (Chu 2002). Usually, in carrying out CS research, the common procedures are to conduct qualitative research to identify a list of attributes, as perceived to be important by respondents (Hanson 1992). This list of attributes is then retained for the subsequent quantitative phase for calculating the Customer Satisfaction Index (CSI). For instance, in a cross-cultural CS study (Spreng and Chiou 2002), slightly different attributes were used across the study samples (US and Taiwan university students) as discussions with industry experts and pre-tests with members of the subject population indicated that the two populations differed in their assessment of what is important in a digital camera. However, according to Chu (2002), this situation may lead to high ratings for most attributes and, the aim of the study–to prioritise the attributes–is undermined. A specific issue in tourism refers to the comparability between tourist holidays. If one compares the purchase of shoes in two countries, with the exception of the product, there would be many differences. However, products and services in tourism are not comparable because they are different, even if they are leisure holidays.

Construct (Instrument) Equivalence

This type of equivalence examines if a given construct serves the same function in different cross-national contexts. The items with the structural equivalence of correlations can be accepted for a further assessment of cross-cultural studies. Otherwise, inferences to be drawn from the findings may be invalid. The following quotation explains this better: "what might appear to be cross-cultural difference could turn out to be solely a reflection of variations in the reliability of the underlying measurements employed in the analysis" (Davis, Douglas and Silk 1981 in Singh 1995: 616). This reports that unequal reliability for the datasets representing different cultures could be a possible reason for the observed difference. VanItemert, Baerweldt and Vermande

(2001), having developed two versions of the same item, tried to test if the difference between the mean scores of such versions gives an indication for the item bias. The findings show that two versions may have two different mean scores and this may damage the structural equivalence of an instrument, and as a result, the findings might be under/over-estimated even though there is no difference between the two groups. Nonetheless, most studies reviewed in the field of tourism and hospitality do not provide detailed information on construct equivalence.

Measurement (Metric) Equivalence

Figure 2 indicates the importance of both objective and subjective variables in carrying out cross-cultural research studies. In a cross-cultural study, perhaps one can expect a little difference between the two groups of people for objective variables, but it might be impossible to observe a neutral structure of a sample group for subjective variables. If this might happen, then there would be no need to carry out a comparative study because no difference would be achieved. Thus, subjective variables can hardly be considered as a control group while objective variables become really a control group. The former is also the main ingredient of a cross-cultural comparative study of CS.

FIGURE 2. Importance of Subjective and Objective Variables

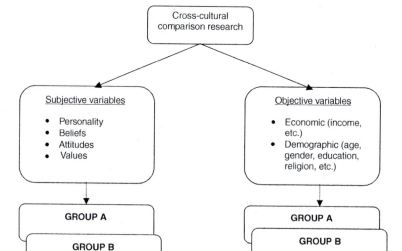

One can suggest that objective variables are not a direct outcome of the term 'culture.' In other words, culture or variances in one's culture can hardly influence their demographic or economic structure. Nevertheless, subjective variables, in comparison with the objective ones, have a much higher possibility of reflecting culture's influence on itself. For example, attitude or belief might be an indicator of cultural differences between various nations or between various groups because such terms are formed as a result of the contact with human beings and reflect one's general view in particular and a nation's cultural structure in general. Berry (1980: 10) notes that measurement equivalence "exists when the psychometric properties of two or more sets of data from two or more cultural groups exhibit essentially the same coherence or structure." To achieve this, a series of steps should be followed.

First, a series of chi-square tests need to be applied in order to ensure that the sample populations are uniform in terms of their socio-demographic and socio-economic characteristics, and as a result, data are comparable. If there is no association among the samples (homogeneous in terms of their socio-demographic profiles), differences in the proportions are meant relating to differences in culture (or nationality). In the case there is any association (heterogeneous in terms of their socio-demographic profiles), it is speculated that the findings for each culture (or nationality) could have been arisen by chance.

Next, the benchmark used to find out if any difference appears between the two cultures is the calculation of mean scores from quantitative data and employing several statistical tests, e.g., "t" or "F" tests. Such tests are used to determine whether significant differences exist between the scores assigned to the individual attributes/factors by those in one culture versus those in another culture. When the probability score of these tests is significant enough ($p<.05$), the result is accepted to be statistically significant. The question mark here is if this is really observed as a result of differences in people's cultural background. Some researchers in the field of psychology argue that data analysis in cross-cultural research is largely dominated by using statistical tests as "t" or "F" (e.g., Matsumoto, Grissom and Dinnel 2001). They draw attention to the risk of fostering stereotypes in research and theory without a meaningful and realistic practical support. These researchers recommend the use of alternative methods (e.g., factor analysis) for analysing the existing data in order to provide valuable information about the magnitude of cultural differences that are not available from the traditional statistical tests. For example, estimating factor structure should be one of the most significant methods to provide construct validity, as well as the use of structural equation modelling for cross-cultural analysis (Turner, Reisinger and McQuilken 2001).

It is also essential to pay attention to the importance of choosing methods on how to collect the comparable data. First, in order to obtain cross-validating evidence, Berry (1980) suggests using various types of research methods to obtain data and to exhibit consistency with test results. Using a combination of methods also helps to develop a more complete theory while using a single method may stop researchers halfway before achieving their objectives. Next, collaboration with researchers living in the prospective partner countries should be needed in order to make the management of data collection procedures easier, faster and more cost-effective. If not, the researcher needs to visit the partner country (or countries). In case the researcher is not so familiar with the environment, s/he might face several bureaucratic problems. Familiarity with the cultural aspects of a community is also essential to discuss the research findings and draw both meaningful and solid implications. Finally, in terms of choosing a correct sample group, sampling frames should be easier to be comparable. Thus, a stratified random sampling may be more useful, e.g., selecting a specific cluster in one culture and comparing this to its akin in another culture.

Spreng and Chiou (2002) conducted a cross-cultural assessment of the satisfaction formation process (i.e., the disconfirmation of expectations model) in the two samples (university students in the US and Taiwan). Their conclusions are three-fold. First, the disconfirmation model (Oliver 1997; Yi 1990) is supported in a cross-cultural test. Second, they evidence the importance of performance on satisfaction and, therefore, this result provides support for the "performance model" of satisfaction in which both disconfirmation and performance have direct effects on CS (Oliver 1997). Third, they indicate that expectations exert a significant positive effect on perceived performance. Overall, although Asian and American cultures are very different (i.e., collectivist culture versus individualistic culture; Hofstede 1983), Spreng and Chiou (2002), the similarity of the relationships of the tested model in both samples, provide confidence in utilizing the disconfirmation model in non-US countries. However, Spreng and Chiou (2002) recognize the limitation of using different measures between US and Taiwan studies. As can be seen in Table 2, while the constructs are the same across the two cultures, the exact measures are not and, consequently, they could not test the invariance of the measures. Further research should develop and use common measures that can be used to test the measurement invariance.

It is important to have equivalence in sample frames and sample selection in order to establish comparability in cross-cultural research. Sampling frames in different cultures, both for qualitative and quantitative research, should rather be purposeful than identical. Ember and Ember (1998) argue that random sampling is preferable and provides less systematic biases when generality is sought. However, probabilistic sampling is not always possible in less developed countries (Craig and Douglas 2000), and other types of sampling methods need to be

TABLE 2. Research Methodology in a Cross-Cultural CS Study

	US sample	Taiwan sample
Sample characteristics	University students	University students
Research design	Laboratory study	Laboratory study
Product used	Digital camera	Digital camera
Attributes	Clarity, sharpness, colour and overall picture quality	The same than US plus colour strength and softness
Expectations	7-point scales ("terrible, very poor" and "excellent quality")	5-point scales ("very poor" and "very good").
Perceived performance	7-point scales ("terrible" and "excellent")	5-point scales ("very poor" and "very good").
Subjective disconfirmation	7-point scales ("worse than I expected" and "better than I expected")	5-point scales ("much worse" and "much better")
Satisfaction at the attribute level	7-point scales ("very dissatisfied" and "very satisfied").	5-point scales ("very dissatisfied" and "very satisfied").
Intentions	2 scales: 11-point scale "0 per cent" to "100 per cent," and 8-point scale "Zero chance than I would buy it" and "Certain that I would buy it"	3-seven point scales, anchored by "possible/impossible," "definitely/definitely not," and "certainly/certainly not"
Data analysis method	Two-group path analyzing using LISREL 8	

Source: Adapted from Spreng and Chiou (2002)

used. Furthermore, identical sampling procedures or methods in each culture are not as important as equivalent levels of accuracy and reliability.

CONCLUSIONS

The increased internationalisation and dynamism of the tourism industry has made it increasingly urgent for market-focussed organizations, and indeed the industry as a collective, to engage in cross-cultural marketing research. The diversity resulting from increased internationalisation, and also a convergence in consumer lifestyles and product category behaviour (e.g., city breaks, rural tourism), has led to a call by practitioners for development of cross-culturally valid instruments for market surveillance. In the best circumstances, the most desirable outcome is for the results of research conducted in different countries to be directly comparable (Askegaard and Brunsø 1999), enabling more coordinated market planning and marketing strategy development.

A cross-cultural CS study needs to take into account several issues as follows. First, the combination of interviews and criteria from existing literature was designed to ensure that the study needs to be based in an ethnic approach as suggested by Berry (1989), i.e., to identify shared categories of selection criteria that are valid for the specific countries involved in the cross-cultural study. Second, interviews need to ensure construct equivalence, i.e., functional, conceptual and categorical equivalence (Frijda and Jahoda 1966; Craig and Douglas 2000). Next, back-translation and the piloting procedures need to be undertaken to insure the instrument equivalence, i.e., item equivalence and translation equivalence (Hui and Triandis 1985; Bhalla and Lynn 1987). Fourth, it is important to try to maintain sampling equivalence, i.e., sampling unit as well as independence and representativeness (Lonner and Berry 1986). Moreover, contextual equivalence, i.e., experimenter-subject relationship and temporal equivalence, is also a step in the methodology to conduct a cross-cultural research (Sekaran 1983). Finally, the issue of measurement equivalence, i.e., metric and calibration equivalence need to be addressed in the cross-cultural research.

It seems obvious from above discussion that one scale or methodology of multicultural comparison developed and applied in one country cannot be replicated losing another without modification. Equivalence among the sample nations or among the sample destinations is really important to enhance the reliability of a multicultural study not only in tourism research, e.g., social and economic indicators, the structure of accommodation capacity and so on. It might be difficult to translate words/terms from one language to another without avoiding its real meaning. "This means that the same term may have different meanings in different countries or even within the same country." As a result, it is highly recommended that researchers be sensitive to the possibility that there might exist interactions between cultural variables and measurement errors/problems which probably make cross-cultural research very difficult to carry out or the research findings to interpret.

Although it is clear from the literature review that cross-cultural research in tourism has received increasing attention, little has been done with regard to the assessment of the possible impact of cultural differences on the level of CS. On the one hand, as tourism businesses and destinations attract visitors from different cultures and countries, it is not reasonable to take into consideration only one specific group of customers. A comparative analysis between groups is required to better understand the importance of understanding the needs and expectations of each segment. Therefore, a comparative analysis of the cultural differences between international tourists and their satisfaction levels becomes a necessity. On the other hand, in a number of empirical studies carried out on CS, the conclusion was reached that there appear to be differences between nations representing different countries. There is one question left here: does this appear to exist as a result of cultural differences or national differences? Or does each country or nation represent a unique culture distinguishing itself from others? This part of tourism research is very new requiring much attention for exploration in the future because it is essential to make sure that there is no bias threatening the validity of the findings in a cross-cultural study.

In summary, a lot has been achieved in the last decade of tourism marketing research. Future research will benefit from a more rigorous, theory-grounded, and model-based approach for assessing cross-cultural differences either particularly in CS or generally in consumer behaviour. There are a number of opportunities for and threats to the further development of cross-cultural CS research. This study has aimed at discussing some special problems observed while undertaking cross-cultural research and to offer methods to eliminate such problems. Thus, some issues, discussed in the context of this paper, require more research effort. It is hoped that this paper will stimulate further advances in this important area of tourism marketing.

REFERENCES

Askegaard, S. and K. Brunsø (1999) "Food-related life styles in Singapore: preliminary testing of a Western European research instrument in Southeast Asia," Journal of Euromarketing, 7 (4): 65-86.

Baker, D. A. and J. L. Crompton (2000). "Quality, Satisfaction and Behavioral Intentions." *Annals of Tourism Research*, 27(3):785-804.

Becker, C. and S. K. Murrmann (2000). "Methodological Considerations in Multicultural Research." *Tourism Analysis*, 5(1):29-36.

Berry, J. W. (1980). "Introduction to Methodology." In H. C. Triandis and J. W. Berry (Eds.) *Handbook of Cross-cultural Psychology: Methodology*. Vol: 2. Boston: Allyn and Bacon, pp.1-28.

Bhalla, G. and L. Y. Lin (1987). "Cross-Cultural Marketing Research: A Discussion of Equivalence Issues and Measurement Strategies." *Psychology and Marketing*, 4(4):275-285.

Bigné, E., X. Font, and L. Andreu (2000). *Marketing de destinos turísticos. Análisis y estrategias de desarrollo*. Esic, Madrid.

Botschen, G., E. M. Thelen, and R. Pieters (1999). "Using Means-end Structures for Benefit Segmentation. An Application to Services." *European Journal of Marketing*, 33(1/2):38-58

Brislin R. (1993). "Some Methodological Concerns in Intercultural and Cross-Cultural Research." In R. Brislin (Ed.). *Understanding Culture's Influence on Behaviour*. Fort Worth: Harcourt Brace College.

Chen, J. S. and D. Gursoy (2000). "Cross-Cultural Comparison of the Information Sources Used by First-Time and Repeat Travelers and its Marketing Implications." *International Journal of Hospitality Management*, 19:191-203.

Choi, T. Y. and R. Chu (2000). "Levels of Satisfaction among Asian and Western Travellers." *International Journal of Quality and Reliability Management*, 17(2):116-131.

Chu, R. (2002). "Stated-importance versus Derived-importance Customer Satisfaction Measurement." *Journal of Services Marketing*, 16(4):285-301.

Churchill, G. A., and C. Surprenant, (1982). "An Investigation Into the Determinants of Customer Satisfaction." *Journal of Marketing Research*, 19(3):491-504.

Clark, T., (1990). "International Marketing and National Character: A review and Proposal for an Integrative Theory." *Journal of Marketing*, 54(4):66-79.

Costa, J.A. and G. J. Bamossy (1995). *Marketing in a Multicultural World*. Sage Publications, USA.

Craig S. C. and S. P. Douglas (2000). *International Marketing Research*. Chichester: John Wiley & Sons.

Crompton, J. L. and L. L. Love (1995). "The Predictive Validity of Alternative Approaches to Evaluating Quality of a Festival." *Journal of Travel Research*, 34(1):11-25.

Cronin, J. J., and S. A. Taylor (1992). "Measuring Service Quality: A Reexamination and Extension." *Journal of Marketing*, 56(1):55-68.

Czepiel, J. A., L. J. Rosenberg and A. Akerele (1974). "Perspectives on Consumer Satisfaction." In *1974 Combined Proceedings Series No: 36*, R. C. Curhan (Ed.). American Marketing Association, pp. 119-123.

Dann, G. (1993). "Limitations in the Use of Nationality and Country of Residence Variables." In D. G. Pearce and R. W. Butler (Eds.) *Tourism Critiques and Challenges*. London: Routledge, pp. 88-112.

Davis H. L., S. P. Douglas and A. J. Silk (1981). "Measure Unreliability: A Hidden Threat to Cross-National Marketing Research?" *Journal of Marketing*, 45(1): 98-109.

Dawar, N. and P. Parker, (1994). "Marketing Universals: Consumers' Use of Brand Name, Price, Physical Appearance, and Retailer Reputation as Signals of Product Quality." *Journal of Marketing*, 58(2):81-95.

Deutscher, I. (1973). "Asking Questions Cross-Culturally: Some Problems of Linguistic Comparability." *In Comparative Research Methods*. D. P. Warwick and S. Osherson (Eds.). NJ: Prentice Hall, pp. 163-185.

Dimanche, F. (1994). "Cross-Cultural Tourism Marketing Research: An Assessment and Recommendations for Future Studies." *Journal of International Consumer Marketing*, 6(3-4):123-134.

Ember C. R. and E. Melvin (1998). "Cross-Cultural Research." In *Handbook of Methods in Cultural Anthropology*. H. R. Bernard (Ed.) Alta Mira Press, pp. 647-687.

Engel, J. F. and R. D. Blackwell (1982). *Consumer Behavior*. 4th Edition, NY: The Dryden Press.

Erkut, S., O. Alarcon, C. G. Coll, L. R. Tropp and H. A. V. Garcia (1999). "The Dual-Focus Approach to Creating Bilingual Measures." *Journal of Cross-Cultural Psychology*, 30(2):206-218.

Fornell, C., (1992). "A National Satisfaction Barometer: The Swedish Experience." *Journal of Marketing*, 56(1):1-21.

Frijda, N. H. and G. Jahoda (1966). "On the Scope and Methods of Cross-Cultural Research." *International Journal of Psychology*, 1:110-127.

Gould, S. J. and N. Y. C. Wond (2000). "The Intertextual Construction of Emerging Consumer Culture in China as Observed in the Movie Ermo: A Post-modern, Sinicization Reading." *Journal of Global Marketing*, 14(1/2):151-167.

Hair, J. F., R. E. Anderson, R. L. Tatham and W. C. Black (1995). *Multivariate Data Analysis with Readings*, 4th Edition, NJ: Prentice-Hall.

Han, S.-P. and S. Shavitt, (1994). "Persuasion and Culture: Advertising Appeals in Individualistic and Collectivistic Societies." *Journal of Experimental Social Psychology*, 30(July):326-350.

Hanson, R. (1992). "Determining attribute importance," *Quirk's Marketing Research Review, http://www.quirks.com/articles/article.asp?arg_ArticleId=430*

Hofstede, G. (1980). *Culture's Consequences: International Differences in Work-Related Values*. Beverly Hills, CA: Sage Publications.

Hofstede, G. (1991). *Cultures and Organizations: Software of the Mind*. London: McGraw-Hill.

Honomichl, J. (1993). "Spending on Customer Satisfaction Continues to Rise." *Marketing News*, 12:17-18.

Hudson, S. and J. R. B. Ritchie (2001). "Cross-Cultural Tourist Behavior: An Analysis of Tourist Attitudes towards the Environment." *Journal of Travel and Tourism Marketing*, 10(2/3):1-22.

Hui, H. C. and H. C. Triandis (1985). "Measurement in Cross-Cultural Psychology, A Review and Comparison of Strategies." *Journal of Cross-Cultural Psychology*, 16(2): 131-152.

Inkeles, A. and D. J. Levinson (1969). "National Character: The Study of Model Personality and Sociocultural Systems." In G. Lindzey and E. Arnson (Eds.), *The Handbook of Social Psychology*. Reading, MA: Addison-Wesley, pp. 418-456.

Kagitcibasi, C. (1997). "Individualism and Collectivism," In J. W. Berry, M. H. Segall and C. Kagitcibasi (Eds.), *Handbook of Cross-Cultural Psychology, Volume 3: Social Behavior and Applications*, 2nd Edition, Boston, MA: Allyn and Bacon, pp. 1-49.

Karlof, B. and S. Ostblom (1993). *Benchmarking: A Signpost Excellence in Quality and Productivity*. West Sussex: Wiley.

Kim, S. S., B. Prideaux and S. H. Kim (2002). "A Cross-cultural Study on Casino Guests as Perceived by Casino Employees." *Tourism Management*, 23(6):511-520.

Kozak, M. (2002). "Comparative Analysis of Tourist Motivations by Nationality and Destinations." *Tourism Management*, 23(3):231-242.

Kozak, M. (2001). "Comparative Assessment of Tourist Satisfaction with Destinations Across Two Nationalities." *Tourism Management*, 22(3):391-401.

Kozak, M. (2000). *Destination Benchmarking: Facilities, Customer Satisfaction and Levels of Tourist Expenditure*. Unpublished PhD Dissertation. Sheffield Hallam University.

Kozak, M., E. Bigné, A. González, and L. Andreu (2003). "Cross-cultural Behaviour Research in Tourism: A Case Study on Destination Image." In G. I. Crouch, R. R. Perdue, H. Timmermans, and M Uysal (Eds.). *Consumer Psychology of Tourism, Hospitality and Leisure, Volume 3*. CABI Publishing, in press.

Lodge, G. C. (1990). *Comparative Business-Government Relations*, NJ: Prentice-Hall.

Lonner, W. and J. Berry (1986). "Sampling and surveying." In Lonner, W. and Berry, J. (Eds.), *Field methods in cross cultural research*, London: Sage, pp. 85-110.

Lynn, M., M. Z. George and J. Harris (1993). "Consumer Tipping: A Cross-Country Study." *Journal of Consumer Research*, 20(4):478-488.

McGuiggan, R. and J. A. Foo (2002). "Do Americans and Australians Play the Same Roles as Tourists?" In Bigné, E.; Johar, J.S. and Hassan, S.S. (Eds.). *Proceedings of the 2002 Multicultural Marketing Conference*. Academy of Marketing Science, Valencia.

Matsumoto, D., R. J. Grissom and D. L. Dinnel (2001). "Do between-culture Differences Really Mean that People are different? A Look at Some Measures of Cultural Effect Size." *Journal of Cross-cultural Psychology*, 32(4):478-490.

Mattila, S.A. (2000). "The Impact of Culture and Gender on Customer Evaluations of Service Encounters." *Journal of Hospitality and Tourism Research*, 24(2):263-273.

Messick, D. M. (1988). "On the Limitations of Cross-Cultural Research in social Psychology." In M. H. Bond (Ed.), *Cross-Cultural Research and Methodology Series Vol. II: The Cross-Cultural Challenge to Social Psychology*, California: Sage, pp. 41-47.

Moser, C. A. and G. Kalton (1971). *Survey Methods in Social Investigation*. 2nd Edition, England: Gower.

Nakata, C. and K. Sivakumar (1996). "National Culture and New Product Development: An Integrative Review." *Journal of Marketing*, 60(1):61-72.

Oliver, R. L. (1980). "A Cognitive Model of The Antecedents and Consequences of Satisfaction Decisions." *Journal of Marketing*, 17:460-469.

Oliver, R. L. (1981). "Measurement and Evaluation of Satisfaction Process in Retail Store." *Journal of Retailing*, 57:25-48.

Oliver, R. L. (1993). "Cognitive, Affective, and Attribute bases of the Satisfaction Response." *Journal of Consumer Research*, 20:418-430.

Oliver, R.L. (1997). *Satisfaction: A Behavioral Perspective on the Consumer*. Boston: McGraw Hill.

Oliver, R. L. (1999). "Whence Consumer Loyalty?" *Journal of Marketing*, 63(Special Issue):33-44.

Pareek, U. and T. V. Rao (1980). "Cross-Cultural Surveys and Interviewing." In H. C. Triandis and J. W. Berry (Eds.), *Handbook of Cross-cultural Psychology: Methodology. Vol: 2*. Boston: Allyn and Bacon, pp. 127-177.

Pearce, P. L. (1982). "Perceived Changes in Holiday Destinations." *Annals of Tourism Research*, 9(2):145-164.

Pizam, A. (1999). "Cross-cultural Tourist Behavior." In A. Pizam and Y. Mansfeld (Eds.) *Consumer Behavior in Travel and Tourism*. NY: The Haworth Press, pp. 393-411.

Pizam, A. and T. Ellis (1999). "Customer Satisfaction and its Measurement in Hospitality Enterprises." *International Journal of Contemporary Hospitality Management*, 11(7):326-339.

Pizam, A. and S. Sussmann (1995) Does Nationality Affect Tourism Behavior? Annals of Tourism Research, 22(4):901-917.

Plog, S. C. (1990). "A Carpenter's Tools: An Answer to Stephen L. J. Smith's Review of Psychocentrism/Allocentrism." *Journal of Travel Research*, 28(4):55-58.

Reisinger, Y. and L. W. Turner (2003). *Cross-Cultural Behaviour in Tourism. Concepts and Analysis*. Oxford: Butterworth-Heinemann.

Richardson, S. L. and J. L. Crompton (1988). "Vacation Patterns of French and English Canadians." *Annals of Tourism Research*, 15(4):430-448.

Roth, M. S. (1995). "The Effects of Culture and Socioeconomic on the Performance of Global Brand Image Strategies." *Journal of Marketing Research*, 32(May):163-175.

Ryan, C. (1995). *Researching Tourist Satisfaction. Issues, Concepts, Problems.* Routledge: London.

Samovar, L. A. and R. E. Porter (1991). *Communication Between Cultures.* Belmont, CA: Wadsworth Publishing Company.

Sechrest, L., T. L. Fay and S. M. H. Zaidi (1972). "Problems of Translation on Cross-Cultural Research." *Journal of Cross-Cultural Psychology*, 3(1):41-56.

Sekaran, U. (1983). "Methodological and Theoretical Issues and Advancements in Cross-Cultural Research." *Journal of International Business Studies*, 14(2):61-73.

Singh, J. (1995). "Measurement Issues in Cross-National Research." *Journal of International Business Studies*, 26(3):597-619.

Spreng, R.A. and J. S. Chiou (2002). "A Cross-Cultural Assessment of the Satisfaction Formation Process." *European Journal of Marketing*, 36(7/8):829-839.

Sussmann, S. and C. Rashcovsky (1997). "A Cross-Cultural Analysis of English and French Canadians' Vacation Travel Patterns." *International Journal of Hospitality Management*, 16(2):191-208.

Turner, L.W., Y. Reisinger, and L. McQuilken (2001). "How Cultural Differences Cause Dimensions of Tourism Satisfaction." *Journal of Travel & Tourism Marketing*, 11(1):47-80.

Warwick, D. P. and S. Osherson (1973). "Comparative Analysis in the Social Sciences." In *Comparative Research Methods*. D. P. Warwick and S. Osherson (Eds.). NJ: Prentice-Hall, pp. 3-41.

Weiermair, K. (2000). "Tourists' Perceptions towards and Satisfaction with Service Quality in the Cross-Cultural Service Encounter: Implications for Hospitality and Tourism Management." *Managing Service Quality*, 10(6):397-409.

Westbrook, R. A. and J. W. Newman (1978). "An Analysis of Shopper Dissatisfaction for Major Household Appliances." *Journal of Marketing Research*, 15(August):456-466.

WTO (1997). *International Tourism: A Global Perspective.* Madrid: World Tourism Organization.

WTO (2003). *Tourism Highlights 2002.* Madrid: World Tourism Organization.

Yi, Y. (1990). "A Critical Review of Consumer Satisfaction." In *Review of Marketing*. V. A. Zeithaml (Ed.). USA: American Marketing Association, pp. 68-123.

Which Comparison Standard Should Be Used for Service Quality and Customer Satisfaction?

Yuksel Ekinci

SUMMARY. The aim of this study is to examine whether consumers use single or multiple comparison standards for the evaluation of service quality and when determining their satisfaction, in the context of the hospitality industry. The data was collected using a convenient student sample. The findings indicate that consumers use multiple comparison standards for the evaluation of service quality and satisfaction. Five of the eight tested comparison standards are found to be significant in predicting service quality and satisfaction. Of these, predictive expectations, deserved expectation, desires congruence and experience-based norm are considered very important. The study also suggests that service quality and customer satisfaction are different constructs and survey instruments should take into account this difference in measurement. *[Article copies available for a fee from The Haworth Document Delivery Service: 1-800-HAWORTH. E-mail address: <docdelivery@haworthpress.com> Website: <http://www.HaworthPress.com> © 2003 by The Haworth Press, Inc. All rights reserved.]*

Yuksel Ekinci is Lecturer in Hospitality Management, School of Management, University of Surrey, Guildford GU2 7XH, United Kingdom (E-mail: Yukselekinci@ hotmail.com).

[Haworth co-indexing entry note]: "Which Comparison Standard Should Be Used for Service Quality and Customer Satisfaction?" Ekinci, Yuksel. Co-published simultaneously in *Journal of Quality Assurance in Hospitality & Tourism* (The Haworth Hospitality Press, an imprint of The Haworth Press, Inc.) Vol. 4, No. 3/4, 2003, pp. 61-75; and: *Current Issues and Development in Hospitality and Tourism Satisfaction* (ed: John A. Williams and Muzaffer Uysal) The Haworth Hospitality Press, an imprint of The Haworth Press, Inc., 2003, pp. 61-75. Single or multiple copies of this article are available for a fee from The Haworth Document Delivery Service [1-800-HAWORTH, 9:00 a.m. - 5:00 p.m. (EST). E-mail address: docdelivery@ haworthpress.com].

KEYWORDS. Expectations, service quality, customer satisfaction, experience based norms, self-concept, and comparison standard

INTRODUCTION

Although use of a comparison standard is central to the measurement of service quality and customer satisfaction, relevant literature reveals that the choice of standard(s) is an issue Customer expectation, desires, equity and experiences are some of the standards most frequently employed in past studies (Woodruff et al., 1991). However, the definition of such standards has not always been clear and their utilisation has varied from one study to another. Some studies treat customer expectation as a single variable, whereas others treat it as multidimensional (Miller, 1977). Some actually reject the use of expectation as a comparison standard for assessing satisfaction (e.g., LaTour and Peat, 1979). Such an approach has caused confusion and some past research has not specified which standard(s) should be used for assessing service quality and customer satisfaction (Liljander and Strandvic, 1993).

Another related issue also emerged from past studies. If customers were to use more than one comparison standard in their evaluation of service quality or satisfaction (e.g., expectation and desires), what would the correct pair be? The outcome of this research may in turn shed light on the conceptual distinction between the two concepts. Some scholars had already addressed this issue, but the outcome of their research had been inconclusive. Tse and Wilton (1988) examined three comparison standards: expectations, ideal brand norm and equity. Spreng et al. (1996) showed that expectation and desires congruence influenced customer satisfaction. Liljander (1994) demonstrated that deserved expectation was the best determinant of customer satisfaction among several alternatives including service excellence, best brand norm, product type norm, brand norm, adequate service, predicted service and equity.

Recognizing the above deficiencies in the measurement of customer satisfaction and service quality in the hospitality literature, the aim of this study is to address three research questions:

1. What is the relationship between different types of expectation and other comparison standards?
2. Do consumers use single or multiple comparison standards for the evaluation of service quality and satisfaction?
3. What is the most relevant comparison standard(s) used for assessing service quality and satisfaction in the hospitality industry?

LITERATURE REVIEW

Expectation

Although expectation is one of the most frequently employed comparison standards in past studies, its conceptualisation is too vague. According to Miller (1977, p. 76), the concept of expectation has four categories: *ideal, expected, minimum tolerable* and *deserved*. The ideal reflects the "desired" performance level of a product. The "expected" is known as *predictive* expectation and reflects what the future performance of a product will be. The "minimum tolerable" is the lowest acceptable performance level of a product and reflects what the minimum level of product performance "must be." The "deserved" expectation reflects what the performance of a product *ought to be* or *should be* according to a given investment (e.g., money paid). The four types of expectation are hierarchical. The desired expectation stands at the top and the minimum tolerable stands at the bottom. The deserved expectation and predictive expectation come somewhere in the middle. However, their exact position (i.e., whether the predictive expectation is above, equal to or below the deserved expectation) may change according to situational factors, such as the consumer's investment in the product or their personality.

Early research on service quality suggested that a "should" type of expectation was appropriate for measuring service quality (Parasuraman et al., 1988). According to the SERVQUAL model, service quality is the gap between customer expectation and perceived performance. Although, in this context, the meaning of a "should" expectation was not entirely clear, it was referred to as the customer's *desired level of product performance*. However, in a subsequent study, Parasuraman et al. (1991) stated that such a "should" expectation was not a useful measure, since the service quality gap always came out negative when the perception score was subtracted from the expectation score.

Therefore, the idea of normative expectation was introduced and the wording of expectation statements was changed from "A company should have . . . " to "An excellent company will have . . . " to capture the new conceptualisation. Parasuraman et al. (1991, pp. 3 and 4) argued that excellent service was similar to the "ideal" standard used in the satisfaction literature. However, Teas (1993; 1994) identified several problems regarding this concept. He pointed out that, according to the gap model, in certain situations the perceived quality may decline even if the perception exceeded the ideal expectation. He also showed that interpretation of the ideal service performance varied among respondents–a point that threatened validity of the survey outputs.

In order to address the above criticisms, Zeithaml et al. (1993) introduced the idea of multiple expectations in service quality measurement. The two most frequently used expectations, namely desired and adequate expectation, are selected for this approach. Desired service expectation is the level of service that a consumer wishes to receive. It corresponds to a mixture of what the customer believes the level of performance *can be* and *should be*. A product that exceeds this type of expectation is recognised as being of excellent quality. Adequate service expectation is the lower level of performance that is just acceptable to consumers.

Zeithaml et al. (1993, p. 6) argue that the adequate service expectation level is comparable to Miller's minimum tolerable expectation. According to them, if a product performed at this level of customer expectation, the customer would be satisfied. The area between the desired service and adequate service is called the *zone of tolerance* (ZOT), which represents the level of service performance a customer would tolerate. At this level of performance a customer may be satisfied with a product, but the outcome of the performance is below the desired expectation and therefore the quality of service will be seen as poor.

However, the new formulation of expectation still seems somewhat ambiguous. For example, Zeithaml et al. (1993) note that the "adequate service" is comparable to Miller's minimum tolerable level (where the performance is better than nothing). And, according to Miller (1977), this level of performance causes dissatisfaction. Hence, if the performance is equal to the minimum tolerable expectation:

> . . . the consumer experiences dissatisfaction. He may attempt to remedy the situation and probably won't purchase that brand (continue patronising that store) but will switch to another. If no alternative is available, he will probably continue to use the product as long as it 'satisfies' or fills a need. (Miller 1977, p. 79)

Based on the above statement consumers will not tolerate a level of performance that is equal to the minimum tolerable level. According to Miller (1977), consumers will only tolerate a service when the actual performance is below the ideal but equal to the predictive or deserved expectation. A ZOT will only occur when the actual performance is below the expected (predicted) but equal to the deserved expectation level. Consumers may be disappointed with this level of performance, but their feelings can best be described as "unsatisfaction" rather than "dissatisfaction." Hence, the bottom line for satisfaction is where the performance is equal to the *deserved expectation*.

Ekinci et al. (2001) argue that a performance only measurement provides limited information to enhance our understanding of service quality and customer satisfaction. Therefore, assessing performance against different types of expectation may be valuable when trying to locate the desired level of service performance from a consumer's point of view. The ideal, predictive or deserved service level may also be used as a *benchmark* by which to control the level of service quality in longitudinal assessments.

Desires Congruence

The use of human values (desires, needs or wants) as comparison standards is theoretically compelling, because they are the centrepiece of human perception (Rokeach, 1973). For example, means-end models suggest that product attributes are linked to consumer values (Olshavsky and Spreng, 1989). However, past research has found little empirical support for the direct relationship between human values and satisfaction.

One of the reasons for this weak link is that values are operationalised at a very abstract level. Spreng et al. (1996) suggest that values should be conceptualised as desires or product benefits. They defined desires congruency as a match/mismatch between a person's desires and actual performance, and their study indicated that the desires congruency had a significant effect on attribute satisfaction, information satisfaction and overall satisfaction. In addition to desires congruence, predictive expectation was also found to have a significant influence on satisfaction.

Experience-Based Norms

Consumers employ previous experiences as a comparison standard for their satisfaction decision. The experience-based norm is suggested to be different from customer expectation because it comes about through experiences (Cadotte et al., 1987). Experiences may be gathered from direct use of product categories or information received. Experiences with other brands in the evoked set or with similar product categories might be employed as a norm, as might brand attitude. Generally speaking, the experience-based norm can be operationalized in three different forms: a best brand norm, a brand-based norm and a product-based norm.

In testing various alternative standards, Cadotte et al. (1987) showed that the best brand norm and the product-based norm explained satisfaction better than the focal brand norm. At the same time, the expectation model failed to predict overall satisfaction. The study also indicated that there was no single comparison standard that best explained satisfaction across different consumption situations.

Self-Concept Congruence

The theory of self-congruence suggests that consumers evaluate products by referring to their self-concept (Sirgy, 1982). Hence, the higher the self-congruence (the match between self-image and the product image), the higher the probability of displaying favourable behaviour, such as intention to purchase or satisfaction. This theory has been applied in various situations to examine the relationship between self-concept and different types of consumer behaviour. Examples have included self-concept and preference for houses (Malhotra, 1988), self-concept and store image (Sirgy and Samli, 1985), self-concept and satisfaction with holiday destinations (Chon, 1992), and self-concept and satisfaction, service quality and attitude towards the service organisation (Ekinci, 2003).

Self-concept is proposed to be multidimensional (consisting of actual, ideal and social self) and thus the relationship between self-concept congruence and consumer behaviour may differ across product categories. The relationship between actual self-congruence and customer satisfaction may not be significant because consumers often superimpose their "ideal" self in their purchasing, particularly when the actual self-concept is perceived to be unfavourable. Therefore, different types of self-concept (e.g., actual or ideal self-concept) should be taken into account when investigating the relationship between self-concept congruence and consumer behaviour.

Malhotra (1988) supports the differential role of self-congruence in product evaluation. His study indicates that ideal self-congruence rather than actual self-congruence has the primary influence on house preferences. Hamm and Cundiff (1969) support only the relationship between ideal self-congruence and product preference. Hong and Zinkhan (1995) show that ideal self-congruence rather than actual self-concept is a better predictor of brand preference among various product categories such as cars and shampoos. Consequently, this study measured actual and ideal self-concept to predict service quality and satisfaction.

METHODOLOGY

Measurement of Variables

The survey questionnaire measured 11 different concepts: desired expectation, predictive expectation, deserved expectation, minimum tolerable expectation, desires congruence, experienced-based norm, actual self-congruence, ideal self-congruence, overall satisfaction, overall service quality and intention to purchase. Table 1 shows descriptions of comparison standards used in this study.

Four types of expectation were measured using seven-point semantic differential scales ranging from -3 to 3. The scale endpoints were as follows:

worse than I wished it to be/better than I wished it to be (desired expectation), *worse than I thought it would be/better than I thought it would be* (predictive expectation), *worse than I paid for/better than I paid for* (deserved expectation), *worse than I would normally tolerate/better than I would normally tolerate* (minimum tolerable expectation).

Desires congruence was measured using a two-item scale developed by Spreng and Mackoy (1996). The first part of the scale questioned to what extent the service experience was different from the desired level. Subjects responded on a seven-point scale, with *exactly as desired* (1) and *extremely different from what is desired* (7) at either end and *somewhat different from what I desired* (4) in the middle. Immediately after this scale, subjects were asked to respond to what extent this difference was good or bad. Their responses were recorded on an eleven-point scale, with *very bad* (-5) and *very good* (5) as endpoints and *neither good nor bad* (0) as the midpoint. Desires congruence was calculated by multiplying the two scores.

Experience-based norm was measured on a seven-point semantic differential scale with (-3) corresponding to *being worse than similar restaurants in this area*, and (3) to *being better than similar restaurants in this area*. Self-concept congruence was measured using a five-point Likert-type scale ranging from (1) *strongly disagree* to (5) *strongly agree*. The following scenario-type introduction was given to obtain the respondents' ratings:

> Please take a moment to think about the kind of customer who typically visits the restaurant you visited. Try to imagine this person using one or more personal adjectives such as organised, classy, friendly, modern, traditional, comfortable or whatever personal characteristic you would use. Once you have done this, indicate your agreement or disagreement with the following statements.

TABLE 1. Descriptions of Comparison Standards

Comparison Standards	Descriptions
Desired Expectation	An ideal performance level.
Predictive Expectation	A performance level which is likely to happen.
Deserved Expectation	A performance level that must happen according to a given investment (e.g. money paid).
Minimum Tolerable Expectation	A lower level of performance that is just acceptable to consumers.
Desires Congruence	A match /mismatch between desires and actual performance.
Experienced-Based Norm	A level of performance in relation to the other firms' performance in the same vicinity.
Actual Self-Congruence	A match /mismatch between actual self image and product image.
Ideal Self-Congruence	A match /mismatch between ideal self image and product image.

Four statements were used to assess actual and ideal self-congruence (e.g., 'The typical customer of this restaurant is very similar to me' and 'The typical customer of this restaurant is the kind of person I admire,' respectively). The respondent's rating was recorded on a seven-point numeric scale, with (1) being extremely unlikely and (7) being extremely likely. Overall satisfaction with services was assessed by two seven-point numeric scales. The scale labels were *delighted/terrible* and *completely dissatisfied/completely satisfied* (Spreng and Mackoy, 1996). Overall service quality was also measured using two seven-point numeric scales. The scale labels were *excellent/awful* and *extremely poor/extremely good* (Cronin and Taylor, 1992). Finally, intention to purchase was measured by a seven-point numeric scale (1) *being extremely unlikely* (7) being *extremely likely*.

The study took place in a US university for reasons of sampling convenience. A total of 250 questionnaires were distributed to second-year undergraduate students who were registered on a business management degree. They were asked to report on a restaurant visit experience within the last four weeks. A total of 182 usable questionnaires were collected (73%) and all respondents were US nationals. The sample was 45% female and 55% male. Fifty-three percent of the respondents were aged between 18 and 20, 43 percent were between 21 and 24, and 3 percent were older than 24. The majority of respondents (48%) mentioned that his was their first visit. Nineteen percent had made one previous visit and 21 percent had made two visits. The visits occurred on different 'types' of occasion (leisure 45%, casual 39%, celebration 25% and business 1%) and at different times of the days (although some 75% were around dinner time).

FINDINGS

The two principal objectives of this study were to check the relationship between the comparison standards and to identify the type(s) of comparison standard used for evaluation of service quality and customer satisfaction. Prior testing of the relationships between the variables was carried out, and the validity and reliability of the measures were established. Reliability of the scales was estimated using Cronbach's alpha statistics (Churchill, 1979). Reliabilities of the overall service quality and overall satisfaction scale were excellent (.94 and .91, respectively). The validity of the self-congruence scale was checked by exploratory factor analysis using Varimax rotation. The result of the factor analysis indicated that the four-item scale measured two types of self-congruence: actual and ideal. The two factorial solution explained 89 per cent of the variance (ideal self-congruence = 62% and actual self-congruence =

27%). Reliabilities of the actual (.87) and ideal self-congruence scales (.88) were very high.

To establish the relationship between service quality and satisfaction linear correlation analysis was conducted. The two variables were strongly correlated ($r = .71$). Past studies have indicated that, although there is a large amount of overlap between the two concepts, they are different (Ekinci, 2003; Dabholkar et al., 2000). Dabholkar et al. (2000) showed that satisfaction mediated the relationship between service quality and intention to purchase behaviour. In the same way, evaluation of service quality leads to satisfaction, which in turn leads to intention to purchase behaviour.

In order to check the mediating effect of satisfaction, Baron and Kenny's (1986) conditions for perfect mediation were used. To do this, three different linear regressions were employed. In the first regression model, service quality was regressed on satisfaction. The data showed a good fit to the model and service quality significantly enhanced satisfaction ($R^2 = .50$, $F_{(1\ df)} = 50.8$, $t = 5.85$, $p < .00$). In the second model, satisfaction was regressed on intention to purchase. The data showed a good fit to the model ($R^2 = .49$, $F_{(1\ df)} = 172.2$, $t = 13.1$, $p = .00$.). The third linear regression model included both service quality satisfaction measures and they were regressed on intention to purchase. Again the data fitted the model ($R^2 = .49$, $F_{(2\ df)} = 86.7$, $p = .00$), but only satisfaction appeared to be a significant predictor of purchase intention ($t = 9.19$, $p < .00$). Service quality became insignificant and its effect was reduced ($t = .06$, $p > .05$). These findings support the mediation effect of satisfaction on purchase intention and the "direction" of consumer evaluation from service quality to satisfaction.

Having established validity of the measures, the study checked the relationship between the comparison standards. Table 1 shows the correlation matrix.

As can be seen from the correlation coefficients in Table 1, the relationships between comparison standards were positive and the strengths of the relationship varied from weak to strong. The actual self-congruence did not correlate with the majority of the comparison standards, except for ideal self-congruence and the experience-based norms.

In summary, the correlation analysis offered three useful findings. Firstly, the expectation measures can be grouped into three categories: predictive expectation, deserved expectation and minimum tolerable expectation. The desired and predictive expectation measures were strongly related. Also the paired samples t-test indicated that the desired expectation was not statistically different from the deserved expectation ($p = .15$). Secondly, the relationship between the three expectations and the other comparison standards (desired congruence, and actual and ideal self-congruence) were weak to moderate. Thirdly, the other comparison standards were not strongly correlated with each other, and thus each provided some unique information in relation to service evaluation.

In order to determine the most significant comparison standard for service quality and satisfaction, ordinary linear regression analysis was employed (see Table 3). The dependent variables were service quality and satisfaction. The independent variables were comparison standards. However, desired expectation was eliminated from the independent variable list because it was strongly correlated with predictive expectation and deserved expectation. The preliminary analysis indicated that this variable caused a multicollinearity problem in the regression models (Hair et al., 1998). Table 2 shows the two regression models that estimate service quality and satisfaction.

As can be seen from the regression results in Table 2, the data supported the service quality and satisfaction model ($p < .00$). The model fit statistics indicated that comparison standards explained 47 per cent of the variance in estimating service quality and 58 per cent of the variance in estimating satisfaction. Not all the independent variables were significant in each model, though there were some similarities between the two models. For example, the four comparison standards (predictive expectation, desires congruence, experienced-based norm

TABLE 2. Relationships Between the Comparison Standards

Comparison Standards	DisEx	PEx	DesEx	MTEx	DCon	Ebn	Asc	Isc	Mean (Sd)***
Desired Expectation (DisEx)	1								0.44 (1.24)
Predictive Expectation (PEx)	.72**	1							0.77 (1.25)
Deserved Expectation (DesEx)	.62**	.54**	1						0.56 (1.14)
Minimum Tolerable Expectation (MTEx)	.59**	.51**	.56**	1					0.80 (1.16)
Desires Congruence (DCon)	.47**	.46**	.34**	.33**	1				1.78 (6.62)
Experienced-Based Norm (Ebn)	.61**	.61**	.60**	.65**	.28**	1			1.07 (1.34)
Actual Self-Congruence (Asc)	.07	.09	.09	.16*	.06	.11	1		3.55 (.84)
Ideal Self-Congruence (Isc)	.25*	.23*	.12	.19*	.09	.18*	.39**	1	2.61 (.98)

*Correlation is significant at the 0.05 level. **Correlation is significant at the 0.01 level. ***Standard deviation.

TABLE 3. Estimating Service Quality and Customer Satisfaction Using Linear Regression

Variables	Service Quality			Customer Satisfaction		
	Standardised Beta Coefficient	t Score	Sig.	Standardised Beta Coefficient	t-Score	Sig.
(Constant)	-	16.11	.00*	-	17.19	.00*
Predictive Expectation	.28	3.53	.00*	.25	3.61	.00*
Deserved Expectation	.08	1.07	.29	.23	3.42	.00*
Minimum Tolerable Expectation	.07	.89	.37	.01	.22	.82
Desires Congruence	.14	2.25	.02*	.13	2.26	.02*
Experienced-Based Norm	.21	2.43	.01*	.27	3.55	.00*
Actual Self-Congruence	.10	1.61	.10	.02	.40	.68
Ideal Self-Congruence	.19	3.13	.00*	.12	2.28	.02*
R^2	.47			.58		
F(df = 7)	21			33		
P	.00*			.00*		

*Significant at the .05 level

and ideal self-congruence) had a positive influence on service quality and satisfaction decision. The minimum tolerable expectation and the actual self- congruence were not significant in predicting service quality and satisfaction.

There were also some differences between the two models. For example, deserved expectation was the only significant comparison standard in the satisfaction model. The order of importance of the significant variables also seemed to vary between the two models. According to the standardised beta coefficient, predictive expectation ((β = .28), experienced-based norm (β = .21) and ideal self-congruence ((β = .19) were found to be the three most important variables in estimating service quality. These were followed by desires congruence (β = .14). In the satisfaction model, the order of the three most important comparison standards was as follows: experienced based norm (β = .27), predictive expectation (β = .25) and deserved expectation (β = .23). These were followed by desires (β = .13) and ideal self-congruence measures (β = .12).

CONCLUSION

Theoretical Contributions

One of the primary contributions of this study is that it provides evidence that consumers use multiple comparison standards for the evaluation of service quality and satisfaction. Predictive expectation, desires congruence, ideal self-concept and experience-based norm were all found to be significant in predicting service quality and satisfaction. In contrast, minimum tolerable expectation and actual self-congruence were not significant. The negative finding regarding minimum tolerable expectation partly refutes Zeithaml et al.'s (1993) expectation model because it was not relevant to the evaluation of service quality and satisfaction. Meanwhile the positive finding regarding desires congruence supports Spreng et al.'s (1996) satisfaction model which emphasises the importance of desires in satisfaction formation.

This research indicates that expectation can be grouped into three categories: predictive, deserved and minimum tolerable. This finding partly supports Miller's (1997) theory of expectation. The expectation measures positively correlated with other comparison standards but the strength of correlation was not too strong, suggesting that the expectation measures provide unique information with respect to service evaluation. The study provides evidence for the differential role of self-concept, as only ideal self-congruence was found to be significant in predicting service quality and satisfaction. This research also offers empirical evidence for the use of experience-based norm as a comparison standard for the evaluation of hospitality services.

The findings of this study indicate that service quality and customer satisfaction are strongly related but are, nevertheless, different constructs. Evaluation of service quality positively influences customer satisfaction, which in turn positively influences purchase intention. These results support a line of research that conceptualises satisfaction as a mediating variable between service quality and purchase intention. The results also provide additional evidence in the debate surrounding whether (and why) these two concepts should be treated differently. Here the regression models show that the use of comparison standards seems to vary for evaluation of service quality and satisfaction. For example, deserved expectation was found to be significant in the satisfaction model but was not significant in the service quality model. Also, the relative importance of the comparison standards varied between the two regression models.

Managerial Implications

This study highlights the importance of service quality for business success. Hence, quality of services should be improved in order to influence customer satisfaction. Eventually customer satisfaction will positively influence purchase intention. The use of different comparison standards can provide managers with further information about the optimum level of service performance. This study suggests that, as long as the service performance comes up to the customer's predictive expectation level and meets the performance level of similar restaurants, it will be considered good quality. The findings for experience-based norm suggest that managers need to continuously be aware of the products and services of similar restaurants in the market. Indeed, they should check out such competitors' services in order to control their own restaurant's quality level. Most importantly, their restaurant's performance level should not be lower than that of competitors.

Managers should also maintain a good balance between what they offer (benefits to customers) and what they charge for their services in order to influence satisfaction, as deserved expectation and desires congruence both positively influence the satisfaction decision. This can be achieved by adopting a value-based pricing strategy, improving service performance or offering new benefits to customers.

We suggest that performance should be congruent with consumers' desired service level and ideal personality. When delivering services, the consumer personality should be taken into account. This can be achieved by two ways: either by employees modifying their service delivery strategy according to the customer's personality or by products being customized according to the customer's ideal personality trait. For example, if a customer would like to be an adventurous person, an exotic restaurant décor may fulfil this desire.

Finally, the results of this study suggest that guest surveys should include different comparison standards and, in particular, the experienced-based norm, deserved and predictive expectation in order to better assess service quality and customer satisfaction.

Limitations

The present study makes important theoretical contributions to our understanding of comparison standards used for the evaluation of hospitality services. Nevertheless, it has certain limitations, which have to be taken into account when interpreting the findings. One of the limitations of the study is the use of non-probability sampling (convenience sampling) to validate the underlying theory. The sample was limited to undergraduate students studying a specific degree in one university, and therefore the findings cannot be generalized to the whole population. In addition, the dimensions of service quality were not investigated.

REFERENCES

Baron, R.M. and Kenny, D.A. (1985). The moderator mediator variable distinction in social psychological research: conceptual, strategic, and statistical considerations. *Journal of Personality and Social Psychology*, 51(6), 1173-1182.

Cadotte, E.R., Woodruff, R.B. and Jenkins, R.L. (1987). Expectations and norms in models of consumer satisfaction. *Journal of Marketing Research*, 24, 305-314.

Churchill, G.A., (1979), A paradigm for developing better measure of marketing constructs. *Journal of Marketing Research*, 16, 64-73.

Chon, K. (1992). Self-image/destination image congruity. *Annals of Tourism Research*, 19, 360-362.

Cronin, Jr., J.J. and Taylor, S.A. (1992). SERVPERF versus SERVQUAL: reconciling performance-based and perception-minus-expectations measurement of service quality. *Journal of Marketing* 58, 15-131.

Dabholkar, P.A., Shepherd, C.D. and Thorpe, D. I. (2000). A comprehensive framework for service quality: an investigation of critical conceptual and measurement issues through a longitudinal study, *Journal of Retailing*, 76(2), 139-173.

Ekinci, Y. Riley, M. and Chen, J. (2001). A review of comparison standards used in service quality and customer satisfaction studies: emerging issues for hospitality and tourism research. *Tourism Analysis*, 5(2/4), 197-202.

Ekinci, Y. (2003). An investigation of the determinants of customer satisfaction, *Tourism Analysis*, (in press).

Hair, J.F.Jr., Anderson, R.E., Tatham, R.L., Black, W.C., (1998). *Multivariate Data Analysis* (5th edit.). London: Prentice Hall.

Hamm B.C. and Cundiff, E.W. (1969). Self-actualisation and product perception. *Journal of Marketing Research*, 6, 470-472.

Hong J.W. and Zinkhan, G.N.M. (1995). Self-concept and advertising effectiveness: the influence of congruence, conspicuousness and response mode. *Psychology and Marketing*, 12(1), 53-77.

LaTour, S.A. and Peat, N.C. (1979). Conceptual and methodological issues in consumer satisfaction research. In: William, L.W., (Eds.), *Advances In Consumer Research* (pp. 431-437), Ann Arbor, MI: Association for Consumer Research.

Liljander, V. (1994). Modeling perceived service quality using different comparison standard. *Journal of Consumer Satisfaction and Dissatisfaction*, 7, 126-142.

Liljander, V. and Strandvik, T. (1993). Different comparison standard as determinants of *service quality. Journal of Consumer Satisfaction and Dissatisfaction*, 6, 118-132.

Malhotra, N.K. (1988). Self concept and product choice: an integrated perspective. *Journal of Economic Psychology*, 9, 1-28.

Miller, J.A. (1977). Studying satisfaction: modifying models, eliciting expectations, posing problems and making meaningful measurements. In H. Keith Hunt (ed.), *Conceptualizations and Measurement of Consumer Satisfaction and Dissatisfaction*, Bloomington: School of Business, Indiana University, 72-91.

Olshavsky, R.W. and Spreng, R.A. (1989). A desires as standard model of consumer satisfaction. *Journal of Consumer Satisfaction Dissatisfaction and Complaining Behavior*, 2, 49-54.

Parasuraman, A., Zeithaml, V.A. and Berry, L.L. (1988). SERVQUAL a multiple-item scale for measuring consumer perception of service quality. *Journal of Retailing*, 64, 13-40.

Parasuraman, A., Berry, L.L. and Zeithaml, V.A. (1991). Refinement and reassessment of the SERVQUAL scale, *Journal of Retailing*, 67, 421-450.

Rokeach, M. (1973). *The Nature of Human Values*, New York: The Free Press.

Sirgy, M.J. (1982). Self-concept in consumer behaviour: a critical review. *Journal of Consumer Research*, 9, 287-300.

Sirgy, M.J. and Samli, A.C. (1985). A path analytic model of store loyalty involving self-concept, store image, geographic loyalty, and socio-economic status. *Journal of the Academy of Marketing Science*. 13(3), 265-291.

Spreng, R.A. and Mackoy, R.D. (1996). An empirical examination of a model of perceived service quality and satisfaction. *Journal of Retailing*, 72(2), 201-214.

Spreng R.A., MacKenzie, S.B. and Olshavsky, R.W. (1996). A re-examination of the determinants of consumer satisfaction. *Journal of Marketing*, 60, 15-32.

Teas, R.K. (1993). Expectations, performance evaluation, and consumers' perceptions of quality, *Journal of Marketing*, 57, 18-34.

Teas, R.K. (1994). Expectations as a comparison standard in measuring service quality. *Journal of Marketing*, 58, 132-139.

Tse, D.K. and Wilton, P.C. (1988). Models of consumer satisfaction formation, an extension. *Journal of Marketing Research*, 25, 204-212.

Woodruff, R.B., Clemons, S.D., Schumann, D.W., Gardial, S.F, and Burns, M.J. (1991). The standard issue in cs/d research: a historical perspective. *Journal of Consumer Satisfaction, Dissatisfaction and Complaining Behavior*, 4, 103-109.

Zeithaml, V.A., Berry, L.L. and Parasuraman, A. (1993). The nature and determinants of customer expectations of service. *Journal of Academy of Marketing Science*, 24(1), 1-12.

"Just Trying to Keep
the Customer Satisfied":
A Comparison of Models Used
in the Measurement of Tourist Satisfaction

Paul Fallon
Peter Schofield

SUMMARY. The paper compares the predictive validity of six models used in the measurement of satisfaction; it is concerned with their application at destination level, with particular reference to Orlando, Florida. Using factor analysis and multiple regression, the 'performance only' model was clearly identified as the best predictor of satisfaction. The incorporation of 'importance' and 'performance' ratings did not improve the predictive power of the 'performance only' solution. From tourists' 'performance' ratings, five 'dimensions' of Orlando's tourism offering were identified: 'primary,' 'secondary' and 'tertiary' attractions, 'facilitators' and 'transport plus.' Notwithstanding Orlando's reputation as the world's theme park capital, Orlando's 'secondary' attractions (such as shopping and dining opportunities) and 'facilitators' (such as accommo-

---

Paul Fallon (E-mail: P.Fallon@salford.ac.uk) and Peter Schofield (E-mail: P.Schofield@salford.ac.uk) are affiliated with the School of Leisure, Hospitality and Food Management, University of Salford, Salford M6 6PU, UK.

[Haworth co-indexing entry note]: " 'Just Trying to Keep the Customer Satisfied': A Comparison of Models Used in the Measurement of Tourist Satisfaction." Fallon, Paul, and Peter Schofield. Co-published simultaneously in *Journal of Quality Assurance in Hospitality & Tourism* (The Haworth Hospitality Press, an imprint of The Haworth Press, Inc.) Vol. 4, No. 3/4, 2003, pp. 77-96; and: *Current Issues and Development in Hospitality and Tourism Satisfaction* (ed: John A. Williams and Muzaffer Uysal) The Haworth Hospitality Press, an imprint of The Haworth Press, Inc., 2003, pp. 77-96. Single or multiple copies of this article are available for a fee from The Haworth Document Delivery Service [1-800-HAWORTH, 9:00 a.m. - 5:00 p.m. (EST). E-mail address: docdelivery@haworthpress.com].

dation and customer service) were identified as having the most influence on overall tourist satisfaction with Orlando. *[Article copies available for a fee from The Haworth Document Delivery Service: 1-800-HAWORTH. E-mail address: <docdelivery@haworthpress.com> Website: <http://www. HaworthPress.com> © 2003 by The Haworth Press, Inc. All rights reserved.]*

KEYWORDS. Tourist satisfaction, destination performance, predictive validity, factor analysis, multiple regression analysis

INTRODUCTION

Customer satisfaction has generally been conceptualised as the 'outcome' for the customer after exposure to the service product (Crompton and Love, 1995; Baker and Crompton, 2000; Kozak, 2001). By comparison, quality refers to the service operation's 'output', i.e., the attributes of the product that are primarily under the control of the operation (Crompton and Love, 1995; Schofield and Fallon, 2000). Nevertheless, satisfaction also represents a potentially significant 'outcome' for the operation; it provides external benefits–such as customer loyalty and positive word-of-mouth recommendation–and its measurement provides internal opportunities–such as facilitation of resource management, product enhancement and differentiation. Given the development of the tourism sector, it is therefore not surprising that the measurement of tourist satisfaction has become a major area of research in the last three decades (Kozak, 2001). Despite this activity, there is still much discussion about the single best method of measuring customer satisfaction (Kozak, 2003) using pre- and post-experience constructs, i.e., 'expectations,' 'importance' and 'performance.' More recently, the debate has centred on a comparison of single construct measurement, i.e., performance-only models and multiple construct measurements, i.e., expectation-performance and importance-performance models. The 'melting pot' of satisfaction is further complicated by the influence of more personal and subjective variables such as needs, disposition, travelling companions and previous experience which accompany the customer in the service encounter (Crompton and Love, 1995; Meyer, 1997; Kozak, 2001).

Comparative analysis of the various models has been conducted in the context of camp sites (Dorfman, 1979; Fick and Ritchie, 1991), events (Crompton and Love, 1995) and restaurants (Yuksel and Rimmington, 1998) but has so far ignored tourist destinations, arguably the underpinning element of the tourism product. This research takes up the metaphorical gauntlet thrown down by this previous empirical research to determine the predictive validity of the various conceptualisations of satisfaction at destination level with respect to Orlando, Florida, currently the UK's leading long-haul tourist destination.

CONCEPTUALISING SATISFACTION

The most widely documented satisfaction constructs are expectation-performance, importance-performance and performance-only (Kozak, 2001).

Expectation-Performance

The expectation-performance paradigm, derived from adaption level theory, has dominated both satisfaction and service quality research. Confirmation and disconfirmation of expectations have been determined using both 'inferred' and 'direct' methods (Prakash and Lounsberry, 1983; Barsky, 1992; Barsky and Labagh, 1992; Pizam and Milman, 1993; Meyer and Westerbarkey, 1996). The most famous exponent of the inferred method has been the SERVQUAL model (Zeithaml, Parasuraman and Berry, 1985). This has been adopted in a number of destination and tourism-related studies (Crompton and Mackay, 1989; Fick and Ritchie, 1991; Saleh and Ryan, 1992; Pizam and Milman, 1993) but despite its intuitive appeal and widespread use, the expectation-performance paradigm has received considerable theoretical and operational criticism on a number of grounds.

Firstly, there is consensus that the conceptualisation of expectations, the comparative standard, is vague. Lack of experience with a destination or service may cause expectations to be tentative or uncertain and therefore unsuitable as a base against which performance judgements are made (Crompton and Love, 1995; Yuksel and Rimmington, 1998). The measurement of expectations may also be adversely affected by the ideal of high expectations (Dorfman, 1979) and the tendency to indicate a maximum score on each attribute (Babakus and Boller, 1992). This would seem particularly relevant to tourist destination research in general, given the high level of tourist investment and involvement. Moreover, consumers may modify their expectations during a destination visit or service encounter because of their actual experiences (Danaher and Mattsson, 1994; Weber, 1997).

A second criticism of the expectancy-performance paradigm calls the timing of expectations measurement into question (Crompton and Love, 1995; Yuksel and Rimmington, 1998). For example, the original SERVQUAL model administered the expectations and performance batteries together at the post-experience stage (Parasuraman, Zeithaml and Berry, 1985). Carman (1990), Gronroos (1993) and Getty and Thomson (1994) propose that expectations should be sought prior to experience in order to prevent contamination by the actual performance. In effect, in the context of tourist destinations, they then cease to be purely pre-visit perceptions when elicited at the post-visit stage. Interestingly, Miller (1977) explored the basis for expectations, resulting in a classification of: *ideal* ('wished for'); *expected* ('predictive' or 'probable'); *minimum tolerable* ('least acceptable'); and *deserved* ('should be, in the light of the sacrifice made'). Consequently, Ekinci, Riley and Chen (2000) suggest that the purpose and timing of the measurement should determine which of these conceptualisations is chosen.

A third criticism centres on the use and interpretation of discrepancy scores in that they represent an 'inferred,' or 'indirect,' measurement because it is the researcher and not the subject who performs the comparison (Oh, 1999). However, the evidence is equivocal and researchers measuring satisfaction in a variety of fields are continuing to use 'difference' scores (Crompton and Love, 1995), although there is no consensus on what the 'difference' score actually represents. Interestingly, Hughes (1991) and Pearce (1991) throw complete doubt on the disconfirmation approach, and particularly the validity of the 'difference' score as an indicator of the level of quality or satisfaction, by arguing that tourists may be satisfied even though the performance did not fulfil their expectations, i.e., there is negative disconfirmation.

Within the framework of expectations-performance, a single measurement, 'non-difference,' or 'direct,' approach (Weber, 1997) has also been adopted. Using summary-judgement scales to measure confirmation and disconfirmation, respondents are asked to directly rate the extent to which the destination exceeded, met, or fell short of expectations; for example, an attribute is 'better than' or 'worse than' expected (Carman, 1990; Crompton and Love, 1995; Yuksel and Rimmington, 1998). This clearly eliminates some of the theoretical and practical problems identified with the 'difference' approach, but is likely to produce a different result (Williams, 1988).

Performance-Only

The 'performance-only' model directly challenges the above paradigm by proposing that evaluations of a destination, in terms of quality and/or satisfaction, are affected only by perceptions of performance, or experience, of the destination. Given the problems related to the measurement of expectations, it is hardly surprising that many researchers have adopted this single construct methodology; they doubt the validity of disparity theories and consider that performance only is a more effective method and indicator of quality and/or satisfaction (Churchill and Surprenant, 1982; Carman, 1990; Cronin and Taylor, 1992). Mannell (1989) posits that quality perceptions are guided by how well the destination fulfills tourists' drives, motives, needs and wants, rather than any performance comparison with pre-visit predictions. Additionally, given that all tourists–even first-timers–become more experienced over the course of their holiday due to its longitudinal nature, they have the potential to refine not only their initial expectations (Danaher and Mattsson, 1994; Weber, 1997) but also these needs and wants on an ongoing basis. Consequently, the performance-only conceptualisation of satisfaction would seem to be a more valid approach than the expectancy-performance one. Moreover, Meyer and Westerbarkey (1996) argue that measurements that focus on perceptions of performance alone are more typical of the cognitive process, and Yuksel and Rimmington (1998: 63) propose that 'performance bears a pre-eminent role in the formation of customer satisfaction because it is the main feature of the consumption experience.'

Importance-Performance

The relative importance of service 'product' attributes has received considerable attention in the consumer behaviour literature within the context of the theory of reasoned action and the measurement of consumer attitudes (*inter alia* Goodrich, 1978; Crompton, 1979; Ryan and Bonfield, 1980; Witter, 1985). Attribute importance has also been measured as an integral part of the analysis of quality and satisfaction within the expectancy-(dis)confirmation paradigm. Research which has considered importance ratings has focused on 'within-brand' importance of attributes or factors and has neglected 'between-brand' comparisons by consumers (Oh and Parks, 1997). 'Within-brand' importance has been measured directly by questioning subjects or asking them to rate items on Likert-type scales in terms of their importance (Barsky, 1992).

On a practical level, Duke and Persia's (1996) research on consumer perceptions of escorted tours demonstrated that an understanding of the relative importance of tour attributes, from the consumer perspective, helped tour designers to change the features of tours in line with consumer needs. Their methodology included an assessment of the importance of tour attributes both before and after the tour. The results showed that tour attributes were rated differently depending on the timing of the survey, suggesting that the timing of the importance rating is an important and perhaps underresearched issue. Despite these findings, and Oh and Parks' (1997) call for further efforts to improve the measuring and modeling of the importance construct, this dynamic nature has so far been neglected.

Performance ratings have been weighted by importance scores using both indirect inferential approaches employing regression analysis and direct methods in which a subjects' attribute rating is weighted by its corresponding importance score. This model is intrinsically weak because it does not distinguish between the relative contributions of the performance and importance scores and often produces results that do not resemble the original ratings from either the performance or importance scales (Crompton and Love, 1995; Duke and Persia, 1996). There is some disagreement about whether or not to include importance measures. On the one hand, the continuing use of importance-performance analysis (IPA) underlines the benefits of knowing the relative importance of product attributes. On the other hand, it has been argued that the inclusion of importance measures can complicate matters from the standpoint of both statistical analysis and the interpretation of the results from a practical management perspective (Oh and Parks, 1997).

COMPARING THE VALIDITY OF ALTERNATIVE CONSTRUCTS

Whilst the pertinent literature has produced a number of measurement tools, it has generally tended to neglect more practical aspects of measurement such as empirical comparisons of the reliability and validity of the methods (Oh and Parks, 1997) in favour of more conceptual issues and underlying processes. However, a small number of comparative analyses have been implemented.

Following early comparative studies by Dorfman (1979) and Fick and Ritchie (1991), in the context of camping and general tourism businesses respectively, Crompton and Love (1995) carried out research on festivals and, more recently, Yuksel and Rimmington (1998) considered restaurants. In all four studies, the results have been unequivocal in finding significant differences between the validity of the models:

- the performance-only approach emerged as the most valid and reliable measure of satisfaction;
- importance-weighting did not improve the predictive power of the measures;
- the disconfirmation-based operationalisations were the least valid and reliable.

The results of these comparative studies suggest that, with regards to satisfaction measurement, the performance-only approach represents the 'winning ticket.' Certainly, its 'single-hit' methodology offers practical benefits to researchers. However, as Crompton and Love (1995) point out, there are a number of conceptualisations of satisfaction and it is unreasonable to assume that they all measure the same aspect or are even highly correlated. Consequently, there may be no single 'best way' and different approaches may be useful for different purposes. Considering performance-only ratings in isolation means that key insights into the broader elements of related tourist behaviour may be lost. Furthermore, Parasuraman, Zeithaml and Berry (1994) note that some organisations have switched to a disconfirmation approach because the information generated has more diagnostic value. For example, expectations are shaped, in part, by promotional activity (Parasuraman et al., 1985) and, therefore, tracking of expectations would give some indication of the effectiveness of this communication. Also, the importance construct, in conjunction with expectations and/or performance, offers major diagnostic and contextual value (Crompton and Love, 1995; Yuksel and Rimmington, 1998; Crompton, 1999).

Whilst expectation, performance and importance constructs underpin quantitative research at destination level, and despite the call for comparative studies in the field of tourist behaviour (Pearce, 1993), no specific comparative analysis has been undertaken with regards to a tourist destination. The focus of this paper is a comparative analysis of alternative methods of measuring satisfaction at tourist destination level in order to assess their predictive validity and reliability and to refine existing measurement instruments. Six models were compared: 'performance only,' 'performance weighted by pre-visit importance,' 'performance weighted by post-visit importance,' 'pre-visit importance minus performance,' 'post-visit importance minus performance' and 'predictive expectation minus performance.' The research can be differentiated from previous comparative studies by Crompton and Love (1995) and Yuksel and Rimmington (1998) on the following bases: the study was focused at destination level and both pre-visit and post-visit measures of importance were used. These issues have been highlighted as important aspects of tourist satisfaction measurement (Oh and Parks, 1997; Kozak, 2001). Based on the theoretical issues outlined above and the empirical findings of previous studies the following hypotheses were established:

H1   The 'performance only' model would explain more of the variance in the overall satisfaction measure than any of the alternative models.

H2   Weighting the 'performance only' model with importance scores would not improve the predictive validity of the model.

H3   The disconfirmation-based operationalisation would be the least valid and reliable.

H4   The multiple-construct models consisting of purely post-experience evaluations would be better predictors of overall satisfaction than the multiple-construct models incorporating pre-experience evaluations.

METHODOLOGY

The Research Instrument

In order to elicit tourists' pre- and post-visit perceptions of Orlando, on expectation and performance constructs, and compare the alternative conceptualised models, the study adopted a longitudinal research methodology comprising two structured, self-administered questionnaires. Subjects were asked to rate the attributes in terms of their expectations (pre-visit) in the first questionnaire and their performance (post-visit) in the second; in addition, they were asked to rate their importance in both questionnaires thereby facilitating a comparison of the alternative models including pre-visit and post-visit importance constructs (after Duke and Persia, 1996).

The attributes on which Orlando was evaluated were generated from the triangulation of primary and secondary methods (Jenkins, 1999; Tribe and Snaith, 1998). Secondary research took the form of a review of both the relevant academic and commercial literature, which included texts and articles on destination image, quality and satisfaction and brochures and travel guides respectively. Preliminary primary research incorporated free elicitation during eight focus groups and an open-ended questionnaire distributed to a stratified random sample of employees at the University of Salford. In both cases, subjects were representative of Orlando's UK market. There was consensus on a relatively parsimonious set of elements on which UK visitors make judgements on Orlando and a distinction between the destination's offering of specific attractions and activities, which were dominated by its primary attractions such as theme parks, and generic facilities needed to enjoy these attractions during the holiday, such as accommodation. This procedure produced 22 attributes which were incorporated into both pre- and post-visit questionnaires.

The first (pre-visit) questionnaire required respondents to rate Orlando's attributes in terms of importance and expectations. It was divided into four sections: the first section elicited information about the respondents' prior experience of Orlando and their current trip; the second section required respondents to indicate the level of the importance of Orlando's attributes on this holiday; Section three required respondents to indicate the level of their expectations of Orlando's attributes on this holiday; and the fourth section gathered respondents' socio-demographic information. In both questionnaires, attribute ratings were made on a 7-point Likert scale with each point carrying both numerical and labelled descriptors (Ryan, 1995). In order to eliminate potential confusion between importance and expectation judgements (Oh, 2001), clear completion instructions were given in the appropriate sections. On the Importance scale, respondents were asked to indicate how important each attribute was to their current holiday; scale anchors were 'Extremely Unimportant' (1) and 'Extremely Important' (7). On the Expectations scale, respondents were asked to indicate how poor or good they expected Orlando to be in terms of the 22 attributes; anchors were 'Extremely Poor' (1) and 'Extremely Good' (7). It was considered that these predictive expectations were most appropriate for the study, bearing in mind their purpose as a comparison standard and the timing of measurement (as per Ekinci et al., 2000). Furthermore, previous comparative studies, i.e., Crompton and Love (1995) and Yuksel and Rimmington (1998) have employed a predictive expectation standard.

The second (post-visit) questionnaire required respondents to rate Orlando's attributes in terms of how important they were and how well they had performed on this holiday. It was also divided into three sections. Section 1 gathered respondents' attribute importance and performance ratings; the Performance scale anchors were 'Extremely Poor' (1) and 'Extremely Good' (7). Section 2 elicited single ratings of overall satisfaction and behavioural intention. The third section educed additional personal details from the subjects.

The construct validity of the 22-attribute instrument was assessed using an overall measure of satisfaction and two behavioural intention measures, i.e., re-visit and recommend (after Yuksel and Rimmington, 1998; Kozak, 2003). The correlation of the 'performance-only' construct with the overall satisfaction measure produced a co-efficient of 0.504, compared with a co-efficient of 0.334 with the measure of intention to return to the destination. This demonstrates convergent and discriminant validity respectively. Further, nomological validity was established with a correlation co-efficient of 0.459 between the construct and the measure of intention to recommend.

The Sample

After an initial pilot study, which resulted in only minor amendments, a sample of UK visitors to Orlando was taken at both Manchester (UK) and Orlando Sanford (USA) airports in September 2001. Orlando was chosen as the destination subject primarily because it is the UK's most popular long-haul holiday destination with 1.31 million UK visitors in 2000; UK visitors account for 43.5% of overseas visitors to Orlando (Orlando CVB Research, 2001). Additionally, it was considered that Orlando's familiarity, in particular the mass appeal of its core attractions, would increase the validity of the pre-visit assessment of attribute importance and predictive expectations, irrespective of whether visitors had previously visited the destination.

A convenience sample was taken at both airports. Respondents at Manchester were required to complete the first, i.e., pre-visit questionnaire before their outbound flight; they were subsequently given the second, i.e., post-visit questionnaire to complete and return to the researchers in a prepaid envelope after their holiday. Clearly, this system was reliant upon the loyalty and endurance of outbound respondents with regards to the completion and postage of the second questionnaire. To compensate for the possibility of non-completed second questionnaires, post-visit importance and performance ratings were also elicited from a further independent sample at Orlando Sanford airport. The questionnaire administered at Sanford airport was identical to the second questionnaire handed to respondents at Manchester, apart from the fact that it also included additional sections regarding respondents' demographic profile, previous experience of Orlando and information on their current holiday. The Manchester study produced 141 complete sets of questionnaires, i.e., pre- and post-visit; the Sanford post-visit sample produced 326 usable questionnaires. In total there were 467 usable questionnaires. There were no significant differences on the post-visit ratings from the two samples ($p > 0.05$). On this basis, the samples from the two locations were merged for the post-visit component of the study. Use of such a multiple sample has been proposed by a number of authors to compensate for the practical problems encountered in similar pre- and post-visit longitudinal surveys (Oliver, 1997; Yuksel and Rimmington, 1998). Screening questions were used to identify the respondents' suitability for the survey. The majority (90%) of tourists in the overall sample were staying in Orlando for two weeks, which, even given the scale of Orlando's offering, gave them a reasonable time to familiarise themselves with the destination. Most (70%) were travelling in parties of four or more; these were mainly family groups.

Data Analysis

The data was analysed using SPSS Version 11. Subjects' attribute ratings were negatively skewed, which was expected given both the likelihood of tourists to be satisfied in general (Ryan, 1995) and Orlando's highly positive reputation. The study adopted the methodology of previous comparative studies, i.e., Crompton and Love (1995) and Yuksel and Rimmington (1998) by using correlation and multiple regression to test the hypotheses regarding the relationships between the models and an overall measure of satisfaction.

Spearman rank order coefficients were employed to compare the correlations of the various conceptualised models with overall satisfaction ratings. A factor analysis, using principal components as the method of extraction, with varimax rotation was conducted on each scale to identify a smaller set of factors with eigenvalues greater than or equal to 1.0 and factor loadings greater than 0.4 (after Stevens, 1992); Cronbach's alpha coefficient, a Kaiser-Meyer-Olkin (KMO) test of sampling adequacy and Bartlett's test of sphericity were computed to determine the factorability of the correlation matrix. Finally, multiple regression analysis, using these factors, was used to examine the ability of each of the alternative conceptualised models to explain variation in overall satisfaction. The factors were ranked in order of importance by their standardised beta coefficients.

RESULTS AND DISCUSSION

A Comparative Analysis of the Alternative Models

Table 1 shows the correlation between the alternative models and overall satisfaction, the ability of the models to explain variation in overall satisfaction, and the reliability scores for the various models. In the case of the regression analysis, the attribute scores from each model were initially factor analysed in order to reduce multi-collinearity; PCA was used to generate the initial solution due to the absence of a normal distribution (Ryan, 1995).

The 'performance-only' model exhibits the highest correlation with the overall satisfaction measure and also explains more of the variation in overall satisfaction than the other models; consequently, H1 and the results of previous research (Dorfman, 1979; Churchill and Surprenant, 1982; Fick and Ritchie, 1991; Cronin and Taylor, 1992; Crompton and Love, 1995; Yuksel and Rimmington, 1998) are

TABLE 1. Spearman Correlations and Multiple R Values of Alternative Conceptualisations of Satisfaction

Alternative Models	Spearman Correlation Coefficients with Overall Satisfaction	Multiple R Value for Regression on Overall Satisfaction (Based on Factors)	Alpha Co-efficient
Performance Only	.504**	.538* (F = 37.535)	.8813
Post-Visit Importance times Performance	.447**	.383* (F = 15.857)	.8737
Pre-Visit Importance times Performance	.300**	.428* (F = 4.264)	.8245
Post-Visit Importance minus Performance	−.247**	.375*** (F = 3.644)	.7555
Pre-Visit Importance minus Performance	−.377**	.350* (F = 10.738)	.8238
Performance minus Expectations	−.456**	.497* (F = 6.245)	.8978

*significant at .000, ** significant at .001, *** significant at .002

supported. An alternative explanation for the 'large' (Cohen, 1988) co-efficient is the possibility of a halo effect relating to individual attribute and overall satisfaction evaluation due to the shared timing of their capture after the experience. Interestingly, the weighting of 'performance' with 'importance' scores–both pre- and post-visit–has not improved the predictive validity of the 'performance' measure, which supports Hypothesis 2. By comparison H3 has not been supported because the disconfirmation-based operationalisation, i.e., 'performance minus expectation' showed the second highest predictive ability. Given the negative correlation between the 'performance minus expectations' model and overall satisfaction, this predictive ability would seem to support the argument that tourists are satisfied despite negative disconfirmation (Hughes, 1991; Pearce, 1991).

The post-visit importance measure appears to be more effective than its pre-visit counterpart with respect to the results of the correlation analysis. However, the regression co-efficients do not follow this pattern. The regression analysis results for the discrepancy-based models, i.e., 'post-visit importance minus performance' and 'pre-visit importance minus performance' show the higher predictive ability of the former. However, the results involving the weighted models, i.e., 'post-visit importance times performance' and 'pre-visit importance times performance' demonstrate the higher predictive ability of the pre-visit measure over its post-visit counterpart. On this basis the null hypothesis for H4 cannot be rejected. The failure of the weighted models to match the predictive ability of the 'performance-only measure' may result from the inability of these models to discriminate between the contribution of individual importance and performance scores (Crompton and Love, 1995), although this weighted approach would seem preferable to the use of discrepancy models producing 'inferred' scores.

Factor Analysis of Performance Ratings

Given the dominance of the 'performance-only' model, it was considered appropriate to examine its dimensions and their relative influence on subjects' overall satisfaction with Orlando. Therefore, subjects' ratings on the 'performance-only' construct were factor analysed. The analysis produced a five-factor solution (with eigenvalues > 1.0) which explained 56.539% of the overall variance before rotation; 15 of the 21 items had loadings greater than 6.0, indicating a good correlation between the items and the factor groupings they belong to. The Kaiser-Meyer-Olkin (KMO) value of .878 was 'meritorious' (Kaiser, 1974) and the Bartlett's Test of Sphericity reached statistical significance, supporting the factorability of the correlation matrix. The results are given in Table 2 and details relating to the regression of overall satisfaction

TABLE 2. Results of the Factor Analysis of Orlando's Attribute Performance Ratings

Orlando's Attributes	Factor 1	Factor 2	Factor 3	Factor 4	Factor 5	Communality
Factor 1: *Facilitators*						
Accommodation	.803					.685
Cleanliness	.763					.660
Pool	.744					.592
Safety	.719					.598
Customer Service	.718					.626
Friendliness of Locals	.513					.465
Factor 2: *Secondary Attractions*						
Goods at Bargain Prices		.802				.679
Shopping Facilities		.770				.665
Restaurant VFM		.753				.670
Variety of Restaurants		.666				.534
Opportunity for Rest & Relaxation		.457				.489
Factor 3: *Tertiary Attractions*						
Natural & Wildlife Attractions & Trails			.780			.629
Cultural & Historic Attractions & Trails			.775			.639
Sports Facilities			.621			.477
Bus Service			.514			.338
Nightlife			.440			.438
Factor 4: *Core Attractions*						
Many Things to See and Do				.808		.736
Something for Everyone				.743		.673
Theme Parks				.675		.535
Factor 5: *Transport*						
Car-hire service					.811	.696
Road Signs that are Easy to Follow					.401	.388
Eigenvalue	6.244	2.007	1.686	1.434	1.067	
Variance (%)	28.381	9.123	7.664	6.520	4.851	
Cumulative Variance (%)	28.381	37.504	45.168	51.688	56.539	
Cronbach's Alpha	.8502	.7896	.7888	.7382	.5224	
Number of Items (Total = 21)	6	5	5	3	2	

against each of the factors are provided in Table 3. The regression model achieved a satisfactory level of goodness of fit in predicting the variance of tourists' overall satisfaction in relation to the five factors, as predicted by the multiple correlation coefficient (R), coefficient of determination (R^2) *and F* ratio. Firstly, the R value of independent variables on the dependent variable is .538, which shows that the tourists had high satisfaction levels with the five factors. Secondly, the R^2 of 0.289 suggests that almost 30% of the variation in overall satisfaction is explained by the five factors. Finally, the F ratio has a value of 37.535 and is significant at .000 indicating that the beta coefficients can be used to explain each factor's relative contribution to the variance in tourist's overall satisfaction.

The results seem to support the findings from the qualitative research at the front-end of the study in terms of the distinction which was made between Orlando's attractions, for example its theme parks, and secondary elements, such

TABLE 3. Regression Results of UK Tourists' Overall Satisfaction Level Bases on the Performance of Orlando's Factors

Dependent variable: Tourists' degree of their overall satisfaction with Orlando (used as a surrogate indicator)

Independent variables: 5 orthogonal factors representing the components of Orlando's perceived quality

Goodness of fit: Multiple R = .538
R^2 = .289
Adjusted R^2 = .282
SE = .5224

Analysis of variance	Df	Sum of Squares	Mean Square
Regression	5	51.212	10.242
Residual	461	125.795	.273

F = 37.535
Significant F = .000

Variable in the equation Independent Variable	B	SE B	Beta	T	Sig. T
Secondary Attractions (Factor 2)	.203	0.24	.330	8.405	.000
Facilitators (Factor 1)	.177	0.24	.287	7.298	.000
Core Attractions (Factor 4)	.148	0.24	.241	6.132	.000
Tertiary Attractions (Factor 3)	.107	0.24	.174	4.425	.000
Transport (Factor 5)	6.206E-02	0.24	.101	2.565	.011
Constant	4.416	0.24		182.676	.000

as accommodation and customer service, which facilitated the enjoyment of the main features. Indeed, there appears to be a good fit between the factors and Kotler, Bowen and Maken's (1999) product level concept in that *core*, *secondary* and *tertiary* attractions, *facilitators* and *transport plus* (see Table 2) were identified. The *core*, *secondary* and *tertiary* attractions represent the 'pull' elements, whilst the *facilitators* and *transport plus* groupings enable the attractions to be experienced and optimised by the tourist.

Factor 1: Facilitators

This factor contains generic and functional attributes which may not be enough in themselves to attract visitors but their presence enables and supplements enjoyment of the destination and its attractions. Furthermore, as such they offer a frame of reference for comparison of one destination with another. The regression results identify that the *facilitators* carried the second heaviest weight for tourists in their overall destination satisfaction; a one unit increase in the performance would lead to a 0.287 unit increase in tourists' overall level of satisfaction, all other variables being held constant. This emphasises the key role of the performance of these 'basic' items in terms of subjects' overall satisfaction, irrespective of Orlando's reputation in terms of its attractions.

Factor 2: Secondary Attractions

Whilst its theme parks remain Orlando's primary attraction, Orlando is becoming increasingly well known for its eating and shopping facilities and their offerings to tourists, which was emphasised in both the initial primary and secondary research. Orlando CVB Research (2001) identified shopping and dining in restaurants as the top two holiday activities, outstripping visiting the theme parks, for UK visitors in 2000. The results of the regression analysis identify secondary attractions as the single most influential factor affecting tourists' overall satisfaction with Orlando; a one unit increase in the performance of the secondary attractions would lead to a 0.330 unit increase in tourists' overall level of satisfaction, all other variables being held constant. Given the general 'experiential' nature of the holiday and the high financial outlay thereon, especially in Orlando, perhaps it is hardly surprising that the performance of 'tangible' purchases, such as food and goods, and locations in which they are purchased make such a contribution to overall satisfaction. The loading of 'opportunity for rest and relaxation' on this factor is interesting given that Orlando is *prima facie* a highly active holiday destination due to the overall scale and scope of its attractions. Consequently, it may be that shopping and dining represent crucial opportunities for visitors to re-charge their batteries.

Factor 3: Tertiary Attractions

These represent attractions for which Orlando is arguably less well-known. Despite their quality and abundance at the destination, they are overshadowed by the core and secondary attractions. A one unit increase in the performance of the secondary attractions would lead to a 0.174 unit increase in tourists' overall level of satisfaction, all other variables being held constant. Interestingly, Orlando is now trying to broaden its appeal by emphasising its less famous resources and in particular to repeat visitors (Brodie, 2000).

Factor 4: Core Attractions

Since Orlando is renowned for the number and variety of its attractions, especially its man-made theme parks, it might be expected that these core attractions would make the greatest contribution to overall destination satisfaction.

Furthermore, focus group research and informal discussion with respondents during the survey proper emphasised that much of Orlando's appeal lay in its ability to meet the diverse needs of large tourist parties including extended families. However, the results of the regression identify that these *core attractions* carried only the third heaviest weight for tourists in their overall destination satisfaction. A one unit increase in the performance would lead to a 0.241 unit increase in tourists' overall level of satisfaction, all other variables being held constant.

Factor 5: Transport Plus

The majority (70%) of respondents used a hire-car to get around Orlando during their holiday. Clearly, hire-cars and road signs are both attributes which enable, or facilitate, the enjoyment and optimisation of Orlando's attractions, and possibly more so than at any other destination. However, the regression analysis identified this factor as the least influential factor affecting tourists' overall satisfaction with Orlando; a one unit increase in the performance of the secondary attractions would lead to a 0.101 unit increase in tourists' overall level of satisfaction, all other variables being held constant. This contrasts with the contribution of the other functional attributes, i.e., the *facilitators*. This may be due to the fact that cars and road-signs represent the least interesting functional element of Orlando's offering, in comparison with hotels, villas, pools and customer service.

CONCLUSION

The study compared the predictive validity of six conceptualised models in relation to tourists' overall satisfaction with Orlando, Florida, the UK's most popular long-haul holiday destination. Using factor analysis and multiple regression, the 'performance only' model was clearly identified as the best predictor of overall satisfaction. The incorporation of 'importance' ratings did not improve the predictive validity of the 'performance only' solution. Both results support previous comparative research. However, unlike previous research, this study focused on comparing models at the destination level and captured both pre-visit and post-visit importance ratings, which enabled a further comparison. The 'pre-visit importance × performance' model was a better predictor of overall satisfaction than its 'post-visit' equivalent. The second best predictor of overall satisfaction was the 'performance-expectation' model, which contrasted with the results of previous comparative research.

Five 'dimensions' of Orlando's tourism offering were identified from visitors' performance ratings on an original 22-attribute scale: core, secondary and tertiary attractions, facilitators and transport. *Secondary attractions*–comprising shopping and dining facilities, their output and the opportunity for rest and relaxation–had the highest influence on overall tourist satisfaction with Orlando. The second most influential factor was *facilitators*, which relates to the functional attributes such as accommodation and customer service. *Core attractions*, the original *raison d'etre* of many holidays in Orlando, made only the third largest contribution to overall satisfaction. The fourth largest influence was due to *tertiary*, and arguably less well-known, attractions, i.e., sports facilities, nightlife, and cultural and wildlife resources. The final factor identified related to *transport*, comprising car-hire and easy-to-follow road-signage, which, like the *facilitators*, also enable tourists to optimise their holiday in Orlando.

Given that destinations are increasingly being challenged to compete for tourists, they need to continually build on their strengths and supplement their offerings in order to both maintain their appeal and also 'keep the customer satisfied.' In effect, these two key objectives for destinations 'book-end' the tourist's holiday decision-making and experience by appealing to tourists in the first instance and subsequently 'sending them home happy,' and hopefully ready to recommend and return. This research has identified that Orlando's *secondary attractions* make the highest contribution to UK visitor satisfaction. Interestingly, two of these–shopping and dining in restaurants–represent the main current activities of UK visitors to Orlando; visiting theme parks is now only the third most popular leisure activity (Orlando CVB Research, 2001). Consequently, it would seem that Orlando is succeeding in keeping its UK customers satisfied, both in general and specifically in terms of their main activities. Furthermore, Orlando also has the basic functional elements, or *facilitators*, in place; these elements make the second highest contribution to overall visitor satisfaction.

REFERENCES

Babakus, E. and Boller, W.G. (1992) An empirical assessment of the SERVQUAL scale. *Journal of Business Research*, 24: 253-268.

Baker, D.A. and Crompton, J.L. (2000) Quality, satisfaction and behavioural intentions. *Annals of Tourism Research*, 27 (3): 785-804.

Barsky, J.D. (1992) Customer satisfaction in the hotel industry: meaning and measurement. *Hospitality Research Journal*, 16: 51-73.

Barsky, J.D. and Labagh, R. (1992) A strategy for customer satisfaction. *Cornell Hotel and Restaurant Administration Quarterly*, 33 (5): 32-40.

Brodie, C., (2000) Telephone Interview with UK/European Marketing Director, Visit Florida UK, London. (March 1).

Carman, J. (1990) Consumer perceptions of service quality: an assessment of the SERVQUAL dimensions. *Journal of Retailing*, 66 (Spring): 32-48.

Churchill, G.A. and Surprenant, C. (1982) An investigation into the determinants of customer satisfaction. *Journal of Marketing Research*, 19: 491-504.

Cohen, J.W. (1988) *Statistical Power Analysis for the Behavioural Sciences* (2nd ed.). New Jersey: Lawrence Erlbaum Associates.

Crompton, J.L. (1979) An assessment of the image of Mexico as a vacation destination and the influence of the geographical location upon that image. *Journal of Travel Research*, 17 (4): 18-23.

Crompton, J.L. (1999) Keynote paper presented at the ATLAS Annual Tourism Conference 'Service Quality and Customer Service in Tourism and Leisure,' Munich. (September 9-11).

Crompton, J.L. and Love, L.L. (1995) The predictive value of alternative approaches to evaluating quality of a festival. *Journal of Travel Research*, 34 (1): 11-24.

Crompton, J.L. and Mackay, K.J. (1989) Users' perceptions of the relative importance of service quality dimensions in selected public recreation programs. *Leisure Services*, 11: 367-375.

Cronin, J.J. and Taylor, S.A. (1992) Measuring service quality: a re-examination and extension. *Journal of Marketing*, 56 (July): 55-68.

Danaher, P.J. and Mattsson, J. (1994) Customer satisfaction during the service delivery process. *European Journal of Marketing*, 28 (5): 5-16.

Dorfman, P.W. (1979) Measurement and meaning of recreation satisfaction: a case study in camping. *Environment and Behaviour*, 11 (4): 483-510.

Duke, C.R. and Persia, M.A. (1996) Consumer-defined dimensions for the escorted tour industry segment: expectations, satisfactions and importance. *Journal of Travel and Tourism Marketing*, 5 (1/2): 77-99.

Ekinci, Y., Riley, M. and Chen, J.S. (2000) A review of comparison standards used in service quality and customer satisfaction studies: some emerging issues for hospitality and tourism research. In J.A. Mazanec, G.I. Crouch, J.R. Brent Ritchie and A.G. Woodside (Eds.) *Consumer Psychology of Tourism, Hospitality and Leisure*, Vol. 2 (pp. 321-332). Oxford: CABI.

Fick, G.R. and Ritchie, J.R.B. (1991) Measuring service quality in the travel and tourism industry. *Journal of Travel Research*, 29 (Fall): 2-9.

Getty, M.J. and Thomson, N.K. (1994) The relationship between quality, satisfaction, recommending behaviour in lodging decisions. *Journal of Hospitality and Leisure Marketing*, 2 (3): 8-14.

Goodrich, J.N. (1978) The relationship between preferences for and perceptions of vacation destinations: application of a choice model. *Journal of Travel Research*, 28 (2): 7-11.

Gronroos, C. (1993) Toward a third phase in service quality research: challenges and future directions. In T.A. Stewart, D.E. Bowen and W.S. Brown (Eds.) *Advances in Service Marketing and Management: Research and Practice*, Vol. 2. Greenwich: JAI Press.

Hughes, K. (1991) Tourist satisfaction: a guided tour in North Queensland. *Australian Psychologist*, 26 (3): 168-177.

Jenkins, O.H. (1999) Understanding and measuring tourist destination images. *International Journal of Tourism Research*, 1: 1-15.

Kaiser, H. (1974) An index of factorial simplicity. *Psychometrika*, 39: 31-36.

Kotler, P., Bowen, J., and Makens, J. (1999) *Marketing for Hospitality and Tourism* (2nd ed.). New Jersey: Prentice-Hall.

Kozak, M. (2001) A critical review of approaches to measure satisfaction with tourist destinations, in J.A. Màzanec, G.I. Crouch, J.R.B. Ritchie and A.G. Woodside (Eds.) *Consumer Psychology of Travel, Hospitality and Leisure*, Vol. 2 (pp. 303-320). Oxford: CABI.

Kozak, M. (2003) Measuring tourist destination satisfaction with multiple destination attributes. *Tourism Analysis*, 7: 229-240.

Leblanc, G. (1992) Factors affecting customer evaluation of service quality in travel agencies: an investigation of customer perceptions. *Journal of Travel Research*, 30 (Spring): 10-16.

Mannell, R.C. (1989) Leisure satisfaction. In *Understanding Leisure and Recreation: Mapping the Past, Charting the Future*, pp 281-301. State College, PA: Venture.

Meyer, M. (1997) The secrets that lay behind improved corporate performance. In *Financial Times Mastering Management*. London: Pitman Publishing.

Meyer, A. and Westerbarkey, P. (1996) Measuring and managing hotel guest satisfaction. In D.M. Olsen, R. Teare and E. Gummesson (Eds.) *Service Quality in Hospitality Organisations* (pp. 185-204). New York: Cassell.

Miller, J.A. (1977) Studying satisfaction: modifying models, eliciting expectations, posing problems, and making meaningful measurements. In *Conceptualisation and Measurement of Consumer Satisfaction and Dissatisfaction* (pp. 72-91). School of Business, Indiana University: Bloomington.

Oh, H. (1999) Service quality, customer satisfaction, and customer value: an holistic perspective. *Hospitality Management*, 18: 67-82.

Oh, H. (2001) Revisiting importance-performance analysis. *Tourism Management*, 22: 617-627.

Oh, H. and Parks, C.S. (1997) Customer satisfaction and service quality: a critical review of the literature and research implications for the hospitality industry. *Hospitality Research Journal*, 20 (3): 36-64.

Oliver, R.L. (1997) *Satisfaction: a Behavioural Perspective on the Consumer*. London: McGraw-Hill.

Orlando CVB Research Department (2001) *2000 Overseas Visitors Profile*. Florida: Orange County Convention and Visitors Bureau Inc.

Parasuraman, A., Zeithaml, V.A. and Berry L.L. (1985) A conceptual model of service quality and its implications for further research. *Journal of Marketing*, 49 (Fall): 41-50.

Parasuraman, A., Zeithaml, V.A. and Berry L.L. (1994) Reassessment of expectations as a comparison standard in measuring service quality: implications for further research. *Journal of Marketing*, 58 (1): 111-124.

Pearce, P.L. (1991) Introduction to the tourism psychology. *Australian Psychologist*, 26 (3): 145-146.

Pearce, D.G. (1993) Introduction. In R. Butler and D. Pearce (Eds), *Tourism Research: Critiques and Challenges*. London: Routledge.

Pizam, A. and Milman, A. (1993) Predicting satisfaction among first time visitors to a destination by using the expectancy disconfirmation theory. *International Journal of Hospitality Management*, 12 (2): 197-209.

Prakash, V. and Lounsberry, W.J. (1983) A reliability problem in the measurement of disconfirmation of expectations. In P.R. Bagozzi and M.A Tybout (Eds.) *Advances in Consumer Research*, Vol. 10 (pp. 244-249). Michigan: Ann Arbor.

Ryan, C. (1995) *Researching Tourist Satisfaction–Issues, Concepts and Cases*. London: Routledge.

Ryan, M. and Bonfield, E.H. (1980) Fishbein's intention model: a test of external and pragmatic validity. *Journal of Marketing*, 44: 82-95.

Saleh, F. and Ryan, C. (1992) Client perception of hotels–a multi-attribute approach. *Tourism Management*, 13 (2): 163-168.

Schofield, P. and Fallon, P. (2000) Measuring the importance of critical factors in restaurant service quality performance evaluation: a triadic perspective. In D. Bowen, E. Wickens, A. Paraskevas and N. Hemmington (Eds.) *Proceedings of Consumer Satisfaction Research in Tourism and Hospitality Conference* (pp. 159-182), Oxford Brookes University. (November 25).

Stevens, J.P. (1992) *Applied Multivariate Statistics for the Social Sciences*, 2nd Edition. Erlbaum, Hillsdale, NJ.

Tribe, J. and Snaith, T. (1998) From SERVQUAL to HOLSAT: holiday satisfaction in Varadero, Cuba. *Tourism Management*, 19 (1): 25-34.

Watson, A.E., Roggenbuck, J.W. and Williams, D.R. (1991) The influence of past experience on wilderness choice. *Journal of Leisure Research*, 23 (1): 21-36.

Weber, K. (1997) The assessment of tourist satisfaction using the expectancy disconfirmation theory: a study of the German travel market in Australia. *Pacific Tourism Review*, 1 (1): 35-45.

Williams, D.R. (1988) Great expectations and the limits to satisfaction: a review of recreation and consumer satisfaction research. In A.H. Watson (Ed.), *Outdoor Recreation Benchmark: Proceedings of the National Recreation Forum* (pp. 422-438). U.S. Forest Service: General Technical Report SE-52.

Witter, B.S. (1985) Attitudes about a resort area: a comparison of tourists and local retailers. *Journal of Travel Research*, 24 (Summer): 14-19.

Yuksel, A. and Rimmington, M. (1998) Customer satisfaction measurement. *Cornell Hotel and Restaurant Administration Quarterly*, December: 60-70.

Zeithaml, V., Parasuraman, A. and Berry, L (1985) *Delivering Service Quality*. New York: Free Press.

Guest Satisfaction
in the U.S. Lodging Industry
Using the ACSI Model
as a Service Quality Scoreboard

Bonnie J. Knutson
Arjun J. Singh
Hung-Hsu Yen
Barbara Everitt Bryant

SUMMARY. This article extracts data from the American Consumer Satisfaction Index (ACSI) for the lodging industry and for the six hotel brands included in the study. Guest satisfaction scores are analyzed for three important standards: overall satisfaction, expectancy-disconfirmation, and customer experience compared to an ideal product. Findings indicate

---

Bonnie J. Knutson (E-mail: Drbonnie@msu.edu) and Arjun J. Singh (E-mail: singharj@msu.edu) are affiliated with The School of Hospitality Business, Eli Broad College of Business, Michigan State University, East Lansing, MI 48824.

Hung-Hsu Yen is affiliated with the Department of Park Recreation and Tourism Resources, 172 Natural Resources Building, Michigan State University, East Lansing, MI 48824 (E-mail: yenhungh@msu.edu).

Barbara Everitt Bryant is affiliated with the National Quality Research Center, University of Michigan Business School, 701 Tappan Street, Ann Arbor, MI 48109-1234 (E-mail: bryantb@umich.edu).

[Haworth co-indexing entry note]: "Guest Satisfaction in the U.S. Lodging Industry Using the ACSI Model as a Service Quality Scoreboard." Knutson, Bonnie J. et al. Co-published simultaneously in *Journal of Quality Assurance in Hospitality & Tourism* (The Haworth Hospitality Press, an imprint of The Haworth Press, Inc.) Vol. 4, No. 3/4, 2003, pp. 97-118; and: *Current Issues and Development in Hospitality and Tourism Satisfaction* (ed: John A. Williams and Muzaffer Uysal) The Haworth Hospitality Press, an imprint of The Haworth Press, Inc., 2003, pp. 97-118. Single or multiple copies of this article are available for a fee from The Haworth Document Delivery Service [1-800-HAWORTH, 9:00 a.m. - 5:00 p.m. (EST). E-mail address: docdelivery@haworthpress.com].

Digital Object Identifier: 10.1300/J162v04n03_07

97

that [1] the lodging industry scores slightly better than the entire service sector and about the same as the national score, and [2] there is significant variation in satisfaction scores among the six brands tested. Implications for management are included. *[Article copies available for a fee from The Haworth Document Delivery Service: 1-800-HAWORTH. E-mail address: <docdelivery@haworthpress.com> Website: <http://www.HaworthPress.com> © 2003 by The Haworth Press, Inc. All rights reserved.]*

KEYWORDS. Customer satisfaction, guest satisfaction, hotels, lodging, American Customer Satisfaction Index, satisfaction model

INTRODUCTION

A 2001 study asked hotel managers to identify key areas of concern in the management of their business. Not surprisingly, hotel managers identified "understanding the customer" as the second most important issue after human resource management. Their concerns in this area fell into three categories, obtaining good customer information, thinking strategically about marketing and customer segments to obtain competitive advantage, and developing measures of guest satisfaction (Enz, 2001). The U.S. hotel industry has matured and market growth has peaked, resulting in slow growth. With the proliferation of brands, U.S. hotels operate in a very competitive environment–both nationally and internationally. In this operating environment, maintaining and increasing market share is a direct function of guest retention and repurchase decisions by these guests. The growth of frequent guest programs offered by the leading hotel chains is evidence of how important customer loyalty is.

A typical business strategy to increase revenue has both offensive and defensive elements. Offensive strategy is involved with guest acquisition and therefore focuses on external promotional tools such as sales, advertising, publicity, and public relations. On the other hand, defense elements rely on operational service quality to maximize guest retention and reduce guests' incentives to switch to a competitor's hotel. There are primarily two forms of defensive or internal elements: (1) increasing switching barriers, which make it costly for customers to change to another hotel brand, and (2) increasing customer satisfaction, which makes it more expensive for the competitor to take away the hotel's current guests (Fornell, 1992). In a mature lodging market, a hotel firm's growth is most likely a result of increasing market share at the expense of the competing hotels in the same market space. As a result, hotel firms that focus on increasing guest satisfaction are more likely to have a stronger defense and less likely to erode their customer base. The hospitality industry has traditionally focused on the assets it best understands–real property and the capital that finances it. And yet what will distinguish the most successful companies for the next century will be the effective management of people, information and customer relationships, the industry's intangible assets (Cline, 1997).

RELEVANT RESEARCH ON GUEST SATISFACTION

Leading hotel companies have an instinctive understanding of the value of a satisfied customer and continuously examine and develop innovative guest relation practices within their organization. The results of a 1999 benchmark study that identified hotel company *Best Practices* show that many of the leading companies have a service culture firmly in place, have built an empowered service delivery system, have facilitated a customer listening orientation, and have developed responsive service guarantees (Enz and Siguaw, 2000; Dube and Renaghan, 1999). The research also showed that the *Best Practices Champion* hotel, has developed its guest service practices to create a satisfactory service experience that delivers customer value, and in turn builds customer loyalty (Dube and Renaghan, 1999).

In a review of customer satisfaction research in the hospitality industry, Oh and Parks (1997) found that most of the studies undertaken by hospitality researchers have focused on identifying the sources of customer satisfaction and discovering effective ways to determine customer wants and needs. While most researchers disagree on the number of key attributes, they all agree that satisfaction must be measured on a multiattribute scale.

Barsky (1992) and Barsky and Labagh (1992) introduced the expectancy and disconfirmation paradigm into hospitality satisfaction research. They tested their model using comment card data and found that those guests who were satisfied or highly satisfied with their stay expressed a willingness to return to the hotel. Pizam and Millman (1993) continued to use the expectancy-disconfirmation paradigm to predict traveler satisfaction.

Gundersen, Morten and Olsson (1996) identified important factors of guest satisfaction for business travelers and created an instrument to measure satisfaction within this segment. They found that the tangible aspects of housekeeping along with the intangible aspects of the front desk were particularly important for overall guest satisfaction for business travelers.

Other studies on guest satisfaction in the hospitality industry include Kirwin (1992), who studied the relationship among guest satisfaction, sales and profits; Reid and Sandler (1992), who reviewed technology as a tool to improve customer satisfaction in hotels; and (Dube, Renaghan and Miller, 1994), who researched the use of customer satisfaction data to identify market-positioning strategies.

Based on an extensive review of customer satisfaction and service quality research in the hospitality industry, Oh and Parks (1997) found that, despite the advancement of customer satisfaction constructs and models in the consumer behavior literature, application in the hospitality industry has been limited. Accordingly, they identified a number of opportunities to modify and apply these models for the hospitality industry. More specifically, they found that there is a lack of industry-specific models designed to measure CS. As customer expectations differ, depending on the target industry or organization, it is difficult to generalize results of studies that use a broad sample. They suggest that researchers should design industry level studies to study customer satisfaction within a particular competitive market structure. Results of these studies can be more revealing, as they would identify differences in satisfaction, and expectations between customers within the given market set.

The American Customer Satisfaction Index (ACSI), which forms the basis of this study, fills these two deficiencies in the hospitality research literature, by applying a well-recognized structural equation model to a hotel market specific research design.

OVERVIEW OF AMERICAN CUSTOMER SATISFACTION INDEX

Established in 1994, the American Satisfaction Index (ACSI) is a national economic indicator of customer evaluations of the quality of goods and services from companies and government agencies that produce approximately half of the Gross Domestic Product (GNP), plus foreign companies with substantial market shares in the United States. It does so by quantifying customer satisfaction and its effects on customer loyalty. The ACSI reports a national satisfaction index on a scale of 0-100. It is updated quarterly, on a rolling basis, with new data for one or two sectors of the economy, replacing data collected the prior year for those sectors. Sector, industry, and agency indices are updated annually. The ACSI currently measures satisfaction for seven economic sectors, 29 industries, 180 companies, two local government services, major customer segments of 30 Federal agencies, and the U.S. Postal Service. The Index is produced and the data housed at the National Quality Research Center (NQRC) at the University of Michigan Business School. For a more in-depth discussion of the American Satisfaction Index, see ACSI Methodology Report (Fornell, Bryant, Cha, Johnson, Anderson and Ettlie, 1998) or visit the ACSI website at http://www.theacsi.org.

Data for the macro ACSI model were collected through phone surveys using a computer-assisted telephone interviewing system (CATI). Customers, ages 18 to 84, were randomly selected from within national and/or regionally probability samples of continental U.S. households. Respondents within the household were selected using the criterion of having the most recent birthday; this provided a representative distribution of respondents by age, gender, and other characteristics. The definition of a " customer" in the American Customer Satisfaction data set is: an individual chosen randomly from a large universe of potential buyers who qualifies by recent experience as the purchaser and user of products of services of specific companies or agencies that supply household consumers in the continental United States. (Fornell, Bryant, Cha, Johnson, Anderson & Ettlie, 1998).

THE ACSI MODEL

Satisfaction should be reflected in a variety of comparison standards (Cadotte, Woodruff and Jenkins, 1987; Johnson & Fornell, 1991; Woodruff, Ernest and Jenkins, 1983). The American Consumer Satisfaction Index is embedded in a set of causal equations (cause-effect) that link customer expectations, perceived quality, and perceived value to customer satisfaction (ACSI). As illustrated in Figure 1, the *index* is the *heart* of the model; it is a weighted average of three critical standards: (1) Overall Satisfaction, (2) Expectancy-disconfirmation (performance that falls short of or exceeds expectations), and (3) Performance versus the customer's ideal product or service in the category.

Part I of the model encompasses three drivers of satisfaction (left side of model), each of which has its own index:

- *Overall Perceived Quality.* Satisfaction is primarily a function of a customer's quality experience with a product or service (Churchill & Suprenant, 1982; Fornell 1992; Tse & Wilton, 1988; Westbrook & Reilly, 1983). According to Deming (1981) and Juran and Gryna (1988), a quality experience provides key customer requirements (customization) and delivers on those requirements reliably (reliability).
- *Perceived Value.* Value is the level of product or service quality experience relative to the price paid. It incorporates price information into the model so consumers can compare brands and categories from a monetary perspective (Johnson, 1984). The concept of perceived value also must control for differences in income and budget constraints across customers (Hauser and Shugan, 1983, Lancaster, 1971), thus allowing comparisons of high- and low-priced products and services.

- *Customer Expectations.* Expectations are the level of quality a customer expects to receive and are based on prior exposure to the product or service–including past experiences, recommendations from others, and corporate promotional activities, such as advertising, public relations, and publicity. Expectations serve as an anchor in the evaluation process, thereby allowing comparisons of high and low priced products and services (Oliver, 1980; van Raaij, 1989). Expectations capture the guest's prior knowledge of the product or service, and are adjusted up and down in light of his or her more recent purchase and consumption experience. Thus, they capture the guest's ability to learn from experience and predict quality and value (Howard, 1977).

Part II (center) is the key to the model and the focus of this research project. It embodies Customer Satisfaction as measured by the three-variable ACSI.

Overall Satisfaction. This variable measures the satisfaction of the respondent's experience with a hotel based on ten-point scale with "1" being very dissatisfied and "10" indicating very satisfied.

- *Expectancy-Disconfirmation.* This variable measures the degree to which the respondent's experience fell short or exceeded his or her expectations on a 10-point scale, with "1" indicating fell short of expectations and "10" exceeding expectations.
- *Comparison to Ideal.* The third variable asked the respondent to imagine their ideal hotel and compare the current hotel with this ideal product. A 10-point scale was used with "1" being not very close to the ideal hotel and "10" indicating close to the ideal.

Part III of this model indicates the outcomes of Satisfaction–i.e., the consequences of the ACSI.

- *Customer Complaints.* Following Hirshman's (1970) exit voice theory, the immediate results of an increase in Customer Satisfaction are decreased Customer Complaints and increased Customer Loyalty (Fornell and Wernerfelt, 1988).
- *Customer Loyalty.* The final relationship in the model is the effect of Customer Complaints on Customer Loyalty, which indicates a firm's customer-handling system (Fornell, 1992). A positive relationship indicates the effectiveness of complaint handling while a negative relationship implies that a deficient customer-handling system may have encouraged customer defection.

FIGURE 1. ACSI Model for the Hotel Industry 2000

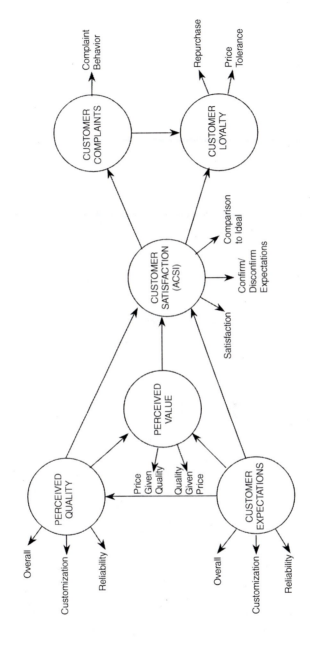

APPLICATION OF THE ACSI MODEL
TO THE U.S. LODGING INDUSTRY

The ACSI model is useful on four levels. The first level is that of a national or macro model of satisfaction with the quality of goods and services consumed in the United States. This national model has been successfully developed and validated at the National Quality Research Center at the University of Michigan Business School (Fornell, Johnson, Anderson, Cha and Bryant, 1996). The second level represents the overall satisfaction with an economic sector, such as the service sector. The third level evaluates performance by an industry as measured and represented in the ACSI. The fourth and final level is a micro measure of customer satisfaction with his or her total purchase and consumption experience, both actual and anticipated, from an individual firm.

To date, data for the hotel industry (level three) have not been extracted, validated, and analyzed using the ACSI framework. This void is also true for the individual hotel brand's (level four) included in the ACSI. Given this fact, the focus of this study was two-fold: (1) To extract data for the hotel industry from the 2000 data set to evaluate consumers' overall satisfaction (Part II of the model) with their hotel experiences, and (2) to compare ACSI scores across those hotel brands included in the index for this bellwether year. The results of this analysis will provide and validate the measurement of a hotel brand's most fundamental revenue-generating assets: it customers. Higher customer satisfaction, should increase loyalty, reduce price elasticities, insulate current market share from competitors, lower transaction costs, reduce failure costs and the costs of attracting new customers, and help build a firm's reputation in the marketplace (Anderson, Fornell, and Lehman, 1994).

HOTEL INDUSTRY SAMPLING FRAME

The Hotel Industry is included in the ACSI as part of the Services Sector. Six hotel companies, representing a broad cross-section of market segments, locations, price tiers, brand affiliations, amenities, represent the industry and services offered. Firms included are those that are considered to have a major impact on their field. The six companies chosen in the hotel industry represents 1,289,883 rooms, which is 31 percent of the total U.S. hotel room inventory. Currently, the ACSI hotel industry database has approximately 14,500 national interviews from 1994-2000. Table 1 outlines a description of the hotel companies and sample size of the hotel data extracted from the ACSI database for the current research.

TABLE 1. Hotel Firms Represented in American Customer Satisfaction Index (2000)

Hotel Firm	Description Of Hotel Firm	N[1]
Ramada	**Franchisor** with three hotel brands: Ramada Limited, Ramada Inn, and Ramada Plaza. Operating in the lower and middle market price segments. Approximately 120,000 rooms and 978 properties. Brand is part of Cendant Hotels.	251
Holiday Inn	**Franchisor** with four hotel brands. Holiday Inn, Holiday Inn Express, Holiday Inn Select, and Sunspree Resort. Operating in the lower and middle price segments and multiple market segments. Approximately 320,000 rooms and 2300 properties. Brand is part of Six Continental Hotels.	250
Marriott	**Franchisor and management company** of multiple brands in the luxury, upper, middle, and lower price segments and multiple market segments. Approximately 436,000 hotel rooms and 2600 properties.	250
Hilton	**Owner, management company, and franchisor** of multiple brands in luxury, upper, middle, and lower price segments and multiple market segments. Approximately 326,000 hotel rooms and 1986 properties.	310
Starwood	**Owner, management company and franchisor** multiple brands in luxury, and upper price segments and multiple market segments. Approximately 224,000 rooms and 743 properties.	253
Hyatt	**Management Company** of multiple Hyatt Brands such as Grand Hyatt, Hyatt Regency, and Park Hyatt primarily focusing in the luxury and upper price segments and mainly in the business and resort market segments. Approximately, 55,000 rooms and 120 properties.	149
Total		1463

[1]N = Number of customers responding to that firm.

ANALYSIS OF RESULTS

As stated earlier, this study focuses on the heart of the ACSI model–the three elements that measure Customer Satisfaction. The principal findings, presented in Tables 2, 3 and 4, summarize and analyze guest satisfaction with hotel industry as whole as well as each of the representative firms included in the study. Specifically, the findings analyze (1) the guest's overall satisfaction with their experience, (2) the degree to which their experience exceeded or fell short of expectations, and (3) the proximity of this experience with the guest's ideal hotel. The summary and dispersion statistics were analyzed and a t-test of equality of means was applied to test for significant differences in these three satisfaction scores between the hotel firms. In other words, we tested for significant differences between hotel firms with regard to their overall satisfaction scores, the degree to which their satisfaction exceeded or fell short of consumer expectations and the proximity of their satisfaction score to their ideal hotel experience.

TABLE 2. Measures of Satisfaction[2] for the Hotel Industry and the Six Selected Hotel Brands Tested in the American Consumer Satisfaction Index (ACSI) in 2000

	Hotel Industry	Hilton	Holiday Inn	Hyatt	Marriott	Ramada	Starwood
☐ **Satisfaction**							
N	1463	310	250	149	250	251	253
Mean[3]	8.17	8.49	8.12	8.33	8.34	7.87	7.85
Std. Deviation	1.85	1.58	1.78	1.56	1.69	2.14	2.10
☐ **Distribution of Satisfaction Scores**							
Score of 10	27.8%	34.5%	24.4%	25.5%	28.8%	26.7%	24.1%
Scores of 7-9	58.6	55.5	61.6	63.7	62.4	53.0	58.1
Scores of 4-6	10.5	8.6	11.6	9.4	6.0	15.2	12.2
Scores of 1-3	3.2	1.3	2.4	1.4	2.8	5.2	5.6
☐ **T-Tests**[4]							
Hilton	---		.009*	.294	.256	.000*	.000*
Holiday Inn	---	.009*		.236	.165	.154	.126
Hyatt	---	.294	.236		.966	.014*	.010*
Marriott	---	.256	.165	.966		.007*	.005*
Ramada	---	.000*	.154	.014*	.007*		.938
Starwood	---	.000*	.126	.010*	.005*	.938	

[2]Measured in the ACSI by Variable #10 (See Table 1): *Overall Satisfaction*
[3]Mean scores are computed on a scale where 10 = Very Satisfied and 1 = Very Dissatisfied.
[4]* = Significant at $p \leq .05$.

OVERALL GUEST SATISFACTION

In the bellwether year studied (2000), the hotel industry had a strong overall guest satisfaction performance, with a mean score of 8.17 on the ACSI 10-point scale (see Table 2).

However, with a standard deviation of 1.87, we may expect about 70 percent of the cases to score between 6.30 and 10.00. This indicates that, while on average, the industry had a higher score, guests are being exposed to a wide range of satisfaction experiences. Individually, Hilton, Marriott, and Hyatt hotels had the highest guest satisfaction experiences, with mean scores of 8.49, 8.34, and 8.33 respectively. They are followed by Holiday Inn (8.12), Ramada (7.87) and Starwood (7.85). Furthermore, the three higher-scoring hotel brands had lower standard deviations, as compared to both the overall hotel industry and lower-scoring hotel firms; this suggests a more predictable range of guest experiences. Both Ramada and Starwood hotels had the highest standard deviations, 2.14, and 2.10 respectively, suggesting a wider range of satisfaction experiences.

TABLE 3. Measures of Expectancy Disconfirmation[5] for the Hotel Industry and the Six Selected Hotel Brands Tested in the American Consumer Satisfaction Index (ACSI) in 2000

	Hotel Industry	Hilton	Holiday Inn	Hyatt	Marriott	Ramada	Starwood
☐ **Meeting Expectation Scores**							
N	1459	310	248	149	250	250	252
Mean[6]	7.24	7.58	7.14	7.29	7.31	6.96	7.08
Std. Deviation	2.09	1.94	2.03	1.91	2.03	2.32	2.19
☐ **Distribution of Expectancy Disconfirmation Scores**							
Score of 10	14.35%	16.8%	10.5%	12.8%	14.0%	16.0%	12.8%
Scores of 7-9	54.3	59.0	58.0	58.3	56.0	45.2	58.3
Scores of 4-6	26.3	20.3	26.2	25.5	26.0	31.2	25.5
Scores of 1-3	5.1	3.9	5.2	3.3	4.0	7.6	3.3
☐ **T-Tests**[7]							
Hilton	---		.009*	.131	.106	.001*	.004*
Holiday Inn	---	.009*		.474	.359	.344	.728
Hyatt	---	.131	.474		.925	.123	.325
Marriott	---	.106	.359	.925		.071	.218
Ramada	---	.001*	.344	.123	.071		.554
Starwood	---	.004*	.728	.325	.218	.554	

[5]Measured in the ACSI by Variable #11 (See Table 1): *Performance that falls short or exceeds expectations.*
[6]Mean scores are computed on a scale where 10 = Exceeds expectations and 1 = Falls short of expectations.
[7]* = Significant at $p \leq .05$.

The distribution of the satisfaction scores revealed that about 28 percent of the guests were very satisfied with the industry (score of 10), with a majority (58.6%) giving a score between 7 and 9. Hilton, the highest-scoring firm, had more than one-third of its guests awarding it 10 points, with about 56 percent selecting 7 to 9 points. An analysis of this distribution across all six lodging firms provides a favorable satisfaction distribution, with 90 percent of guests at the high-performing firms, Hilton, Hyatt and Marriott, and 80-85 percent of guests at Ramada, Starwood, and Holiday Inn choosing scores of 7 to 10 points. Even though the large proportion of satisfied guests points to strong service quality, differences in dissatisfaction scores between hotel firms are even more informative. Ten percent of the guests staying at Hilton, the strongest-performing brand in the study, indicated low satisfaction scores, while at the other extreme, 20 percent of Ramada customers indicated low satisfaction with their experience. In an increasingly competitive market, where growth in market share is often dependent upon retaining present customers coupled with convincing customers to switch from other brands, even small differences in satisfaction scores between competitors is critical for the brand's performance.

TABLE 4. Measures of Performance Compared to Ideal[8] for the Hotel Industry and the Six Selected Hotel Brands Tested in the American Consumer Satisfaction Index (ACSI) in 2000

	Hotel Industry	Hilton	Holiday Inn	Hyatt	Marriott	Ramada	Starwood
☐ **Comparison to Ideal**							
N	1453	309	247	149	249	250	249
Mean[9]	6.75	7.17	6.62	7.21	6.97	6.44	6.17
Std. Deviation	2.27	2.11	2.16	1.90	2.10	2.51	2.53
☐ **Distribution of Comparison to Ideal Scores**							
Score of 10	11.9%	14.6%	11.3%	10.7%	10.8%	14.0%	8.8%
Scores of 7-9	49.0	53.1	47.0	61.0	53.4	40.8	42.6
Scores of 4-6	29.2	25.9	33.6	22.9	28.1	30.8	32.8
Scores of 1-3	9.9	6.4	8.0	5.4	7.6	14.4	16.0
☐ **T-Tests[10]**							
Hilton	---		.003*	.858	.265	.000*	.000*
Holiday Inn	---	.003*		.007*	.069	.372	.033*
Hyatt	---	.858	.007*		.261	.001*	.000*
Marriott	---	.265	.069	.261		.010*	.218
Ramada	---	.000*	.372	.001*	.010*		.244
Starwood	---	.000*	.033*	.000*	.218	.244	

[8]Measured in the ACSI by Variable #12 (See Table 1): *Performance versus the customer's ideal product and service in the category.*
[9]Mean scores are computed on a scale where 10 = Very close to ideal and 1 = Not very close to ideal.
[10]* = Significant at $p \leq .05$.

Our analysis of satisfaction scores across the six hotel brands found interesting differences among firms. Based on a t-test of equality of means, we identified significant differences in satisfaction scores among Hilton, Holiday Inn, Ramada, and Starwood. As Hilton had the highest satisfaction scores, they appear to be better positioned to gain or retain market share. Similarly, satisfaction scores at Hyatt were significantly different as compared to Ramada and Starwood. While there is no relevance with regard to the Ramada scores (Hyatt and Ramada are not competing brands), Hyatt appears better positioned to compete against Starwood, which is a competitor with its Sheraton, W, Westin, and St Regis brands. Similarly, satisfaction scores for Marriott were significantly different compared to Ramada and Starwood. As Marriott is a widely-diversified hotel firm and has brands ranging from Fairfield, in the limited service segment, to Ritz Carlton, in the luxury segment, both Ramada and Starwood may be adversely affected.

While the preceding analysis focuses on the differences in satisfaction scores among hotel firms, an interesting observation regarding similarity of satisfaction performance between two dissimilar operating formats may be in order.

While Hyatt Hotels is purely a management company with hotels in the upper tier, Marriott operates in multiple market segments and has multiple operating formats (franchisor, management company, and corporate owned), yet their satisfaction scores are almost identical (8.33 and 8.34). This may dispel a popular notion that when companies franchise their operations, they necessarily lose quality.

ACTUAL SATISFACTION EXPERIENCE COMPARED TO GUEST EXPECTATIONS

Whereas overall satisfaction scores measured the guest's experience with their hotel stay, the second central component of customer satisfaction is a comparison of guest expectations with their actual experience. Customers measure their satisfaction based on the degree to which the hotel industry and individual firms exceed, meet, or fall short of their expectations. While the overall guest satisfaction score for the hotel industry was 8.17, the industry's ability to meet guest expectations was lower, with a mean score of 7.24 (see Table 3).

With a standard deviation of 2.09, the industry suffers from a wide range of customer expectancy-confirmation scores, with about 70 percent of the cases likely to score between 5.15 and 9.38. While earning lower scores than for overall satisfaction (7.58, 7.31 and 7.29), guests staying at a Hilton, Marriott and Hyatt are more likely to have their expectations met than at a Holiday Inn, Starwood and Ramada hotel, with mean scores of 7.14, 7.08 and 6.96, respectively. Despite differences in mean expectation scores, variability in scores was high across all hotel firms, with standard deviations ranging from 1.91 to 2.32. This establishes the fact that guests staying at these hotels experience a high degree of unpredictability with regard to their expectations being met.

A review of the distribution of expectation scores shows that these hotels exceed guest expectations 14 percent of the time (score of 10), while either meeting or coming close to meeting expectations for about 54 percent of their guests. Alarmingly, however, for a little over 30 percent of guests, hotels do not meet their expectations. While industry seminars, company newsletters, trade publication articles, and best practice research all tout the importance of "delighting the customer," "showering them with surprises," "the WOW factor" and "exceeding guest expectations," results do not reflect this purported high level of service. Even the high-performing hotel brands exceeded guest expectations only in 17 percent of the cases. All the firms either meet or come close to meeting expectations in about 60 percent of the cases (Ramada, was the only exception with 45%). Equally important to note is that most firms fell short of meeting guest expectations in 25-30 percent of the cases, with the lowest-performing firm (Ramada) not meeting guest expectations in about 40 percent of the cases.

Our analysis found significant differences in meeting guest expectations among Hilton, Holiday Inn, Ramada, and Starwood. To the degree to which guests' hotel choice is based on the perception that the brand will meet their expectation, differences in expectation scores between hotel firms is important. Based on this analysis, Hilton has a competitive advantage over other hotels. Once again, there is a remarkable similarity between Hyatt and Marriott, two dissimilar firms, in their ability to meet guest expectations (7.29 and 7.31).

ACTUAL GUEST EXPERIENCE COMPARED TO IDEAL HOTEL

A third frame of reference used by customers to gauge their satisfaction is comparison of a product or service to an ideal. The ideal in this case serves as a benchmark against which a product or service is compared to form a positive or negative impression. A customer's ideal hotel is one which meets all her or his expectations, satisfies the customer's requirements for customization and reliability, and has the highest perceived value.

As an industry, hotels fall short of meeting the guest's requirements from a guest's image of an ideal hotel. Whereas a score of 10 would indicate that the hotel is very close to the guest's ideal, the hotel industry scored 6.75, with a wide standard deviation of 2.27 (see Table 4).

Hyatt hotels had the highest mean score of 7.21, followed by Hilton (7.17) and Marriott (6.97). At the low end were Holiday Inn (6.62), Ramada (6.44) and Starwood (6.17). As with the expectation-disconfirmation scores, there was a wide dispersion of scores, with standard deviations ranging from a low of 1.91 to a high of 2.51.

The hotel industry was very close to the guest's ideal hotel only in 12 percent of the cases, with about 49 percent of the times being fairly or close to the guest's ideal hotel. The low-scoring hotels (Ramada, Starwood and Holiday Inn) achieved proximity to the guest's ideal hotel in about 40 to 47 percent of the cases, while the high-scoring hotels (Hyatt, Hilton and Marriott) achieved proximity in about 65 to 72 percent of the cases. The wide gap between the hotel's service delivery and the guest's ideal benchmark points to an opportunity to further understand guest preferences.

Testing for differences among brands shows that the high-performing hotels, Hyatt, Hilton were significantly different than the low-performing hotels, and Marriott was significantly different from Ramada. Even among the low-performing hotels, Holiday Inn was significantly different from Starwood. In a competitive marketplace, when the closest competitor has a closer ideal fit, low-scoring hotels are in danger of eroding their market share.

COMPARISON OF HOTEL ACSI SCORES WITH SERVICE SECTOR AND US NATIONAL SCORES

An *individual* hotel brand's ACSI score represents an evaluation of the total purchase and consumption experience by its customers; an *industry* ACSI score represents the industry customer's overall evaluation of its market offering. On the other hand, a *sector* score is an overall evaluation of all service industries while the *national* ACSI gauges the nation's total consumption experience (Fornell, Johnson, Anderson, Cha & Bryant, 1996).

In addition to looking at the three measures outline in Tables 2, 3, and 4, we found it very useful to analyze two other findings. First, we wanted to look at the overall ACSI score for each of the six hotel brands. The rankings, shown in Table 5, mirror those found in each of the component measures.

Hilton is the clear leader with a 77. Hyatt and Marriott, tie for second place at 74, and are closely followed by Starwood with a 73. Holiday Inn scores two points lower, while Ramada exhibits the lowest score of 69. While only eight ranking points separate these brands, this represents a significant range in satisfaction.

Secondly, we needed to look at how the hotel industry fares when compared to industries in the Service Sector, as well as the national whole. For the year 2000, hotel customers reported higher satisfaction scores (72) as compared to the consumption experience of service sector customers as a whole (69.4) and slightly lower than the national total of 72.6. This indicates that hotel firms are

TABLE 5. Comparison of Overall ACSI Scores: National Total, Service Sector, Hotel Industry, Six Hotel Brands in 2000[11]

National	72.6
Service Sector	69.4
Hotel Industry	72.0
☐ Hilton	77.0
☐ Holiday Inn	71.0
☐ Hyatt	74.0
☐ Marriott	74.0
☐ Ramada	69.0
☐ Starwood	73.0

[11]The ACSI scores represent the econometric computation of Variables 10, 11, and 12 shown in Table 2.

doing a somewhat better job in satisfying their guests than are other service organizations, but are not out-performing the national set of US organizations.

CONCLUSIONS

This study extracts the hotel industry scores from the overall ACSI in order to analyze guest satisfaction using three important standards: (1) overall satisfaction, (2) expectancy-disconfirmation, and (3) customer experience compared to an ideal product. Findings from this research study reveal meaningful information about satisfaction at multiple levels.

- First, results show that customer satisfaction with the hotel industry product is clearly different based on the standard used. While overall satisfaction scores were relatively high, when measured against guest expectations, the scores were lower. Furthermore, the scores were the weakest when guests were asked to compare their experience with an ideal hotel stay.
- Second, even though the summary ACSI scores for the hotel industry were relatively high for overall satisfaction and the majority of the guests were either satisfied with their stay, had their expectations met or found their hotel experience fairly proximate to their ideal, the dispersion of these scores was very wide. Also, the results show that in only a small percentage of cases, guest experiences matched their ideal hotel or exceeded their expectations.
- Third, a comparison of satisfaction, across the different firms and brands indicated a number of significant differences in satisfaction scores, which implies a heterogeneity of guest experiences across brands.
- Finally, when compared with the service sector and national customer satisfaction for the year 2000, the hotel satisfaction scores are slightly ahead of the service sector and virtually even with national customer satisfaction.

IMPLICATIONS AND RECOMMENDATIONS FOR THE HOTEL INDUSTRY

In an overly-saturated and branded hotel market, the results of this research have many important implications for hotel managers and brand management in general. Combining the results of our research with related research, we highlight these implications and offer recommendations for management to consider.

At a very fundamental level, the results of this study show that it is imperative for hotel managers to focus on increasing overall guest satisfaction levels as a guest retention strategy. As previously noted, studies have shown a relationship between customer satisfaction and loyalty. While a loyal customer is not necessarily satisfied, satisfied customers tend to be loyal. In a competitive marketplace where market growth depends more on increasing market share than on creating new demand, high satisfaction levels are the hotel brand's anchor to promote guest retention. The growth of Internet-based distribution channels has further increased the threat of customers migrating to the competition.

Guests generally choose a branded hotel over an unbranded hotel because of the expectation that the brand offers–i.e., a predictable level of service, consistent with that brand. This study shows that, in general, the hotel industry displays low expectancy scores that were highly varied, indicating unpredictability. At the individual brand level, the variation in scores between the firms will benefit the higher-scoring firms at the expense of their lower-scoring peers. However, at the industry level the unpredictability of expectation scores erodes the implicit promise of a brand, namely to create a product designed for a particular market niche, providing a predictable level of service. In an environment in which the proliferation of hotel brands is reducing the distinction between them, and the threat of "commoditization," (a phenomenon that equates hotel rooms with commodities, differentiated primarily by their price, rather than their unique selling proposition) looms over brand managers, an increasing gap between guest expectations and actual service delivery at branded hotels will continue to pose a serious challenge to brand equity.

In 1999, a comprehensive study at Cornell University titled, a "Key to Best Practices in the U.S. Lodging Industry," (Dube and Reneghan, 1999) identified functional best practices in the industry. A key finding showed that effective branding decisions means that hotels must translate promised benefits into detailed operating functions, the service delivery systems, and the structural aspects of the property. The best practice leaders in the study were those who had functional practices in place that matched its brand promise. Except for these few industry leaders, the Cornell study found little evidence to show that hoteliers are establishing links between what the brand promises and what the functional areas of hotel operations deliver. The results of our research reached a similar conclusion, showing a gap between expectations, and actual experience.

During the past fifteen years, the hotel brands have attempted to penetrate different market segments by implementing a corporate brand extension strategy. Corporate extension occurs when a parent brand (such as Holiday Inn) launches sub-brands (such as Holiday Inn Express). Examples of these prolific extensions include Holiday Inn's introduction of Holiday Inn Express, SunSpree Resorts, and the upscale Holiday Inn Crowne Plaza. Marriott added Marriott Courtyard as an extension and Hilton added Homewood suites after its acquisition of Promus in 2000. Jiang, Dev and Rao (2002) state that the creation of multiple sub-brands may reduce brand equity by their inability to maintain brand-specific customer-service standards. In fact, the empirical results of their research show that hotel firms with more than three brand extensions will promote customer switching by straining the brand's credibility, confusing and alienating customers, and by reducing the company's support of each individual brand. The six firms, which were part of the ACSI data set used in this study, include 65 brands, with an average of about 11 sub-brands per firm. At the high end, Marriott International has 23 sub-brands, and Hyatt is at the low end with 4 sub-brands. It should be noted that Ramada, one of the brands in this study is part of Cendant, which has a total of 12 brands. Ramada, in turn, has extended itself into three sub-brands (Ramada Inn, Ramada Limited, and Ramada Plaza). Furthermore, Holiday Inn is part of Six Continents, which as a total of 10 brands.

This analysis only provides partial support for the contention that more than three brands affect satisfaction scores, since the overall scores of Hilton (7 brand extensions), Marriott (23 brand extensions) and Hyatt (4 brand extensions) are the highest in the sampled industry subset. On the other hand, Holiday Inn (10 brand extensions) and Ramada (12 brand extensions) are the lowest. An explanation of this anomaly may be because a larger percentage of hotels are corporate-managed (management contract), in the high-scoring companies, while the low-scoring companies are mostly franchised (with no direct corporate management control).

As the hotel market becomes more crowded, brand offerings become less distinct and the hotel room moves closer to commoditization. While most hotels focus on improving the functionality of service attributes (as in the case of the best practice leaders), Gilmore and Pine (2002) feel that hotels need to go a step further. The key to providing a distinct service experience is not by merely being functionally efficient, such as consistently providing a wake-up call on time, but making the routine wake-up call into a memorable experience, something that the guest will share with colleagues, friends and family members later in the day, week, month or even year. Bruce Laval, a former vice president with Disney, coined the term, *guestology* (Ford, Heaton and Brown, 2001). The purpose of the term is to focus everyone's attention on guest behavior and expectations. Guestology forces the firm to look systematically at the customer experience from the guest's point of view. It identifies the key factors that determine quality and value for the guest, modeling them for study, measuring their impact on the customer experience, testing various strategies that might improve quality of that experience, and then providing the combination of factors that increases repeat visitation. Disney used guestology to identify that cleanliness was one of the most important drivers of customer satisfaction at theme parks. They have, therefore, designed their service systems around this factor, which is now one of its greatest assets.

Services inherently require a human performance or deed, often in real time and in the presence of a demanding customer. As the production and consumption in a service setting are simultaneous, hotels have little or no opportunity to detect or correct a service failure. The results of our study indicate this unreliability in satisfaction performance across all brands. While improving service quality and the consistency of service delivery should be at the heart of any recommendation to management, we recommend the implementation of service guarantees to overcome customer skepticism and regain their confidence. However, many service guarantee programs are poorly implemented, and, therefore, lack appeal to the customer. Marmorstein, Sarel and Lasser (2001) state that to be effective, service guarantees should be stated in a clear and straightforward manner, be easy for the customer to use and should include service aspects of importance to the customer. Promus was the first hotel to institute a 100 percent customer satisfaction guarantee in 1989. The guarantee promised the guest a free room night if they were not satisfied for any reason. Carlson Hospitality also provides a guarantee, but only if certain conditions apply (Enz & Siguaw, 2000). In September 2002, Sheraton (a Starwood brand) launched the Sheraton Service Promise, which provides either an instant discount, money back or frequent stay points for service lapses. Only a few hotel firms provide service guarantees, and they remain largely an unused resource. A study conducted by Evans, Clark and Knutson (1996) found that only 25 percent of the hotel respondents had some form of satisfaction guarantee program. Those who opposed the program cited a variety of reasons including problems with implementation and potential guest abuse of the guarantee. Given the results of this study, we strongly suggest that hotel firms reevaluate this premise and consider implementing satisfaction guarantee programs.

Finally, a research study conducted at the University of Michigan's National Quality Research Center found that a one percent increase in information technology labor investment in the service sector resulted in a 0.27 percent increase in customer satisfaction (Mithan, Krishnan, & Fornell, 2002). Interestingly, they also found that from 1999-2000, investment in Information Technology (IT) by service industries actually had a negative impact on customer satisfaction. They theorize that this may result from the firm investing too much in the latest IT technologies, without gauging the true customer needs. This has direct implications for the hotel industry, which tends to view IT tools, such as in-room technologies, property management tools and Internet distribution channels, as ways to get close to customers and provide them with added value. The authors of the research point out that, while IT applications have the potential to enhance customer experience when implemented correctly, an overemphasis on IT in automating customer touch points without specific knowledge of individual customer needs may have adverse effects on customer satisfaction (Mithas, Krishnan & Fornell, 2002). Another implication for the hotel industry of this research is that investment in IT labor earns a higher return in satisfaction scores, as compared to investment in equipment. Therefore, investments in IT support services (which improves reliability), technology literacy, and training of guest touch-point employees (bellman, front desk, and telephone operators) are more important considerations for hotels seeking to invest in technology to improve guest satisfaction.

IMPLICATIONS FOR FURTHER RESEARCH

This study is the first step towards extracting and mining the rich hospitality database that is in the ACSI model. In subsequent steps, we need to study both the drivers and outcomes of Customer Satisfaction in the lodging industry–i.e., Parts I and II of the ACSI model. Once they are examined, trend data for the entire model should be analyzed from 1994 to the present to identify changes and understand their root causes. Finally, using the hotel industry research as a template, research into other hospitality industries that are included in the ACSI study can be extracted and similarly studied.

REFERENCES

Anderson, E.W., Fornell, C., & Lehman, D.R.(1994, July). Customer satisfaction, market share, and profitability: Findings from Sweden. *Journal of Marketing*, 58 (3), 53-67.

Barsky, J.D. (1992). Customer satisfaction in the hotel Industry: Meaning and Measurement. *Hospitality Research Journal*, 16 (1), 51-73.

Barsky, J.D., & Labagh.R. (1992, October). A strategy for customer satisfaction. *Cornell Hotel and Restaurant Administration Quarterly*, 33 (5), 32-40.

Cadotte, E.R., Woodruff,R.B., Jenkins,R.L. (1987). Expectations and norms in models of consumer satisfaction. *Journal of Marketing Research*, 24 (3), 305-314.

Churchill, G.A., & Suprenant, C. (1982). An investigation into the determinants of customer satisfaction. *Journal of Marketing Research*, 19 (4), 491-504.

Cline, R.S. (1997, October). The value of human capital. *Lodging Hospitality*, 53 (10), 20-24.

Deming, W.E. (1981). *Management of Statistical Techniques for Quality and Productivity*. New York: New York University, Graduate School of Business.

Dube, L., & Renaghan, L.M. (1999, October). How hotel attributes deliver the promised benefits. *Cornell Hotel and Restaurant Administration Quarterly*, 40 (5), 89-95.

Dube, L., Reneghan, L.M., Miller J. M. (1994) Measuring Customer Satisfaction for strategic management. *Cornell Hotel and Restaurant Administration Quarterly*. 35 (1), 39-47.

Enz, C.A., & Siguaw, J.A. (2000, October). Best Practices in Service Quality. *Cornell Hotel and Restaurant Administration Quarterly*, 41 (5), 20-29.

Enz, C.A. (2001, April). What Keeps You Up at Night? *Cornell Hotel and Restaurant Administration Quarterly*, 42 (2), 38-45.

Evans, M.R., Clark, J.D., & Knutson, B.J. (1996, December). The 100 percent, unconditional, money-back guarantee. *Cornell Hotel and Restaurant Administration Quarterly*, 37 (6), 56-61.

Ford, R.C., Heaton, C.P., Brown, S.W. (2001, Fall). Delivering excellent service: Lessons from the best firms. *California Management Review*, 44 (1), 39-56.

Fornell, C. (1992). A national customer satisfaction barometer: The Swedish experience. *Journal of Marketing*, 56 (1), 6-21.

Fornell, C., & B. Wernerfelt (1988). A model for consumer complaint management. *Marketing Science*, 7 (3), 271-286.

Fornell, C., Bryant, B.E. Cha, J., Johnson, M.D., Anderson, E,W, & Ettlie, E.W. (1998). *American Customer Satisfaction Index: Methodology Report*. University of Michigan Business School: Ann Arbor, Michigan, National Quality Research Center.

Fornell, C. Johnson, M.D., Anderson, E.W., Cha, J., & Bryant, B.E.(1996, October). The American Customer Satisfaction Index: Nature, Purpose, and Findings. *Journal of Marketing*, 60 (4), 7-18.

Gilmore, J. H., & Pine, J.B. (2002, June). Differentiating hospitality operations via experiences. *Cornell Hotel and Restaurant Administration Quarterly*, 43 (3), 87-96.

Gundersen, M.G., Heide, M., & Olssen, U.H. (1996, April). Hotel guest satisfaction among business travelers. *Cornell Hotel and Restaurant Administration Quarterly*, 37 (2), 72-83.

Hauser, J.R., & Shugan, S.M. (1983). Defensive marketing strategies. *Marketing Science*, 2 (4), 319-360.

Hirschman, A.O. (1970). *Exit Voice, and Loyalty-Responses to Decline in Firms, Organizations and States*. Cambridge, MA: Harvard University Press.

Howard, J. A. (1977). *Consumer Behavior: Application of Theory*. New York: McGraw Hill.

Jiang, W., Dev, C.S., & Rao, V.R. (2002, August). Brand extension and customer loyalty: evidence from the lodging industry. *Cornell Hotel and Restaurant Administration Quarterly* 43 (4), 5-16.

Johnson, M.D. (1984). Consumer choice strategies for comparing noncomparable alternatives. *Journal of Consumer Research*, 11 (3), 741-753.

Johnson,M.D., & Fornell, C. (1991). A framework for comparing customer satisfaction across individuals and product categories. *Journal of Economic Psychology*, 12 (2), 267-286.

Juran, J.M., & Gryna, F.M. (1988). *Juran's Quality Control Handbook* (4th ed.). New York: McGraw Hill.

Kirwin, P. (1991, June). The satisfaction of service. *Lodging Hospitality*. 47 (6), 66-68.

Lancaster, K. (1971). *Consumer Demand: A New Approach*. New York: Columbia University Press.

Marmorstein, H., Sarel, D., Lasser, W.M., (2001). Increasing the persuasiveness of a service guarantee: the role of service. *Journal of Services Marketing*, 15 (2), 147-163.

Mithan, S., Krishnan, M.S., & Fornell, C. (2002). *Effect of IT Investments on Customer Satisfaction: An Empirical Analysis*. Unpublished Manuscript, University of Michigan, Ann Arbor. Working Paper series 02-012.

Oh, H., & Parks, S.C. (1997). Customer satisfaction and service quality: A critical Review of the literature and research implications for the hospitality industry. *Hospitality Research Journal*, 20 (3), 35-64.

Oliver, R. L. (1980). A Cognitive model of the antecedents and consequences of satisfaction decisions. *Journal of Marketing Research*, 17 (4), 460-469.

Pizam, A., & Milman, A. (1993). Predicting satisfaction among first time visitors to a destination by using the expectancy-disconfirmation theory. *International Journal of Hospitality Management*, 12 (2), 197-209.

Reid, R. D., Sandler, M. (1992) The use of technology to improve service quality. *Cornell Hotel and Restaurant Administration Quarterly*. 33 (3), 68-73.

Tse, D.K., & Wilton, P.C. (1988). Models of consumer satisfaction formation: An extension. *Journal of Marketing Research*, 25 (2), 204-212.

van Raaij, F.W. (1989). Economic news, expectations, and macro-economic behavior. *Journal of Economic Psychology*, 10 (4), 473-494.

Westbrook, R.A., & Reilly, M.D. (1983). Value-Percept Disparity: An alternative to the disconfirmation of expectations theory of consumer satisfaction. In Richard P.Bagozzi & Alice M. Tybout (eds.). *Advances in consumer research* (pp. 256-261). Ann Arbor, MI: Association for Consumer Research.

Woodruff, R.B., Ernest, R.C., & Jenkins, R.L. (1983). Modeling consumer satisfaction processes using experience-based norms. *Journal of Marketing Research*, 20 (3), 296-305.

An Investigation
into the Perceived Importance
of Service and Facility Attributes
to Hotel Satisfaction

Tekle Shanka
Ruth Taylor

SUMMARY. In a complex service environment such as the hotel sector, assessing the perceived importance of services and facility attributes provides management with information not only to benchmark their service level provision, but also to retain and increase their customer base. The present study examines the perceived importance of the service and facilities attributes provided by a 3-star hotel. Results of the self-administered survey of 101 guests of three 3-star hotel properties in Perth (Western Australia) indicated that 13 of the 18 attributes were perceived as important. The 18 services and facility attributes were factor-analysed and three components emerged: *physical facilities, service experienced* and *services provision*. These three components were found to significantly contribute to the overall importance rating of the hotel attributes.

Tekle Shanka (E-mail: shankat@cbs.curtin.edu.au), Research Coordinator, School of Marketing, and Ruth Taylor (E-mail: taylorr@cbs.curtin.edu.au), Lecturer, School of Management, Curtin Business School, Curtin University of Technology, GPO Box U1987, Perth, WA 6845, Australia.

[Haworth co-indexing entry note]: "An Investigation into the Perceived Importance of Service and Facility Attributes to Hotel Satisfaction." Shanka, Tekle, and Ruth Taylor. Co-published simultaneously in *Journal of Quality Assurance in Hospitality & Tourism* (The Haworth Hospitality Press, an imprint of The Haworth Press, Inc.) Vol. 4, No. 3/4, 2003, pp. 119-134; and: *Current Issues and Development in Hospitality and Tourism Satisfaction* (ed: John A. Williams and Muzaffer Uysal) The Haworth Hospitality Press, an imprint of The Haworth Press, Inc., 2003, pp. 119-134. Single or multiple copies of this article are available for a fee from The Haworth Document Delivery Service [1-800-HAWORTH, 9:00 a.m. - 5:00 p.m. (EST). E-mail address: docdelivery@haworthpress.com].

119

Statistically significant differences were noted for age and residence on the physical facilities and services provided components. Results were discussed and implications with further research opportunities were suggested. *[Article copies available for a fee from The Haworth Document Delivery Service: 1-800-HAWORTH. E-mail address: <docdelivery@haworthpress. com> Website: <http://www.HaworthPress.com> © 2003 by The Haworth Press, Inc. All rights reserved.]*

KEYWORDS. Attributes, 3-star hotel, importance, perceptions, satisfaction

INTRODUCTION

In a post-modern society, tourism is often conceptualised as a highly-complex series of production-related activities (Cohen, 1996; Pretes, 1995; Munt, 1994). Changes in post-industrial society have seen an increase in leisure time, changing work modes, increase in disposable income, growth of consumer credit, expansion of services, and with the emergence of a post-modern culture have all led to an increase in tourism activity (Strinati, 1995). The changes in available income and leisure time have provided the medium for people to consume, with the associated economic shift from production-driven markets to information-based and service-driven markets (Johnson, Menor, Roth and Chase, 2000). It is therefore of interest to understand and identify the characteristics of the tourism consumer, as the pleasures of tourism originate from complex systems and processes of production and consumption (Laws, 2003; Urry, 1990). Thus, the vast range of attributes, characteristics and images used by tourism and hospitality professionals to promote their services and products requires research so as to facilitate the quality tourism experience for the consumer.

As an integral part of the tourism product, the role of accommodation providers is to understand the motivators and expectations of their target audiences. Recognising that hotel experiences have both tangible and intangible elements, the challenge for hoteliers is to understand and identify how hotel managers define and create enjoyable and effective experiences for their guests. Thus, hoteliers need to establish what aspects of their property their target audience considers to be important when evaluating the hotel experience (Carneiro and Costa, 2001). Once these attributes have been identified, it is then a secondary challenge for management to develop reliable techniques for measuring the quality of the experience (Gundersen, Heide and Olsson, 1996). Thus, this paper examines the importance levels of hotel attributes with significance to satisfaction.

The aim of this research project was to determine which attributes guests of three-star hotel properties perceived as important, that is to determine the importance level of the nominated attributes. It then sought to investigate the satisfaction with the nominated attributes (Wilensky and Buttle, 1988). Whilst many five-star or leading hotels of the world have iconic status, or distinctive historic links, or perhaps outstanding physical attributes or locations, many three-star hotels tend to have lesser tangible attributes to compete with. Thus, it is of interest to investigate this mid-range band of hotels within the hospitality sector in regards to customers' perceptions. In a complex service environment such as the hotel sector, assessing the guests' perception of the facilities and services provides management with information not only to benchmark their service level provision, but also to retain and increase their customer base.

Whilst tourism products are tangible and hence readily identifiable, services are unique in that they are highly intangible. They frequently have high levels of perishability and heterogeneity, and can differ in attributes due to the fact that they may be provided by different service providers. Another key characteristic of services is that of simultaneity, that is, it may be consumed only when the customer is present (Lovelock, Wirtz, and Keh, 2002). With the increased expectation of tourism experience in service delivery systems and process has developed an increase in consumer participation in the service process (Baron and Harris, 2003; Irons, 1994). This has led to changes in structure, control and outputs in many hotel practices and operations. Many of the outputs are transient experiences, memories and promises (Irons, 1994). Irons (1994) explains the service process with his Discontinuity theory, which presents the idea that customers see the service as a continuum punctuated by significant events or key points, which he identifies as discontinuities of importance in the service delivery. The key then is for management to identify these key points or critical discontinuities as identified by the customer, not as identified by management, with the end result being that these are the attributes that can transform the business and the business results in terms of customer satisfaction.

One method of investigating the service system is to consider the nature of customer satisfaction (Baron and Harris, 2003; Kotler Adam, Brown and Armstrong, 2003; Zeithaml and Bitner, 2003). Indeed, service providers have focused on customer satisfaction as a competitive edge over their direct competitors. Kotler et al. (2003) define customer satisfaction as "the extent to which a product's perceived performance matches a buyer's expectations." That is, if a customer places a particular expectation or value on a service performance and if expectation is not met, the customer is either satisfied (the expected level is superseded) or dissatisfied (if the expected level falls below the bar) (Zeithaml and Bitner, 2003). It is therefore necessary not only to identify the attributes which collectively add to generate customer satisfaction, it is also necessary to identify the importance levels of these attributes to enable not only overall satisfaction quality, but excellence in total experience in the provision of these attributes.

Much of the literature links customer satisfaction with the concept of quality (Kandampully, 2002; Irons, 1994). From this basis has developed the premise that attributes are variably valued by a consumer. This variation in importance levels of attributes needs to be identified by an organisation, for management to maximise a customers' overall satisfaction. This is done by providing these attributes at an appropriate level of quality within the organisation. These attributes can be bundled into dimensions to measure overall customer satisfaction based on those important dimensions, which then become the organisations' selling propositions or competitive advantages.

Thus, the investigation into the perceived importance of attributes can be developed through a number of steps. Initially, an investigation between customer and organisational perceptions of attribute provision needs to be established. After the identification of these attributes, the perceived importance of the attributes can then be determined. Measurement of consumer satisfaction of these key attributes is then required to establish the significance of the attributes, and finally, strategies can then be developed for the management of these attributes (Kotler et al., 2003; Morrison, 2002; Irons, 1994). Once the important variables have been identified, they can be grouped or bundled according to product or service provision based on the key satisfaction outcomes perceived by service industry customers. These products and services can then be aligned to organisation capabilities, and included in management strategies. Whilst there has been a strong emphasis from the services marketing literature (Lovelock et al., 2002; Kotler et al., 2003; Baron and Harris, 2003) for organisations to provide all the necessary wishes/needs of the customer to generate satisfaction, it is necessary to also consider the context within which organisations' management operates. It is imperative that organisations recognise that resources are finite and management has to work within the internal capabilities of the organisation and the external environment conditions, both at the operational and strategic level to sustainably generate customer satisfaction (Figure 1).

Recent studies have attempted to validate the relationship between the services provided by hotels and the way in which customers evaluate their levels of satisfaction derived from using these services (Tsaur, Chiu and Huang, 2002; Getty and Thompson, 1994). Customers are likely to view the services as a bundle of attributes that may differ in their contributions from the product or service evaluation and choice (Choi and Chu, 2001; Gundersen, Heide, and Olsson, 1996; Kivela, 1996; Fornell, 1992; Halstead and Page, 1992). These attributes arouse consumers' purchase intention and help to differentiate from

FIGURE 1. Sequential Approach of Importance Levels of Attributes with Significance to Satisfaction

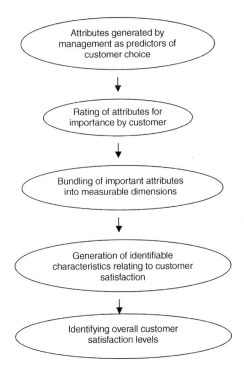

competitors' offerings. Wuest, Tas, and Emenheiser (1996) discuss the perception of hotel attributes as being the extent to which visitors may find the various facilities and services as being important in generating customer satisfaction for staying in a hotel.

From a literature review investigating hotel attributes within the hospitality industry, it has been suggested that attributes such as cleanliness, location, room rate, guest rooms, service quality, security, employee attitudes, and reputation/brand name of the hotel or chain are regarded as important for hotel guests (Choi and Chu, 2001; Dube and Renaghan, 2000; Worcester, 1999; Verespej, 1994; Ananth, deMicco, Moreo and Howey, 1992; Barsky and Labagh, 1992; Atkinson, 1988; Cardotte and Turgeon, 1988). Atkinson (1988) adds that cleanliness, security, value for money, courtesy, and helpfulness of staff were found to be important attributes for travellers in their selection of hotels.

However, Barsky and Labagh (1992) suggest that employee attitude, location of the hotel, rooms, price, and hotel facilities were the attributes that ranked highly when guests were considering choice of hotels. Attitudes of employees, cleanliness and neatness of rooms, quality of service, and employee knowledge of service were the most frequent factors raised by guests in a survey consisting of 26 categories of compliments (Cardotte and Turgeon, 1988). Ananth et al. (1992) surveyed a total of 510 guests to rate the importance of 57 attributes in their hotel choice selection. Price and quality were rated as the most vital attributes, followed by security and convenience of location. Heung, Wong, and Qu (2002) studied tourists' satisfaction and concluded that employee attributes were found to be the most important factor contributing to tourists' overall satisfaction, thus impacting on repeat visitation and recommendation intentions of guests. The Marriott Corporation team conducted a survey of hotel factors that influenced guest satisfaction and identified cleanliness, friendliness of personnel, value, and check-in speed to be the key attributes (Verespej, 1994). Frequent leisure travellers identified the physical properties, interpersonal service, guest rooms, quality standards, and location as the most important attributes driving their decision to book their most recent hotel stay (Dube and Renaghan, 2000).

In view of this, it would be of considerable worth for hoteliers to investigate which attributes are most likely to influence customer's valuing of these characteristics and how to measure the resultant levels of satisfaction which customers derive from these attributes (Richard and Sundaram, 1993). Guest comment cards, satisfaction surveys, focus groups (Withiam, 1995), and systematic registration of customer complaints and compliments are just some of the examples of instruments that have been used to track customer satisfaction (Gundersen, Heide, and Olsson, 1996). However, in most cases, such studies experience low response rates and the information yielded is insufficient to provide actionable feedback for managers. Moreover, there is the potential of biases while guest comments are being collated. Responses collected from guests, especially voluntary comments, can also be subject to statistical error (Jones and Ioannou, 1993). This is due to the fact that most guests offer feedback voluntarily for two main reasons–when they either have to make a complaint or to commend the hotel for excellent service delivery (Heymann and Schall, 2002).

Due to the intangibility of many of the attributes, and subjective nature of value, information that is provided by guests is subjective and relates to the individual respondents, temporal, spatial and psychological state at the time of evaluation. The information does not take into account the perceptions and satisfaction of other guests who are either neutral or who do not make a habit of voicing their comments (Heymann and Schall, 2002). Neutral guests are those who have had no poor experiences during their hotel stay and the hotel has not made an impression on them. This group of guests makes up a large component of total customers who make purchase decisions based on price, facilities, amenities, and experiences. Therefore, if the perceptions and needs of 'neutrals' are not met or excelled, there is the possibility that they will not become repeat customers. In order to excel and emerge as the best in the industry, 3-star hotels must know how they measure up against guest expectations and how their performance compares against the competition (Worcester, 1999).

Industry surveys are regarded as highly significant sources of information that provide customers with an outlet for feedback, and hotel managers with an understanding of their customers. Surveys also provide hotels with a diagnostic tool from which both guests and management stand to gain. Customers will get what they want out of the hotel and these hotels can improve upon their service performances (Worcester, 1999). Lewis and Pizam (1981) concurred with the importance of guest surveys in their ability to generate vital information to aid management decisions, however, including the proviso that the surveys are actually addressing the questions that are required. Wilensky and Buttle (1988: 29) comment that marketing research within the hotel sector " . . . is generally limited to the analysis of guest related data," they suggest that to "enable management . . . to predict customer choice with some degree of confidence," the degree of analysis will determine the value of the feedback. Lewis and Pizam (1981) were also aware and discussed the problems hoteliers face when interpreting survey data. This presents the need for rigor in research within the hotel sector, and for diligent analysis of the findings. Reliable information is then generated for high-quality management and marketing strategies. Thus, this highlights the need for not only the collection of data from various stakeholders, but the implicit advantage of a high level of analysis to be used in the data analysis stages of all research.

STUDY METHODS

The present study attempts to determine which of the services and facilities provided by a 3-star hotel to their guests were considered by the latter as important attributes and the overall satisfaction with these services with likelihood of future stay in the hotel. Self-administered survey was therefore conducted to: (a) measure the level of importance each attribute in the hotel plays in determining hotel guests' choice intentions, (b) determine what constructs (dimensions) can be explained by these attributes, and examine whether there are statistically significant differences between the demographic variables on the perceived importance of particular attribute/s, and (c) determine the overall satisfaction levels of the guests and their likelihood of repeat stay in the hotel. The paper is organised in the following structure: methodology, questionnaire design and survey, analysis and discussion (factor analysis, t-tests and ANOVA, linear regression), and implications and conclusion.

This study was conducted on a 3-star hotel located within the Perth metropolitan area of WA. Permission was sought in writing from the general managers of 3-star hotels who showed keen interest to participate in the survey. The three 3-star hotels were privately owned and collectively, had an estimated 80 rooms on average. The study was conducted over a week's duration based on the consensus of the hotel general managers. The target population chosen was randomly selected from guests staying at all of the three hotels. Given the total of 200 rooms available and an average hotel stay of 3.8 days in Perth (Western Australian Tourism Commission, 2002), the target population for the three 3-star hotels was 368 guests for the duration of one week (Shanka and Quintal, 2003). The questionnaires were made available to guests in their hotel rooms and at the checkout counters. In total, 300 questionnaires were distributed over one week. One hundred and six (106) questionnaires were completed and returned, representing a response rate of 35%. From the 106 questionnaires, five questionnaires were excluded from the analysis due to incomplete information. The remaining 101 questionnaires (34% effective response rate) were analysed using SPSS Version 11.0 for Windows.

The number of attributes used for this study was eighteen (18) as agreed by all three managers of the 3-star hotels concerned in addition to information gleaned through literature review. These 18 attributes were selected by reviewing literature, SERVQUAL scale and by consulting the three 3-star hotel managers under study. This was done to capture all attributes that were regarded as important by all three hotels, notwithstanding that there may be some other relevant attributes that are perceived as important for other hotel guests staying in different star-grade hotels.

The questionnaire of this survey consisted of two parts. The first part consisted of 18 pre-specified and pre-tested hotel service attributes measuring their perceived importance to hotel guests. The 18 hotel service attributes were grouped into three categories: *hotel facilities*, *room amenities*, and *front office (reception)*. The sets of questions were measured on a 5-point Likert scale where 5 denoted 'most important' attributes and 1 denoted 'least important' attribute. To reduce the potential bias of forced responses from respondents, the option 'not applicable' was included for each question. The last section of the questionnaire collected socio-demographic information of the respondents.

PROFILES OF RESPONDENTS

The demographic structure of the respondents revealed that the number of female respondents was marginally higher (51.5%) than their male counterparts (48.5%). Over 33% of respondents were aged 51 years or over, 39% of respondents were interstate visitors (intrastate and overseas visitors accounted for 26% and 35%, respectively), and about 44% were holidaymakers. Eighty-eight percent of respondents indicated that they were fairly satisfied or very satisfied with the hotel services and 66% indicated their likelihood of stay in the same hotel during their future travel to Perth.

RESULTS AND DISCUSSIONS

The 18 attributes used to measure perceived importance of hotel amenities were subjected to a reliability test to determine the internal consistency of the scale ($\alpha = 0.84$). The mean scores, standard deviations and ranking (based on mean scores) are presented in Table 1. The most important attributes with the highest mean scores of 4.0 or more included *friendly front office staff* (item #16), *efficient check-in/checkout* (item #17), *restaurant & bar* (item #8), and *lobby ambience* (item #18). On the other hand, the least important attributes with mean scores 3.0 or less included *dry cleaning services* (item #2), *sauna and gym* (item #3), *business facilities* (item #6), *Internet connection facilities*

TABLE 1. Mean Scores, Standard Deviations and Ranking Based on Mean Scores

		Mean Score *	Std. Deviation	Ranking
1.	24 hour reception	3.8	1.1	4
2.	Dry cleaning	2.5	1.2	13
3.	Sauna & gym	2.6	1.2	12
4.	Taxi booking	3.6	1.3	5
5.	On-site parking	3.9	1.4	3
6.	Business facilities	2.6	1.3	12
7.	Safe deposit boxes	3.3	1.3	7
8.	Restaurant & bar	4.2	0.9	2
9.	Tour bookings	3.3	1.3	7
10.	Mini bar	3.0	1.3	10
11.	Internet connection	2.8	1.3	11
12.	In-house movies	3.2	1.3	8
13.	Personal safe	3.4	1.3	6
14.	Long bath	3.1	1.4	9
15.	IDD	3.2	1.4	8
16.	Friendly front office staff	4.7	0.8	1
17.	Efficient check-in/out	4.7	0.7	1
18.	Lobby ambience	4.2	0.9	2

*On a scale 1 = Least important and 5 = Most important

(item #11) and *mini bar* (item #10). Hence, all attributes with mean scores of 3.0 and less were excluded from further analyses and the resulting coefficient α was at the acceptable level of 0.71.

Factor Analysis

The 13 items that were retained were factor-analysed to reduce them to a smaller set of underlying dimensions (factors) that summarise the essential information contained in the 12 items. Factorability of the scale items was confirmed by the KMO measure of sampling adequacy result of 0.759 and significant Bartlett's test of sphericity ($\chi^2 = 586.785$, df = 123, sig. 0.000). One item, restaurant and bar (item #8) with factor loadings of less than 0.55 was eliminated during the analysis (Hair, Anderson, Tatham and Black, 1998).

Three components explaining 60.6% of total variances were extracted (Table 2). The first component, labelled *physical facilities*, consisted of five attributes namely personal safe (item #13), safe deposit box (item #7), IDD (item #15), en-suite long bath (item #14), and in-house movies (item #12). This component had eigenvalue of 3.33 and accounted for 27.2% of total variances. Its coefficient alpha was 0.82. The second component, labelled *services experienced*, consisted of three attributes including friendly front office staff (item

TABLE 2. Results of Principal Component Analysis with Varimax Rotation

Components/Items		Factor Loadings	Eigenvalue	Percent of Variance	Cumulative Percent	Scale Mean	Cronbach's α
1. Physical facilities			*3.33*	*27.2*	*27.2*	*16.3*	*0.82*
Item 13.	Personal safe	0.878					
Item 7	Safe deposit boxes	0.858					
Item 15	IDD	0.772					
Item 14	Long bath	0.667					
Item 12	In-house movies	0.657					
2. Service experienced			*2.74*	*21.3*	*48.5*	*13.2*	*0.73*
Item 16	Friendly front office staff	0.910					
Item 17	Efficient check-in/ check-out	0.888					
Item 1	24 hour reception	0.616					
3. Services provided			*1.57*	*12.1*	*60.0*	*14.8*	*0.53*
Item 4	Taxi booking	0.743					
Item 18	Lobby ambience	0.619					
Item 9	Tour bookings	0.595					
Item 5	On-site parking	0.594					

#16), efficient check-in/check-out (item #17), and 24-hour reception (item #1). It had eigenvalue of 2.74 and accounted for 21.3% of total variances with coefficient alpha of 0.73. The third component, labelled *services provided*, consisted of four attributes, namely taxi booking (item #4), lobby ambience (item #18), tour bookings (item #9), and on-site parking (item #5). Its eigenvalue, percent of variance and coefficient alpha were 1.57, 12.1% and 0.53, respectively. The scale means for the three components were 16.3, 13.2, and 14.8, respectively (Table 2).

Independent Samples T-Tests and One-Way Analysis of Variance (ANOVA) Tests

The Independent Samples *t-test* results showed no statistically significant differences between female and male respondents on the three components. One-way ANOVA tests were conducted to determine statistically significant differences for respondents' age group, purpose of visit, usual place of residence and intention to stay. Test results revealed no significant differences on any of the components for purpose of visit and intention to stay in future visit; however, statistically significant differences were reported for age group and usual place of residence.

Age Group

Statistically significant differences were reported (F = 9.973, p < 0.01) for age groups on two of the three components, physical facilities and services provided. On the physical facilities, significant differences were reported between three age groups. The mean score for 51+ group was significantly lower than those for 30 or younger group and 31-50 age group. The former group's mean score for the physical facilities was 2.59 compared with that of: (a) 30 or younger group (mean = 3.54), and (b) 31-50 years (mean = 3.52). The older group did not consider physical facilities as an important dimension, whereas for the two younger age groups, this component was important. For the services provided component, statistically significant difference (F = 3.646, p < 0.05) was reported between 30 or younger age group and 51+ age group. The older group considered this component more important (mean = 3.98) while the younger age group mean was 3.41.

Usual Place of Residences

Statistically significant difference (F = 4.609, p < 0.05) were reported between interstate and overseas visitors on the physical facilities component only. Overseas visitors perceived this component more important (mean =

3.61) compared with interstate visitors, whose mean score of 2.87 suggested this group attached less importance to the physical facilities.

Multiple Regression Analysis

Hierarchical multiple regression was conducted to determine, (a) the contribution made by each of the three components physical facilities, service experienced, and services provided (as independent variables) individually and collectively to the overall importance of the attributes (as dependent variable), and (b) to identify which of the three components best predict the overall importance. Assumption testing indicated no violations.

The *Model Summary* section in Table 3 indicates that all three components together explained 90% of the variance in overall importance, which was highly significant. Physical facilities component on its own contributed 69.2% of the variance in overall importance and is significant predictor. At the second step, both physical facilities component and service encountered ac-

TABLE 3. Hierarchical Regression Model Summary and Coefficients

Model Summary

Model	R	R Square	Adjusted R Square	Std. Error of the Estimate	Change Statistics R Square Change	F Change	df1	df2	Sig. F Change
1	.832	.692	.689	.365	.692	222.835	1	99	.000
2	.887	.787	.783	.305	.095	43.624	1	98	.000
3	.949	.900	.897	.210	.113	110.271	1	97	.000

Coefficients

Model		Unstandardized Coefficients B	Std. Error	Standardized Coefficients Beta	t	Sig.
1	(Constant)	1.896	.114		16.590	.000
	Physical facilities 13,7,15,14,12	.503	.034	.832	14.928	.000
2	(Constant)	.721	.202		3.571	.001
	Physical facilities 13,7,15,14,12	.467	.029	.772	16.272	.000
	Service experienced 16,17,1	.292	.044	.314	6.605	.000
3	(Constant)	8.421E-02	.151		.556	.580
	Physical facilities 13,7,15,14,12	.439	.020	.725	22.019	.000
	Service experienced 16,17,1	.216	.031	.231	6.896	.000
	Services provided 4,18,9,5	.281	.027	.352	10.501	.000

Predictors: (Constant), Physical facilities (Items 13, 7, 15, 14, 12)
Predictors: (Constant), Physical facilities (Items 13, 7, 15, 14, 12), Service experienced (Items 16, 17, 1)
Predictors: (Constant), Physical facilities (Items 13, 7, 15, 14, 12), Service experienced (Items 16, 17, 1), Services provided (Items 4, 18, 9, 5)
Dependent Variable: Overall importance

counted for 78.7% of the variance in overall importance as evidenced by the significant F change (R Square change = 9.5%). At the third step, physical facilities, service experienced and services provided together explained 90% of the variance in overall importance as evidenced by significant F change (R Square change = 11.3%).

The *t*-values in Table 3 (under *Coefficients section*) indicated that all three components individually and in conjunction with the other components/s contributed significantly to the overall importance. The standardized coefficients showed that physical facilities contributed significantly higher to the overall importance followed by physical facilities + service provided and physical facilities + service experienced + services provided. The individual component contribution in the overall model was physical facilities, services provided and service experienced, respectively.

IMPLICATIONS AND CONCLUSION

The importance of being able to offer high-quality experiences which are meaningful to hotel guests is unquestionable. For hotels to ensure customer satisfaction requires knowledge of what guests deem as important when evaluating the hotel experience which is being provided. The results of this study indicate that guests in 3-star hotels rank the importance of hotel attributes in physical facilities, service experienced and services provided. To attract and maintain their customers, 3-star hotels could enhance their existing services to provide guests with the best of what the hotel already has to offer, that is a quality provision and delivery of products and services. This would be more feasible than developing a new range of services that might stretch budgets and make service delivery even more difficult to perform. Hotel management would do well in ensuring that their hotel lobbies are well maintained, their front office procedures are in place, and that their in-room services meet quality standards derived from customer expectations.

The results of this exploratory study have identified statistically significant differences between age groups and between guests based on their country of residence on the dimensions of the *facilities* and *services provided* components. This suggests that existing hotel facilities should be maintained and where possible, upgraded. This may prove to be crucial for 3-star hotels which have a significant interstate and international traveller audience, as these guests have ranked facilities as an important component in their choice of hotels.

In conclusion, the findings in this study are based upon a specific study setting, therefore in order to assess the external validity of this data, it is suggested that the study should be replicated and conducted in other 3-star hotel settings located elsewhere, with larger sample sizes. It is conceivable that given the different settings and locations, guests might have different perceptions of the service attributes offered by 3-star hotels or these variables may be validated as being the important variables across the tourism population per se.

The development of a valid list of important attributes would enable individual hotels to bundle these into identifiable characteristics to enhance their overall customer satisfaction. Additionally, it could also provide a discrete list relevant across a hotel chain or group of particular hotels which would allow management to identify their individual chains' offerings at a quality level appropriate to the targeted hotel audience based on the bundled attributes meaningful to their guest, which fit with the strategic goals of the organisation.

Thus, the ability to identify important attributes would allow management to manage and market accordingly the quality development of these bundled products and services which are meaningful to guests. In fact, it would enable management to concentrate on these important attributes thus ensuring quality experiences through purposeful financial support (Kimes, 2001), by developing attributes whose importance levels have been identified by, and thus are significant to, both the customer and organisation for satisfaction.

REFERENCES

Ananth, M., DeMicco, F. J., Moreo, P. J. and Howey, R. M. (1992). Marketplace lodging needs of mature travellers. *Cornell Hotel and Restaurant Administration Quarterly, 33* (4): 12-24.

Atkinson, A. (1988). Answering the eternal question: what does the customer want? *Cornell Hotel and Restaurant Administration Quarterly, 29* (2): 12-14.

Barsky, J. D. and Labagh, R. (1992). A Strategy got Customer Satisfaction. *Cornell Hotel and Restaurant Administration Quarterly, 33* (5): 32-38.

Baron, S. and Harris, K. (2003). *Services Marketing: Texts and Cases.* (2nd ed) London: Palgrave.

Cardotte, E. R. and Turgeon, N. (1988). Key factors in guest satisfaction. *Cornell Hotel and Restaurant Administration Quarterly, 29* (1): 45-51.

Carneiro, M. and Costa, C. (2001). The influences of service quality on the positioning of five-star hotels–the case of the Lisbon Area. *Journal of Quality Assurance in Hospitality & Tourism, 1* (4): 1-20.

Choi, T. Y. and Chu, R. (2001). Determinants of hotel guests' satisfaction and repeat patronage in the Hong Kong hotel industry. *International Journal of Hospitality Management, 20* (3): 277-297.

Cohen, E. (1996). "A Phenomenology of Tourist Experiences" in *The Sociology of Tourism–Theoretical and Empirical Investigations,* Ed. Apostolopoulos, Leivadi and Yiannakis, London: Routledge.

Dube, L. and Renaghan, L. M. (2000). Creating visible customer value: How customers view best-practice champions. *Cornell Hotel and Restaurant Administration Quarterly, 41* (1): 62-72.

Fornell, C. (1992). A national customer satisfaction barometer: The Swedish experience. *Journal of Marketing, 56* (1): 6-21.

Getty, J. M., and Thompson, K.N. (1994). The relationship between quality satisfaction and recommending behaviour in lodging decision. *Journal of Hospitality and Leisure Marketing, 2* (3): 3-22.

Gundersen, M. G. Heide, M. and Olsson, U. H. (1996). Hotel guest satisfaction among business travellers: What are the important actors? *Cornell Hotel and Restaurant Administration Quarterly, 37* (2): 72-81.

Hair, J. F., Anderson, R. E., Tatham, R. L. and Black, W. C. (1998). *Multivariate Data Analysis,* 5th edition. Upper Saddle River, New Jersey: Prentice Hall.

Halstead, D. and Page Jr., T. J. (1992). The effects of satisfaction and complaining behaviour on consumers repurchase behaviour. *Journal of Satisfaction, Dissatisfaction and Complaining Behaviour, 1*: 1-11.

Heymann, K. J. and Schall, M. (2002). Make money from guest satisfaction. *Lodging Hospitality, 58* (7): 13.

Heung, V. C., Wong, M. Y. and Qu, H. (2002). A study of tourists' satisfaction and post-experience behavioural intentions in relation to airport restaurant services in the Hong Kong SAR. *Journal of Travel Research, 12* (2/3): 111-135.

Irons, K. (1994). *Managing Service Companies: Strategies for Success.* England: Addison-Wesley Publishing Company.

Johnson, S., Menor, A., Roth, A. and Chase, R. (2000). "*A critical evaluation of the new service development process,*" in Fitzsimmons, J.A. and Fitzsimmons, M.J. (eds) New Service Development: Creating Memorable Experiences. California: Sage.

Jones, P. and Ioannou, A. (1993). Measuring guest satisfaction in UK-based international hotel chains: Principles and practice. *International Journal of Contemporary Hospitality Management, 5* (5): 27-32.

Kandampully, J. (2002). Services Management: The new paradigm in hospitality. Australia: Pearson Education.

Kimes, S. (2001). How product quality drives profitability: The experience at Holiday Inn. *The Cornell Hotel and Restaurant Administration Quarterly,* June: 25-29.

Kivela, J. (1996). Marketing in the restaurant business: A theoretical model for identifying consumers' determinant choice variables and their impact on repeat purchase in the restaurant industry. *Australian Journal of Hospitality Management, 3* (1): 13-23.

Kotler, A., Adam, S., Brown, L. and Armstrong, G. (2003). *Principles of Marketing.* (2nd ed) Melbourne: Prentice Hall.

Laws, E. (2003). Towards an analysis of complex tourism service systems, *Proceedings of the CAUTHE 2003 Conference, Riding the Waves of Tourism & Hospitality Research,* Coffs Harbour, 5-8 Feb.

Lewis, R. and Pizam, A. (1981). Guest surveys: A missed opportunity. *The Cornell Hotel and Restaurant Administration Quarterly,* (Nov):37-44.

Lovelock, C. Wirtz, J., and Keh, H.T. (2002). *Services Marketing in Asia*. United States: Prentice Hall.

Morrison, A. (2002). *Hospitality and Travel Marketing*. (3rd ed). United States: Thomson Learning.

Munt, I. (1994). The 'Other' post modern tourism: culture, travel and the new middle classes. *Theory, Culture and Society, 11*:101-123.

Pretes, M. (1995). Post-modern tourism: The Santa Claus industry. *Annals of Tourism Research, 22*: 1-15.

Richard, M. D. and Sundaram, D. S. (1993). Lodging choice intentions: A causal modelling approach. *Journal of Hospitality and Leisure Marketing, 1* (4): 81-98.

Shanka, T. and Quintal, V. (2003). Hotel facilities perceived importance–hotel guests' perceived views: An exploratory study. *Proceedings of the CAUTHE 2003 Conference, Riding the Waves of Tourism & Hospitality Research*, Coffs Harbour, 5-8 Feb.

Strinati, D. (1995). *An Introduction of the Theories of Popular Culture*. London: Routledge.

Tsaur, S. H., Chiu Y. C., and Huang CH. H. (2002). Determinants of guest loyalty to international tourist hotels–a neural network approach. *Tourism Management, 23* (4): 397-405.

Urry, J. (1990) *The Tourist Gaze: Leisure and Travel in Contemporary Societies*, London: Sage.

Verespej, M. A. (1994). How the best got better. *Industry Week, 243* (5): 27.

Western Australian Tourism Commission. (April 2002). *Research Brief on Tourism*. Perth: WATC.

Willensky, L. and Buttle, F. (1988) A multivariate analysis of hotel benefit bundles and choice trade-offs. *International Journal of Hospitality Management, 7* (1): 29-41.

Witham, G. (1995). Measuring guest perceptions: Combine measurement tools. *Cornell Hotel and Restaurant Administration Quarterly, 36* (6): 16.

Worcester, B. A. (1999). Industry leaders find value, satisfaction in surveys. *Hotel and Motel Management, 214* (13): 33-36.

Wuest, B., Tas, R. F. and Emenheiser, D. A. (1996). What do mature travellers perceive as important hotel/motel customer service? *Hospitality Research Journal, 20* (1): 77-93.

Zeithaml, V. and Bitner, M. (2003) *Services Marketing: Integrating Customer Focus Across the Firm*. New York: McGraw Hill.

Categories of Participants
Based on Their Expectations
of Instructor-Led Training

Candice E. Clemenz
Pamela A. Weaver
Jiho Han
Ken W. McCleary

SUMMARY. Trainees' expectations of training are important considerations in the development of training programs, yet a lack of research exists to understand the expectations of trainees as they relate to various
training delivery methods. To investigate the underlying dimensions or
factors that determine trainees' expectations in instructor-led training
sessions, 164 surveys were collected from attendees at six different hospitality industry instructor-led training sessions. Utilizing a factor analytic procedure, the following five dimensions of trainees' expectations
were identified: courtesy, entertainment, climate, tangibles, and rele-

Candice E. Clemenz (E-mail: clemenz@vt.edu) is Assistant Professor, Pamela A.
Weaver (E-mail: weaver@vt.edu) and Ken W. McCleary (E-mail: mccleary@vt.edu)
are Professors, and Jiho Han (E-mail: jihan1@vt.edu) is a Doctoral Candidate, all at the
Department of Hospitality and Tourism Management, Virginia Polytechnic Institute
and State University, 362 Wallace Hall, Blacksburg, VA 24061-0429.

[Haworth co-indexing entry note]: "Categories of Participants Based on Their Expectations of Instructor-Led Training." Clemenz, Candice E. et al. Co-published simultaneously in *Journal of Quality Assurance
in Hospitality & Tourism* (The Haworth Hospitality Press, an imprint of The Haworth Press, Inc.) Vol. 4, No.
3/4, 2003, pp. 135-148; and: *Current Issues and Development in Hospitality and Tourism Satisfaction* (ed:
John A. Williams and Muzaffer Uysal) The Haworth Hospitality Press, an imprint of The Haworth Press, Inc.,
2003, pp. 135-148. Single or multiple copies of this article are available for a fee from The Haworth Document
Delivery Service [1-800-HAWORTH, 9:00 a.m. - 5:00 p.m. (EST). E-mail address: docdelivery@
haworthpress.com].

http://www.haworthpress.com/web/JQAHT
Digital Object Identifier: 10.1300/J162v04n03_09

vance. These expectations of training dimensions were then used to cluster analyze trainees into three groups: "the good-timers," "the high hopes," and "the serious students." *[Article copies available for a fee from The Haworth Document Delivery Service: 1-800-HAWORTH. E-mail address: <docdelivery@ haworthpress.com> Website: <http://www.HaworthPress.com> © 2003 by The Haworth Press, Inc. All rights reserved.]*

KEYWORDS. Training, instructor-led training, expectations, quality of training

INTRODUCTION

Training is a huge business. Noted for being a change agent that promises improved employee attitude, job satisfaction, productivity, and work quality, training costs American companies an estimated $200 billion a year (Wiley, 1993). In spite of the fact that executives repeatedly ask for feedback pertaining to the effectiveness and/or return on the investment of their training programs, less than ten percent of companies in the hospitality industry conduct formal assessments of their training programs (Conrad, Woods, & Ninemeier, 1994). Practitioners frequently address this statistic by pointing to a lack of training research on the part of academics, and the subsequent absence of proven evaluation techniques and tools.

The purpose of this study is to further research the area of training evaluation by viewing training effectiveness as a function of meeting trainees' expectations. Based upon the works of Hoiberg and Berry (1978), Hicks and Klimoski (1987), and Tannenbaum, Mathieu, Salas and Cannon-Bowers (1991), expectations have been shown to play an important role in determining training effectiveness. Therefore, by using a training evaluation scale developed by Clemenz (2001), this research seeks to understand the underlying dimensions of trainees' expectations regarding the quality of instructor-led training programs. Following factor analysis, the identified dimensions are cluster analyzed to classify trainees by their expectations of training.

LITERATURE REVIEW

Individuals enter training with varying expectations (Hoiberg & Berry, 1978). Understanding trainees' expectations of training is important because, as Hoiberg and Berry (1978) and Hicks and Klimoski (1987) suggest, unmet expectations can affect training outcomes. Noe (1986) concurred that the expectations of trainees may either limit or enhance the effectiveness of training. Yet, per Feldman (1989), training expectation research is limited and additional exploration is needed. Tannenbaum and Yukl (1991) also called for further examination of training expectations, indicating that individual differences in trainees' attitudes and expectations may be central influences on training effectiveness.

In 1991, Tannenbaum et al. defined the extent to which training meets a trainee's expectations as training fulfillment. In their study of 666 navy recruits, Tannenbaum et al. (1991) examined the role of expectations in the development of employee attitudes. They measured navy recruits' expectations about training and their perceptions of what actually occurred during training. The researchers found that the extent to which training met trainees' expectations was related to training motivation, physical self-efficacy, academic self-efficacy, and organizational commitment. However, the relationship between met expectations was strongest with the post-training attitudes of training motivation and organizational commitment. Tannenbaum et al. (1991) found that unmet expectations had negative consequences on sailors' performance in technical school and on their fleet assignments, consistent with Hoiberg and Berry's (1978) research that revealed sailors' expectations were significantly related to graduation from training school.

The link between expectations and motivation is notable since training motivation is viewed as "an important antecedent of training effectiveness" (Tannenbaum et al., 1991, p. 760). Noe (1986) described motivation in a training environment as the force that influences trainees' enthusiasm about the program, and a stimulus that directs participants to learn and attempt to master the content of the program. Training practitioners agree that motivated trainees engage more actively with training and get more out of it than do trainees who are not motivated (Tracey & Tews, 1995). Further, a study by Mathieu, Tannenbaum, and Salas (1992) indicated a positive, direct link between trainees' motivation and their learning during training.

Kirkpatrick's (1959) taxonomy of training evaluation criteria, a frequently referenced model, identifies four hierarchical levels of training evaluation: reactions, learning, behavior, and results. Reactions refer to a measure of customer satisfaction; learning pertains to changes in attitudes, skills, or knowledge that result from training; behavior is synonymous with training transfer or the implementation of training on-the-job; results address the outcomes or impacts of training (Kirkpatrick, 1959). Within this context, expectations are classified as reactions to training. Alliger and Janak (1989) observed low correlations between reaction-level criteria and learning. However, when Mathieu et al. (1992) explored non-linear relationships, they found support for the role of reactions to training as moderators between training motivation (a reaction-level criteria) and learning.

Scales that measure expectations of training are difficult to find, however, Clemenz (2001) developed one such scale in the course of a study regarding training quality. Operating from the paradigm that training is a service, Clemenz initiated a rigorous scale development process in a study that revealed the dimensions of perceived quality of training based upon trainees' impressions of training. The research borrowed Parasuraman, Zeithaml, and Berry's (1985) definition of service quality as the difference between perceptions and expectations, and a scale was developed that was composed of 30 items. Each item was evaluated by trainees as an expectation and a perception of instructor-led training (Clemenz & Weaver, 2003).

METHODOLOGY

Research Questions

Three research questions were proposed for this study:

1. What are the dimensions or primary factors that underlie trainees' expectations of training?
2. Is it possible to group trainees in instructor-led training sessions based on their expectations of training?
3. Do specific demographic characteristics affect trainees' expectations of training?

Sample

The sampling frame for this research consisted of six instructor-led training sessions conducted in the hospitality industry. Four training sessions were sponsored by hospitality companies (food service and hotels) for their respective employees while one training session was hosted by an industry association; the other session was offered by a professional hospitality training organization. Trainees were supervisory or management-level employees, and all attendees at each of the training sessions were asked to complete surveys. A total of 172 surveys were distributed and 164 completed surveys were returned for a 94.5% response rate. This method of convenience sampling was deemed appropriate for exploratory-level research (Zikmund, 1997).

The majority of the respondents were male (64%) and the remaining thirty six percent were female (see Table 1). The greatest percentage of respondents,

TABLE 1. Demographic Information Regarding Questionnaire Respondents (n = 164)

Characteristics	Percentage	Frequency
Gender		
Female	35.6	57
Male	64.4	103
Age		
18 to 25	9.4	15
26 to 35	35.0	56
36 to 45	41.3	66
46 to 55	11.9	19
56 and older	2.5	4
Time with current company		
One year or less	21.3	34
More than 1 year but less than 3 years	23.1	37
3 to 6 years	31.9	51
More than 6 years	23.8	38
Time in current position		
One year or less	30.6	49
More than 1 year less than 3 years	26.9	43
3 to 6 years	25.6	41
More than 6 years	16.9	27
Number of instructor-led training sessions attended in the past five years		
None	11.3	18
2 sessions	15.6	25
3 sessions	13.8	22
4 sessions	15.6	25
5 sessions	6.9	11
more than 5 sessions	36.9	59
Required or elective attendance at training		
Required	36.7	58
Elective	63.3	100

Note. Percentages that do not equal 100 are due to rounding.

41%, were in the 36 to 45 year old age category. Thirty-two percent had been with their respective companies three to six years and twenty-seven percent had been in their current positions more than one but less than three years. Thirty-seven percent of the respondents replied they attended more than five instructor-led training sessions in the past five years; eleven percent reported they had not participated in an instructor-led training session in the past five years; and more than half of the respondents (52%) had attended two to five instructor-led training sessions in the past five years. The majority of the respondents (63%) chose to attend the training sessions while the others were required to attend.

Instrument Development

The expectation scale developed by Clemenz (2001) was incorporated into a survey instrument that consisted of two sections. Section 1 of the questionnaire consisted of the 30-item scale that measured trainees' expectations of training quality using a five-point Likert scale (1 = strongly disagree and 5 = strongly agree). The second section included demographic information regarding respondents' gender, age, time with current company, time in current position, number of instructor-led training sessions attended, and whether they were required to attend or elected to attend the training.

Data Collection

The process of gathering information from trainees was facilitated through a self-administered questionnaire (Zikmund, 2000). Although the researcher offered to travel to each of the six training sites to conduct the survey, in all cases the respective trainers preferred to administer the surveys themselves. Therefore, the researcher mailed overnight packages to each trainer in advance of the scheduled session. According to the instructions provided, each trainer administered the questionnaires to the trainees prior to the beginning of training.

Statistical Tests

Exploratory factor analysis was performed to find the underlying dimensions of trainees' expectations towards quality training, and Principal Component Analysis utilizing Varimax rotation was adapted to factor-analyze 30 expectation items. Reliability tests were done to compute the coefficient alphas for each factor to examine the internal consistency of each dimension. ANOVAs, Kruskal-Wallis tests, and cross-tabulations with chi-square tests were performed to examine the factors. Then, using cluster analysis, respondents were grouped based on factor scores of expectations. Summated scales that are average mean scores of the variables in each factor were used. Also, clusters were examined to determine demographic and other job-related characteristics by utilizing ANOVAs, Kruskal-Wallis tests, and cross-tabulations with chi-square tests.

RESULTS

Exploratory Factor Analysis

Although factor analysis has critical assumptions that are more conceptual than statistical (Hair, Anderson, Tatham & Black, 2002), a visual inspection of the data matrix was used to verify that a substantial number of correlations were greater than .30, thereby indicating an appropriateness to continue with factor analysis. Bartlett's test of sphericity rejected the null hypothesis that the data matrix was an identity matrix, therefore suggesting that significant correlations existed between at least some variables. Another test of the underlying structure assumption, the Kaiser-Meyer-Olkin Measure of Sampling Adequacy (MSA), scored .771 or in the "middling" range of acceptability according to Hair et al. (2002).

In the course of eleven iterations of factor analysis, eleven items were eliminated due to factor loadings less than .50 or because they loaded on two factors. Nineteen items, all with Eigenvalues that exceeded 1.0, from the original 30-item scale were found to comprise five dimensions of expectations of training quality (see Table 2). Based upon the supporting items, the dimensions were labeled and defined as follows:

1. Courtesy–respect, recognition, and on-going concern for trainees by trainer.
2. Climate–the surrounding condition or mood of the training environment.
3. Entertainment–the infusion of excitement and fun into training.
4. Tangibles–the physical facilities and structure of training.
5. Relevance–the relationship of training to trainees' needs and job performance.

The five factors/dimensions explained 60.3% of the variance in trainees' responses regarding expectations (see Table 3). One dimension (Courtesy) was supported by six items, one dimension (Climate) had four related items, and three dimensions (Entertainment, Tangibles, and Relevance) were composed

TABLE 2. Items Found to Comprise the Training Expectation Scale Per Exploratory Factor Analysis

Items
1. Training should directly relate to trainees' jobs
2. Training should realistically mirror the trainees' jobs
3. Trainer should be knowledgeable regarding the content
4. Training should incorporate humor
5. Training should be fun
6. Trainer should be enthusiastic
7. Quality food and beverage service should be provided during training
8. Training should be conducted in a quality facility
9. Training room should be geared to the physical comfort of trainees
10. Trainees should be informed regarding the sequence of training
11. Trainees should feel relaxed during training
12. Mood during training should be supportive of trainees
13. Training should provide a safe (e.g. free from criticism) environment
14. Trainer should remember trainees' names
15. Trainer should show a personal interest in the trainees
16. Trainer should express appreciation for the work experience of trainees
17. Training should be designed to follow-up with trainees after they return to work
18. Training should outline the rewards for using training on the job
19. Training should include a test of learning

of three items each. The coefficient alpha of each dimension produced reliability ratings ranging from .56 to .84. In descending order of variance explained, the dimensions of expectation of training quality are Courtesy, Entertainment, Climate, Tangibles, and Relevance.

Cluster Analysis

Summated scales for each factor in the factor analysis were created and used as the input data for a cluster analysis. Summated scales are formed by combining several individual variables into a single composite measure. In simple terms, all of the variables loading highly on a factor are combined, and the total, or more commonly the average score of the variables, is used as a replacement variable (Hair et al., 2002). The average mean scores of all variables in each factor were computed and used as summated scales.

TABLE 3. Varimax Rotated Component Factor Matrix for Trainees' Expectations of Instructor-Led Training, Including Factor Loadings, Cronbach Alpha Scores, Eigenvalues, and Percentages of Variance Explained (n = 164)

Factor Analysis Based on Trainees' Expectations of Training Quality

Variables	Factor 1 Courtesy	Factor 2 Entertainment	Factor 3 Climate	Factor 4 Tangibles	Factor 5 Relevance	α
e26-Trainer should show a personal interest in the trainees	0.741					0.7439
e27-Trainer should express appreciation for the work experience of trainees	0.703					
e28-Training should be designed to follow-up with trainees after they return to work	0.672					
e29-Training should outline the rewards for using training on the job	0.610					
e25-Trainer should remember trainees' names	0.594					
e30-Training should include a test of learning	0.529					
e10-Training should be fun		0.792				0.8375
e9-Training should incorporate humor		0.785				
e11-Trainer should be enthusiastic		0.742				
e23-Mood during training should be supportive of trainees			0.752			0.7089
e21-Trainees should feel relaxed during training			0.700			
e20-Trainees should be informed regarding the sequence of training			0.673			
e24-Training should provide a safe (e.g. free from criticism) environment for trainees			0.660			
e16-Training should be conducted in a quality facility				0.810		0.6964
e15-Quality food and beverage service should be provided during training				0.809		
e17-Training room should be geared to the physical comfort of trainees				0.513		
e3-Training should realistically mirror the trainees' jobs					0.800	0.5568
e1-Training should directly relate to trainees' jobs					0.737	
e5-Trainer should be knowledgeable regarding the content					0.514	
Eigenvalue	4.69	2.21	1.75	1.56	1.25	
Cumulative variance explained (%)	24.7	36.3	45.5	53.7	60.3	

Extraction Method: Principal Component Analysis.
Rotation Method: Varimax with Kaiser Normalization.
Entires are factor loadings. Factor loadings less than .50 are not shown.
α = Coefficient alpha

Based on the summated scales of the five dimensions of training expectations, respondents were grouped into three clusters. First, a hierarchical cluster analysis was conducted with a random sample of 25 respondents from the total of 164, and then the cluster seed that was obtained from the hierarchical cluster analysis was used to run K-mean cluster analysis with the total sample of 164 respondents. ANOVA results from the K-mean cluster analysis indicated that all five factors were useful to identify clusters.

Each cluster was labeled according to the expectations of its members regarding quality training (See Figure 1 for cluster profiles). As noted, summated scales for each factor were used to distinguish clusters from one another. The total number of respondents in all three clusters equals only 158 due to some missing data. The first cluster (N = 56) was labeled "The Good Timers" because the respondents had high expectations on the Entertainment dimension but relatively low expectations on the other four factors (especially Relevance). Members of the second cluster (N = 42) were called "The High Hopes" because members indicated relatively high expectations for every aspect of training. Cluster 2 members indicated the highest expectations of all three clusters for all dimensions of training expectations except for factor 5, Relevance.

FIGURE 1. A Comparison of Clusters of Trainees, Based upon Their Ratings of the Five Dimensions of Training Expectations

Comparison of Clusters Based on Factors

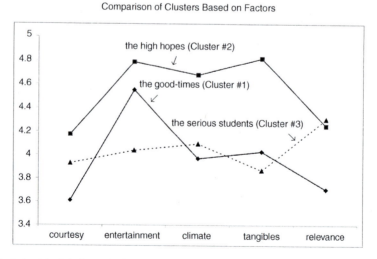

Note. The horizontal axis indicates the five dimensions of training expectations, and the vertical axis represents trainees' responses on a 5-point Likert scale (1 = strongly disagree and 5 = strongly agree).

Members of Cluster 3 (N = 60) were referred to as "The Serious Students" since they had the highest expectations for the dimension of Relevance. Members in Cluster 3 showed higher expectations on Courtesy and Climate and Relevance than "The Good-Timers." As Figure 1 indicates, members of Cluster 1 ("The Good Timers") and Cluster 2 ("The High Hopes") roughly parallel each other except that Cluster 2 is at a higher expectation level on all dimensions of training, and Cluster 1 peaked more sharply on the Entertainment factor. The pattern of Cluster 3 is dissimilar to the expectation ratings of Clusters 1 and 2.

To find the characteristics of each Cluster, ANOVAs and Kruskal-Wallis tests were used with the demographic and job-related variables of gender, age, time in current position, number of instructor-led training sessions attended in the last five years, and whether attendance was voluntary or mandatory. There were no significant differences in gender (p = .15), time in current position (p = .19), number of instructor-led training sessions attended in the last five years (p = .13), and whether attendance was voluntary or mandatory (p = .39) among clusters. The Kruskal-Wallis test on age revealed significant differences in age among clusters (p < .05). Forty-six percent of respondents who are in the age group of 26 to 35 belonged to "The Serious Students." Fifty-three percent of 46 to 55 year olds are in "The Good-Timers" group along with 75% of respondents who are 55 or older (see Table 4).

DISCUSSION AND IMPLICATIONS

Understanding what trainees expect when they attend training programs is essential to designing effective training (Noe, 1986). This study revealed important information about five underlying factors that define trainees' expectations of instructor-led training sessions, and it also identified three classifications of trainees based upon their expectations of training.

In descending order of influence, the five factors that shape trainees' expectations of instructor-led training sessions are (1) Courtesy, (2) Entertainment, (3) Climate, (4) Tangibles, and (5) Relevance. It is important for trainers to realize that trainees expect to be treated courteously above all other considerations; perhaps this is because trainees are adults and therefore wish to be respected and recognized for the knowledge and experience they bring to the training environment. Two other intangibles, Entertainment and Climate, influence trainees' expectations more strongly than either Tangibles or the Relevance of the training to a trainee's job. This information can help trainers to design and execute more effective training that meets the expectations of trainees.

TABLE 4. Cross Tabulation of Age of Cluster Members
Crosstabulation on Age

			18 to 25 years	26 to 35 years	36 to 45 years	46 to 55 years	56 years or older	Total
Cluster	1	Count	4	14	25	10	3	56
Good-Timers		% within Cluster	7%	25%	45%	18%	5%	
		% within age	29%	26%	38%	53%	75%	
		% of Total	3%	9%	16%	6%	2%	
	2	Count	5	16	16	4	1	42
High Hopes		% within Cluster	12%	38%	38%	10%	2%	
		% within age	36%	29%	24%	21%	25%	
		% of Total	3%	10%	10%	3%	1%	
	3	Count	5	25	25	5	0	60
Serious Students		% within Cluster	8%	42%	42%	8%		
		% within age	36%	46%	38%	26%		
		% of Total	3%	16%	16%	3%		
Total		Count	14	55	66	19	4	158

The discovery that trainees in instructor-led training sessions can be categorized according to their expectations is important. For example, trainers now know to anticipate that trainees in their instructor-led sessions are likely to be either "The Good Timers," "The High Hopes," or "The Serious Students." Age was found to be a distinguishing variable among the three clusters. Younger trainees tended to belong to "The Serious Students" while older trainees fell into "The Good Timers" category. This seems to intuitively make sense since younger trainees are in a learning, growing, climbing-the-ladder mode, while older employees are perhaps more comfortable with their accumulated knowledge/skills and more likely to treat training lightly. By understanding the types of trainees based upon their expectations, trainers will be able to execute more effective training sessions.

LIMITATIONS

Sampling issues present limitations for the research under review. The following factors limit the generalizeability of the results: (1) the research was conducted solely within the hospitality industry, (2) the research addressed only instructor-led training sessions, and (3) questionnaire respondents were supervisory or management-level employees. Also, the use of non-probability convenience sampling in this research limited the range of statistical options.

SUGGESTIONS FOR FURTHER RESEARCH

Testing of the expectation scale as it applies to different types of training and/or varying levels of employees within an organization seems to be a logical next step for future research. The scale also needs to be tested in industries other than hospitality, and testing of the scale in countries other than the United States would be an interesting extension of the current research. Finally, research is needed to explore the relationship between expectations and training effectiveness.

CONCLUSION

To recap the answers to the three research questions posed in this study:

1. What are the dimensions or primary factors that underlie trainees' expectations of training? Courtesy, Entertainment, Climate, Tangibles, and Relevance.
2. Is it possible to group trainees in instructor-led training sessions based on their expectations of training? Yes, and the categories, as determined through this study, are "The High Hopes," "The Good-Timers," and "The Serious Students."
3. Do specific demographic characteristics affect trainees' expectations of training? Age is the only variable found to affect trainees' expectations of quality training.

The results of this research build upon the findings of previously cited studies to more fully understand trainees' expectations within the instructor-led training environment.

REFERENCES

Alliger, G. M. & Janak, E. A. (1989). Kirkpatrick's levels of training criteria: Thirty years later. *Personnel Psychology, 42,* 331-341.

Clemenz, C. E. (2001). *Measuring perceived quality of training in the hospitality industry.* Dissertation, Virginia Polytechnic Institute and State University.

Clemenz, C. E. & Weaver, P. A. (in press). Dimensions of perceived training quality: a comparison of measurements. *The Journal of Quality Assurance in Hospitality and Tourism.*

Conrad, G., Woods, R. H., & Ninemeier, J. D. (1994). Training in the U.S. lodging industry: perception and reality, *Cornell Hotel and Restaurant Quarterly*, *35* (5), 16-21.

Feldman, D. C. (1989). Socialization, resocialization, and training: Reframing the research agenda. In I.L Goldstein (Ed.), *Training and development in organizations* (pp. 376-416). San Francisco: Jossey-Bass.

Hair, J.F. Jr., Anderson, R.E., Tatham, R.L., Black, W.C. (2002). *Multivariate data analysis*, (6th ed.). Englewood Cliffs, NJ: Prentice-Hall.

Hicks, W. D. & Klimoski, R. J. (1987). Entry into training programs and its effects on training outcomes: A field experiment. *Academy of Management Journal*, *30*, 542-552.

Hoiberg, A. & Berry, N. H. (1978). Expectations and perceptions of navy life. *Organizational Behavior and Human Performance*, *21*, 130-145.

Kirkpatrick, D. L. (1959). Techniques for evaluating training programs. *Journal of the American Society of Training Directors*, *13* (59), 3-9.

Mathieu, J. E., Tannenbaum, S. I, & Salas, E. (1992). Influences of individual and situational characteristics on measures of training effectiveness. *Academy of Management Journal*, *35*, 828-847.

Parasuraman, A., Zeithaml, V. A., & Berry, L. L. (1985). A conceptual model of service quality and its implications for future research. *Journal of Marketing*, *49*, 41-50.

Tannenbaum, S. I., Mathieu, J. E., Salas, E., & Cannon-Bowers, J. A. (1991). Meeting trainees' expectations: The influence of training fulfillment on the development of commitment, self-efficacy and motivation. *Journal of Applied Psychology*, *76* (6), 759-769.

Tannenbaum, S. I., & Yukl, G. (1991). Training and development in work organizations. *Annual Review of Psychology*, *43*, 399-441.

Tracey, J. B. & Tews, M. J. (1995). Training effectiveness. *Cornell Hotel and Restaurant Administration Quarterly*, *36* (6), 36-42.

Wiley, C. (1993). Training for the '90s. How leading companies focus on quality improvement, technological change, and customer service. *Employment Relations Today*, *20* (1), 79-96.

Zikmund, W.G. (2000). *Business research methods*, (6th ed.). Orlando, Florida: The Dryden Press, Harcourt College Publishers.

The Relationship
Between Destination Performance,
Overall Satisfaction,
and Behavioral Intention
for Distinct Segments

Seyhmus Baloglu
Aykut Pekcan
Shiang-Lih Chen
Joceline Santos

SUMMARY. Destination performance, visitor satisfaction, and favorable future behavior of visitors are key determinants of destination com-

Seyhmus Baloglu is Associate Professor and Joceline Santos is PhD Candidate, University of Nevada Las Vegas.

Aykut Pekcan is affiliated with Bilkent University, School of Tourism and Hotel Management.

Shiang-Lih Chen is Assistant Professor, Widener University, School of Hospitality Management.

Address correspondence to: Seyhmus Baloglu, PhD, Associate Professor, University of Nevada Las Vegas, William F. Harrah College of Hotel Administration, Department of Tourism and Convention Administration, 4505 Maryland Parkway, Box 456023, Las Vegas, NV 89154-6023 (E-mail: baloglu@ccmail.nevada.edu).

A condensed version of this article was published in the proceedings of Eleventh Annual World Business Congress of IMDA, which was held in Antalya, Turkey, July 10-14, 2002.

[Haworth co-indexing entry note]: "The Relationship Between Destination Performance, Overall Satisfaction, and Behavioral Intention for Distinct Segments." Baloglu, Seyhmus et al. Co-published simultaneously in *Journal of Quality Assurance in Hospitality & Tourism* (The Haworth Hospitality Press, an imprint of The Haworth Press, Inc.) Vol. 4, No. 3/4, 2003, pp. 149-165; and: *Current Issues and Development in Hospitality and Tourism Satisfaction* (ed: John A. Williams and Muzaffer Uysal) The Haworth Hospitality Press, an imprint of The Haworth Press, Inc., 2003, pp. 149-165. Single or multiple copies of this article are available for a fee from The Haworth Document Delivery Service [1-800-HAWORTH, 9:00 a.m. - 5:00 p.m. (EST). E-mail address: docdelivery@haworthpress.com].

petitiveness. Most empirical work, assuming that overall tourist population is homogenous, investigates the relationships among product performance, satisfaction, and/or behavioral intentions in an aggregated manner. This study investigates these linkages for different segments of Canadian visitors of Las Vegas. The findings confirmed the mediating role of overall satisfaction for both segments and aggregated sample, and revealed variations in linkages and explanatory power of the models. The study concludes that the segment-based approach is more pragmatic because it provides segment-specific implications for destination management and marketing. *[Article copies available for a fee from The Haworth Document Delivery Service: 1-800-HAWORTH. E-mail address: <docdelivery@ haworthpress.com> Website: <http://www.HaworthPress.com> © 2003 by The Haworth Press, Inc. All rights reserved.]*

KEYWORDS. Destination performance, satisfaction, behavioral intention, segmentation, path analysis, Canadian visitors

INTRODUCTION

The performance of a tourist destination and satisfaction of visitors with the destination are of paramount importance to the destination competitiveness since the pleasantness of the experience is more likely to influence visitors' future behavior. There has been a noticeable increase in the number of studies focusing on destination performance and satisfaction and how they are related to revisitation intention and word-of-mouth behavior of travelers (Pizam, Neumann & Reichel, 1978; Pearce, 1980; Chon, 1992; Pizam & Milman, 1993; Ryan, 1995; Danaher & Arweiler, 1996; Yuksel & Rimmington, 1998; Kozak & Rimmington, 2000).

Most empirical work on tourist satisfaction, however, investigates the relationships among product (attribute) performance, satisfaction, and behavioral intentions, in an aggregated manner (i.e., assuming that overall tourist population is homogenous). Tourist destinations often offer a variety of products and tourists appealed to a destination are not a homogenous market. It is very likely that not only perceived importance of destination attributes, but also the perceived performance of the attributes and future behavior may differ from one segment to another. Pizam and Milman (1993) argued that when investigating tourist satisfaction, the analysis should be conducted separately for different segments because the importance of destination attributes may vary with market segments. The authors, using expectancy-disconfirmation paradigm, examined the relationship between attribute-based satisfaction and overall satisfaction for three segments based on reasons for travel such as sun and sea, culture, and friends and relatives, and found that different destination attributes contributed to overall satisfaction for each segment. Their analyses also showed that the segment-specific approach increased the explanatory power of the model in predicting overall satisfaction.

The purpose of this study is to investigate the relationship among attribute-based destination performance, overall satisfaction, and behavioral intention (return intention and recommendation) for Canadian visitors to Las Vegas. The study, however, examines these relationships for distinct benefit (socio-psychological motivations)-visitor status (first-time and repeat visitors) segments separately to understand variations and similarities in hypothesized linkages due to unique nature of the segments. It also compares the model tested on aggregate data to the models tested for distinct segments in terms of similarities and differences, as well as the explanatory power of the models.

This study follows a procedure similar to the work of Pizam and Milman (1993), but it differs from it from several perspectives. First, it uses socio-psychological (push) motivations rather than destination attributes sought (pull motivations) to reveal the benefits segment. Second, the model includes attribute-based performance, operationalized by performance-only measures, and behavioral intention. Compared to Oliver's (1980) expectancy disconfirmation theory, performance-only measure appears to be the lesser of the devil in the literature. The performance-only measure also outperformed other alternative operationalizations in terms of predicting overall satisfaction and behavioral intention (Crompton & Love, 1995; Baker & Crompton, 2000; Yuksel & Rimmington, 1998; Yuksel & Yuksel, 2001). Therefore, in this study, destination performance was assessed by performance-only measures. Finally, the model is tested for both first-time and repeat visitors rather than first-time visitors only.

LITERATURE REVIEW

The relationships among perceived (attribute-based) performance, satisfaction, and behavioral intention have been investigated to a great extent in the literature and linkages are well-established by empirical studies (see Yi, 1990; Cronin & Taylor, 1992; Tse & Wilton, 1988; Fornell, Johnson, Anderson, Cha, & Bryant, 1996; Baker & Crompton, 2000; Szymanski & Henard, 2001). Therefore, they will not be repeated here in detail. The model in Figure 1 shows the hypothesized linkages among destination performance, overall satisfaction and behavioral intention. The literature reviews on customer satisfaction and perceived performance conducted by several

FIGURE 1. The Relationship Among Performance, Overall Satisfaction, and Behavioral Intention

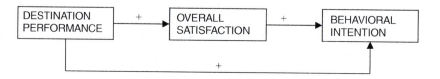

researchers have suggested that satisfaction is positively related to behavioral intent measures such as recommendation (positive word-of-mouth) and return intention (e.g., Yi, 1990; Oh & Parks, 1997). The empirical work on tourist satisfaction also demonstrated the usefulness of examining the effect of experience attributes on overall satisfaction to understand the relative contribution of product/service attributes to overall experience and/or behavioral intention (Pizam & Milmann, 1993; Yuksel & Rimmington, 1998; Kozak & Rimmington, 2000).

The Relationship Among Model Variables

The perceived performance strongly influences customer satisfaction (Churchill & Surprenant, 1982; Tse & Wilton, 1988; Patterson, 1993). According to proposed framework for linkages between trust, satisfaction, and loyalty by Singh and Sirdeshmukh (2000), post-purchase performance perceptions/evaluations positively influence satisfaction. Understanding the effect of attribute-based performance on overall satisfaction enables firms to identify determinants of the overall satisfaction (Mittal, Katrichis, & Kumar, 2001). The attribute-based performance also directly and positively influences behavioral intention (Yuksel & Rimmington, 1998; Baker & Crompton, 2000). The model proposed by Baker and Crompton (2000) posited that attribute-based performance positively influences both satisfaction and behavioral intention. The findings showed that performance influences behavioral intention both directly and indirectly through satisfaction. Therefore, the following hypotheses are proposed:

Hypothesis 1: Destination performance has a positive impact on overall satisfaction with destination.

Hypothesis 2: Destination performance has a positive impact on behavioral intention for destination.

Szymanski and Henard (2001) conducted a detailed meta-analysis of the customer satisfaction literature. The authors confirmed that performance positively influences satisfaction, and overall satisfaction has a positive impact on repurchase intentions. The overall satisfaction has been found a good and strong predictor of repurchase intention because it represents a global evaluation and general attitudinal construct (Anderson, Fornell, & Lehmann, 1994; Mittal, Katrichis, & Kumar, 2001; Jones & Suh, 2000). The American Customer Satisfaction Index (ACSI) model of Fornell et al. (1996) posited overall satisfaction as key mediating variable between performance and repeat behavior. This leads to following hypothesis:

Hypothesis 3: Overall satisfaction with destination has a positive impact on behavioral intention for destination.

The Influence of Market Segments on Model Linkages and Segmentation Base

The segments have varying preferences and benefits sought. For different customer segments, varying destination attributes would determine overall satisfaction and behavioral intention. The socio-psychological motivations for travel (benefits-sought) and visitor status (first-time and repeat visitors) have been the most frequently used segmentation base in travel and tourism and found useful and effective by both academicians and practitioners. First-time and repeat visitors often represent two distinct segments to a destination and their evaluation of destinations attributes is different (Fakeye & Crompton, 1991). The level of tourist experience with a destination would be different for first-time and repeat visitors because of their expertise and expectations. For example, Crompton and Love (1995) have found that correlations between attribute-based evaluations and overall assessment were higher for the first time visitors. Likewise, the benefits sought or push motivations to visit destinations have tremendous impact on visitors' attitudes, satisfaction and future behavior of their inherent effect on cognitive and affective process as well as behavior (Woodside & Jacobs, 1985; Uysal & Hagan, 1993, Baloglu & Uysal, 1996, Baloglu, 2000; Frochot & Morrison, 2000). The benefit segmentation potentially provides wide implications for product development and revision, product bundles and packaging, promotion, and performance assessment (Baloglu & Uysal, 1996; Frochot & Morrison, 2000).

These all suggest that the relative contribution of destination performance attributes to global evaluations would be different for distinct segments. The segment-specific satisfaction, whether distinct segments develop their satisfaction and behavioral intentions based on different service aspects, has also been emphasized in recent literature review of customer satisfaction conducted in hospitality and tourism (Yuksel & Yuksel, 2001, p. 101). Recently, Uysal and Williams (2003) found that different benefit segments moderate the impact of expressive (core attributes) and instrumental (facilitating attributes) on visitor satisfaction. Accordingly, the following hypotheses were derived:

> Hypothesis 4: The destination performance attributes influencing overall satisfaction will differ by visitor status–benefit segments.

> Hypothesis 5: The destination performance attributes influencing behavioral intention will differ by visitor status–benefit segments.

METHODOLOGY

Research Design

The study utilized en route survey methodology. The major advantages of en route methodology are (1) it is cost effective, therefore, it is a preferred methodology by many travel managers; and (2) it reduces response errors (memory bias) because information is sought right after trip experience (Hurst, 1994; Danaher & Arweiler, 1996). The data was collected at Las Vegas McCarran International Airport departure gates while respondents were waiting for their flight to home. The study utilized a multi-stage sampling based on time/schedule domain through randomization. The flight schedules provided by the airport administration included all charter flights to Canada for the period of October 1999 through May 2000. The flights were mostly twice a week (Thursday and Sunday). The study focused on the October through December cluster. First, nine dates were randomly selected (five Sundays and four Thursdays). Then, flight schedules were randomly selected on each day from morning, afternoon, evening, and late night flights. This procedure resulted in sixteen flights to be covered.

A questionnaire was developed based on discussions with selected university faculty, marketing managers of Las Vegas Convention and Visitors Authority and McCarran International Airport, print media and literature review, questionnaires used by the former USTTA and Tourism Canada for international travelers. The questionnaire was then pre-tested on 60 Canadian visitors from two separate flights at departure gates. The pre-test was conducted by two trained graduate students (one American and one Canadian) for wording, layout, content validity, and determining main data collection method. Two versions of the questionnaire were used during the pre-test: self-administered and personal interview with response category cards. The pre-test showed that personal interviews took 25-30 minutes and created response fatigue whereas the respondents completed self-administered questionnaires in 10-15 minutes. Therefore, the self-administered questionnaire was judged a more appropriate data collection method for this study. The final questionnaire included sections on trip information, importance of socio-psychological travel motivations and destination attributes, performance of Las Vegas and the airport, and demographics.

Socio-psychological (push) motivations were measured by 16 items on a 7-point scale, 1 being "Not At All Important" and 7 being "Extremely Important." The performance items included 18 attributes measured on a 7-point scale, 1 being "Terrible" and 7 being "Excellent." A "Don't Know" option was also provided. Respondents were asked to indicate their overall satisfaction with Las Vegas on this trip on a 7-point scale (1 = Extremely Dissatisfied, 7 = Extremely Satisfied). Behavioral intention was measured by three items asking revisitation intention for pleasure next year, revisitation intention for pleasure in the next 3 years (1 = Definitely Will, 7 = Definitely Will Not), and recommending Las Vegas to their friends and/or relatives (1 = Definitely Will, 7 = Definitely Will Not).

The airport authority provided all logistics for data collection, including name badges for the graduate students. The students approached the visitors who were waiting for their flight, identified themselves, explained the purpose of the study, and emphasized that participation was confidential and voluntary. They also mentioned that only one person would be filling the questionnaire in case of couples, families or groups. This condition was also written in large and boldface letters on cover page of the questionnaire.

Data Analysis

Data analysis included several stages. First, a hierarchical clustering procedure by employing Ward's method and squared Euclidean distance was utilized on socio-psychological motivations to identify the number of benefit segments. This was followed by a discriminant analysis to assess the internal consistency of the benefits segments identified. The clusters (segments) were validated by activities participated. Third, a principal component analysis of the performance attributes reduced them into fewer meaningful dimensions. The varimax rotation procedure and eigenvalue/scree plot were utilized to identify the number of components. A cut-off value of 0.40 was used for item inclusion in each component. Fourth, the model variables were prepared by averaging the multi-item scores. Finally, the path model was tested for each visitor status-benefit segments by partial least squares and freeing all possible paths in the recursive model.

RESULTS AND DISCUSSION

Response Rate and Profile of Respondents

The visitors were very participatory and exhibited a high level of interest as only 9% of the travelers approached rejected to participate. The required sample size was determined as about 400 based upon proportion of first-time and repeat visitors at 95% confidence interval. A total of 412 questionnaires were generated, 36 of which were not usable because they had excessive missing data or response bias (i.e., consistently checking a particular number on a scale). Of the remaining 376, 307 respondents indicated that the main purpose of their visit was pleasure/vacation/gaming and were focus sample for this study.

The genders of respondents were 54.3% female and 45.7% male. The majority of respondents (31.2%) reported an age 55 or above, which was followed by 24.3% who belonged to the 45-54 age bracket. Twenty-one percent of them were in the age group 35-44. Twenty-eight percent of the respondents held a university degree; 23.2% of them had some college, and 23% reported an education level of high school or less. The majority of the participants (71.7%) were currently married; 15.2% were never married. Forty-two percent of the respondents reported that their annual household income before taxes (in Canadian $) was $80,000 or more. This was followed by 22% in the income group of $40,000 to $59,999, and 20.3% $60,000 to $79,999. In addition, twenty two percent of the respondents had a professional occupation; 14.5% of them were self-employed or business owner; 13.7% were retired, and 10.7% of them were in skilled/technical category.

Sixty percent traveled with spouse and 34.5% traveled with friends. About 53% had 2 persons in the immediate travel party and another 18% had four people. The majority spent 3 nights in Las Vegas (46.4%) while about 36% spent 4 nights. Only 14.1 spent a week in Las Vegas.

Benefit Segments and Validation

The cluster analysis, computed from two to four cluster solutions, suggested that two-clusters solution was more appropriate and revealed two benefit segments: "Excitement/Fun/Adventure Seekers" (n = 96, 36.1%) and "Relaxation/Novelty Seekers" (n = 164, 63.1%). The discriminant analysis showed that 95% of the cases were correctly classified, indicating good internal consistencies of the two segments (97.9% and 93.3%, respectively). Aldenderfer and Blashfield (1984) pointed out that high classification accuracy is a strong evidence of the internal consistency (reliability), but not validity. The authors suggested that, although not used frequently, a better approach to validate a clustering solution is to perform significance tests that compare clusters on some theoretically relevant criteria that are not used to generate the cluster solution. Therefore, the clusters generated were validated by activities participated. The "Excitement/Fun/Adventure Seekers" were more likely to participate in Thrill Rides, Special Concerts, Nightclubs and Dancing, and Regularly Scheduled Las Vegas Shows than the "Relaxation/Novelty Seekers" (p < .05).

Performance Dimensions

The principal component analysis of performance attributes resulted in three components: "Variety of Activities/ Entertainment," "Quality of Product/Environment," and "Value/Diversity" after excluding two attributes ("golf courses and facilities" and "outdoor activities") from the analysis due to extensive "don't know" responses and low communalities. These three dimensions explained 55.2% of the total variance in the performance attributes (Table 1). One attribute, "resort atmosphere," was cross-loaded on two dimensions and retained in the factor where its loading was higher and more meaningful. The descriptive statistics and reliabilities (Cronbach's alpha) for model variables were shown in Table 2. The reliability scores for multi-item measures were all satisfactory, ranging from 0.76 to 0.82.

The Model and Hypotheses Tests

The model was first tested for the aggregate data (Table 3). The results showed that only "Variety of Activities/Entertainment" had a positive impact on Canadian visitors' overall satisfaction with Las Vegas (p < 0.05). When behavioral intention was regressed on three performance dimensions and the overall satisfaction, the overall satisfaction positively influenced the behavioral intention and none of the performance dimensions was significant at 0.05 probability level. In other words, the overall satisfaction was an intervening or mediating variable between destination performance evaluations and the behavioral intention.

In the next stage, the model was tested separately for each segment (Table 4). For "First-Time Visitors–Excitement/Fun/Adventure Seekers," the performance dimensions of "Value/Diversity" and "Variety of Activities/Entertain-

TABLE 1. Principal Component Analysis of Performance Attributes

Attributes	Variety of Activities/ Entertainment	Quality of Product/ Environment	Value/Diversity
Variety of activities	.815		
Shopping facilities	.709		
Entertainment	.675		
Sightseeing opportunities	.630		
Quality of restaurants	.609		
Spectator events	.564		
Quality of gaming facilities	.787		
Standard hygiene and cleanliness		.684	
Quality of lodging		.670	
Safety and security		.554	
Reliable weather		.522	
Resort atmosphere		.482	.480
Variety of natural attractions			.792
Affordable room rates			.752
Value for money			.678
Suitability for different types of vacations			.620
Eigen-value	5.84	1.64	1.34
Variance explained (%)	36.5	10.2	8.4
Cumulative Variance (%)	36.6	46.8	55.2

Kaiser-Meyer-Olkin Measure of Sampling Adequacy: .809
Bartlett's Test of Sphericity: 516.2 (120 df., .000)

TABLE 2. Descriptive Statistics and Reliability Coefficients for Model Variables

Variables	Mean	Standard Deviation	Number of Items	Cronbach's Alpha
Variety of Activities/Entertainment	5.49	.66	7	.7943
Quality of Product/Environment	5.77	.70	5	.7629
Value/Diversity	5.06	.89	4	.8023
Overall Satisfaction	5.48	1.13	1	NA
Behavioral Intention	5.45	1.41	3	.8252

Note: All variables were measured on a 7-point scale.

ment" were positively related to overall satisfaction ($p < 0.05$). The overall satisfaction had a positive impact on behavioral intention. For "First-Time Visitors–Relaxation/Novelty Seekers," only "Value/Diversity" was positively related to overall satisfaction which, in turn, positively influenced behavioral intention ($p < 0.05$). For "Repeat Visitors–Excitement/Fun/Adventure Seekers," "Quality of Product/Environment" and "Value/Diversity" had a positive im-

TABLE 3. Results of Path Model for Aggregate Data (N = 256)

Endogenous Variables

	Overall Satisfaction			Behavioral Intention		
	(β)	B	VIF	(β)	B	VIF
Variety of Activities/Entertainment	.233*	.596*	1.31	.116	.297	1.36
Quality of Product/Environment	.123	.273	1.20	−.023	−.009	1.31
Value/Diversity	.129	.343	1.29	−.016	−.004	1.42
Overall Satisfaction				.557*	.655*	1.52
F-value (significance level)	13.9 (.000)			33.1 (.000)		
R^2	.142			.345		
Adjusted R^2	.131			.335		

(β): Standardized coefficient
B: Unstandardized coefficient
VIF: Variance Inflation Factor
*: Significant at 0.05 or better probability level

pact on overall satisfaction. Again, overall satisfaction was positively related to behavioral intention ($p < 0.05$). Finally, for "Repeat Visitors–Relaxation/Novelty Seekers," "Quality of Product/Environment" was the only performance dimension that positively influenced overall satisfaction which, in turn, had a positive impact on behavioral intention ($p < 0.05$).

Hypothesis 1, destination performance positively influencing overall satisfaction, was supported for the whole sample and across segments. Hypothesis 2, destination performance positively influencing behavioral intention, was not supported either for the whole sample or across samples. This also led to finding no support for Hypothesis 5, which stated that the destination performance attributes (dimensions) influencing behavioral intention will differ by visitor status–benefit segments. Hypothesis 3, overall satisfaction significantly influencing behavioral intention, was supported both for the whole sample and across segments. Finally, the results showed support for Hypothesis 4, which stated that the destination performance attributes (dimensions) influencing overall satisfaction will differ by visitor status–benefit segments.

It should also be noted that the models tested for segments had higher explanatory powers (R^2) than that for the aggregate sample. In terms of predicting overall satisfaction, the explanatory power (R^2) of the whole sample model was 0.141 whereas the explanatory powers for the segment models were 0.508 (first-time visitors seeking excitement, fun, and adventure), 0.493 (first-time visitors seeking relaxation and novelty), 0.512 (repeat visitors seeking excitement, fun, and adventure), and 0.259 (repeat visitors seeking relaxation and

TABLE 4. Results of Path Model for Visitor Status–Benefit Segments

First-Time Visitors–Excitement/Fun/Adventure Seekers (n = 38)

| | Endogenous Variables | | | | | |
| | Overall Satisfaction | | | Behavioral Intention | | |
	(β)	B	VIF	(β)	B	VIF
Variety of Activities/Entertainment	.472*	.990*	1.15	.207	.501	1.60
Quality of Product/Environment	.083	.199	1.03	.110	.304	1.04
Value/Diversity	.367*	.951*	1.17	−.045	−.134	1.44
Overall Satisfaction				.531*	.612*	2.03
F-value (significance level)	11.7 (.000)			7.2 (.000)		
R^2	.508			.467		
Adjusted R^2	.464			.403		

(β): Standardized coefficient   B: Unstandardized coefficient   VIF: Variance Inflation Factor
*: Significant at 0.05 or lower probability level

First-Time Visitors–Relaxation/Novelty Seekers (n = 36)

| | Endogenous Variables | | | | | |
| | Overall Satisfaction | | | Behavioral Intention | | |
	(β)	B	VIF	(β)	B	VIF
Variety of Activities/Entertainment	.191	.379	1.39	.200	.504	1.47
Quality of Product/Environment	.173	.382	1.42	−.278	−.782	1.48
Value/Diversity	.472*	.870*	1.62	−.050	−.117	2.06
Overall Satisfaction				.598*	.761*	1.97
F-value (significance level)	10.4 (.000)			4.2 (.008)		
R^2	.493			.354		
Adjusted R^2	.446			.270		

(β): Standardized coefficient   B: Unstandardized coefficient   VIF: Variance Inflation Factor
*: Significant at .05 or lower probability level

novelty). Similarly, in terms of predicting overall satisfaction, the explanatory power in the whole sample was 0.34. The explanatory power of segment-based models, on the other hand, ranged from 0.35 to 0.46.

The findings demonstrate that the impact of destination performance evaluations on overall satisfaction show variations from one segment to another. Therefore, any model including attribute-based performance should be tested for specific samples to provide more effective practical implications for the

TABLE 4 (continued)

Repeat Visitors–Excitement/Fun/Adventure Seekers (n = 54)

	Overall Satisfaction			Behavioral Intention		
	(β)	B	VIF	(β)	B	VIF
Variety of Activities/Entertainment	.179	.424	1.69	.266	.691	1.35
Quality of Product/Environment	.406*	.677*	1.29	−.058	−.105	1.63
Value/Diversity	.322*	.718*	1.43	.096	.235	1.41
Overall Satisfaction				.429*	.470*	1.51
F-value (significance level)	17.5 (.000)			8.7 (.000)		
R^2	.512			.417		
Adjusted R^2	.483			.370		

(β): Standardized coefficient   B: Unstandardized coefficient   VIF: Variance Inflation Factor
*: Significant at 0.05 or lower probability level

Repeat Visitor–Relaxation/Novelty Seekers (n = 128)

Endogenous Variables

	Overall Satisfaction			Behavioral Intention		
	(β)	B	VIF	(β)	B	VIF
Variety of Activities/Entertainment	.139	.325	1.16	−.053	−.136	1.19
Quality of Product/Environment	.362*	.655*	1.16	−.059	−.118	1.34
Value/Diversity	.161	.393	1.22	−.014	−.030	1.25
Overall Satisfaction				.662*	.730*	1.35
F-value (significance level)	14.5 (.000)			19.2 (.000)		
R^2	.259			.385		
Adjusted R^2	.241			.365		

(β): Standardized coefficient B: Unstandardized coefficient VIF: Variance Inflation Factor
*: Significant at .05 or lower probability level

tourist destinations. If destinations do not have the understanding of how different destination attribute performances influence global evaluations or future behavior of different segments, the implications generated by "one-for-all" models would not be useful for marketing activities. As a matter of fact, the destination marketing organizations or bodies would be wasting their resources. A segmented approach is more pragmatic than aggregated approach because it provides segment-specific implications for destination management and marketing. This approach, however, requires a careful identification of the segments for a tourist destination. In other words, the destinations should first identify the most effective segmentation base to group their visitors, and then, examine how attribute-based performance is related to overall satisfaction and future behavior for the segments identified.

From a practical standpoint, the findings can be utilized in marketing efforts of Las Vegas to target specific Canadian visitors and to develop sound promotion and packaging tactics as well as product enhancement tactics. To serve this purpose, the segments were further profiled by employing a series of chi-square tests at 0.05 probability level. The results indicated that first-time visitors seeking excitement and adventure are more likely to be ages between 21 and 34. On the other hand, the first-time visitors seeking relaxation and/or novelty are more likely to belong to 35-44 age bracket. The repeat visitors seeking relaxation and/or novelty are more likely to be 55 or older. The first-time and repeat visitors seeking relaxation and or novelty are more likely to be married. They are also more likely to travel with their spouse. The first-time visitors seeking excitement are less likely to travel with family or relatives, but more likely to travel with friend(s). The first-time and repeat visitors seeking excitement and adventure are more likely to take thrill rides. The repeat visitors seeking excitement and adventure are more likely to attend special concerts and go to nightclubs whereas the first-time visitors seeking the same benefits are more likely to go to regularly scheduled Las Vegas shows.

CONCLUDING COMMENTS

This article tested a model involving destination performance, overall satisfaction, and behavioral intention in a path-analytic framework. It clearly demonstrated differences and similarities in model linkages when aggregate data and segment-based data were utilized. The findings strongly indicated that the overall satisfaction is an intervening variable between attribute-based destination performance and behavioral intention for destinations. In other words, the destination performance indirectly influences behavioral intention through overall satisfaction. This finding was in line with the most previous research on customer satisfaction (i.e., Fornell et al., 1996; Szymanski & Henard, 2001). The model was also tested for each segment by treating re/visitation intention and recommendation behavior separately. They both produced consistent results and were not different from when a composite measure of the two was used. This suggests that, if no other information is on hand, the global evaluations seems to be a good predictor of future visitations and word-of-mouth.

The segment-specific findings also help to reveal the destination attributes critical to ensure a pleasant experience for each segment. Therefore, it provides a more pragmatic approach. As pointed out earlier, the segmentation basis (or base) used by a destination is equally important in this approach. Future study would utilize some other segmentation base appropriate for the destination of interest to advance our understanding on the nature of relationship between attribute-based performance, satisfaction, and behavioral intention for distinct markets. The findings are limited to linear relationships among model variables because non-linear or asymmetric relationships were not investigated (please see Mittal at al., 1998). The destination performance may have direct and asymmetric impact on behavioral intention. That would be an interesting future research area.

The model assumed unidirectional relationships between the variables and constructs. Therefore, the findings are limited to recursive model because bi-directional linkages were not investigated. The results are limited to the time period of data collection and destination attributes included in the study. The study measured overall satisfaction by a single-item global measure. Although the single-item overall satisfaction measure has also been used in most recent customer satisfaction research and justified in large-scale surveys (see LaBarbera & Mazursky, 1983; Fornell et al., 1996; Mittal, Ross, & Baldasare, 1998; Kozak & Rimmington, 2000; Yuksel & Rimmington, 1998; Mittal, Katrichis, & Kumar, 2001), future research would use multiple measures as several authors argue that the satisfaction construct has both cognitive and affective dimensions (see Oliver, 1993). The findings are also limited to period when data were collected and to those Canadian travelers who use air travel as their mode of transportation. Therefore, the findings would not be generalizable over Canadian visitors to Las Vegas.

REFERENCES

Aldenderfer, M. S. & Blashfield, R. K. (1984). *Cluster Analysis*, Newbury Park: Sage Publications.

Anderson, E.W., Fornell, C., & Lehmann, D. R. (1994, July). Customer satisfaction, market share, and profitability: Findings from Sweden. *Journal of Marketing*, 58, 53-66.

Baker, D. A. & Crompton, J. L. (2000). Quality. Satisfaction and behavioral intentions. *Annals of Tourism Research*, 27(3), 785-804.

Baloglu, S. & Uysal, M. (1996). Market segments of push and pull motivations: a canonical correlation approach. *International Journal of Contemporary Hospitality Management*, 8(3), 32-38.

Baloglu, S. (2000). "A path-analytical model of visitation intention involving information sources, socio-psychological motivations and destination images" in Woodside et al. (Eds). *Consumer Psychology of Tourism, Hospitality and Leisure* (pp. 63-90). Oxon:CABI Publishing.

Chon, K. S. (1992). Self-image/destination image congruity. *Annals of Tourism Research*, 19(2), 360-76.

Churchill, G. & Surprenant, C. (1982, November). An investigation into the determinants of customer satisfaction. *Journal of Marketing Research*, 19, 491-504.

Crompton, J. L. & Love, L. L. (1995). The predictive validity of alternative approaches to evaluating quality of festival. *Journal of Travel Research*, 34(1), 11-24.

Cronin, J. J. & Taylor, S. A. (1992). Measuring service quality: A reexamination and extension. *Journal of Marketing*, 56(3), 55-68.

Danaher, P. J. & Arweiler, N. (1996). Customer satisfaction in the tourist industry: A case study of visitors to New Zealand. *Journal of Travel Research*, 35(1), 89-93.

Fakeye, P.C. & Crompton J.L. (1991). Image differences between prospective, first-time, and repeat visitors to the Lower Rio Grande Valley. *Journal of Travel Research*, 30 (Fall): 10-16.

Fornell, C., Johnson, M. D., Anderson, E. W., Cha, J., & Bryant, B. E. (1996, October). The American customer satisfaction index: Nature, purpose, and findings. *Journal of Marketing*, 60, 7-18.

Frochot, I. & Morrison, A. M.(2000). Benefit segmentation: A review of its applications to travel and tourism research. *Journal of Travel and Tourism Marketing*, 9(4), 21-45.

Hurst, F. (1994). "En route surveys." In J.R.B Ritchie and C. R. Goeldner (Eds.) *Travel, Tourism, and Hospitality Research: A Handbook for Managers and Researchers*, 2nd ed. (pp. 453-471). New York: John Wiley & Sons, Inc.

Jones, M. A. & Suh, J. (2000). Transaction-specific satisfaction and overall satisfaction: An empirical analysis. *Journal of Services Marketing*, 14(2), 147-159.

Kozak, M. & Rimmington, M. (2000). Tourist satisfaction with Mallorca, Spain as an off-season holiday destination. *Journal of Travel Research*, 38 (February), 260-269.

LaBarbera, P. A. & Mazursky, D. (1983, November). A longitudinal assessment of consumer satisfaction/dissatisfaction: The dynamic aspect of the cognitive process. *Journal of Marketing Research*, 20, 393-404.

Mittal, V., Ross, W. T., & Baldasare, P. M. (1998, January). The asymmetric impact of negative and positive attribute-level performance on overall satisfaction and repurchase intentions. *Journal of Marketing*, 62, 33-47.

Mittal, V., Katrichis, J. M., Kumar, P. (2001). Attribute performance and customer satisfaction over time: Evidence from two-field studies. *Journal of Services Marketing*, 15(5), 343- 356.

Oh, H. & Parks, S. C. (1997). Customer satisfaction and service quality: A critical review of the literature and research implications for the hospitality industry. *Hospitality Research Journal*, 20(3), 35-64.

Oliver, R. L. (1980, November). A cognitive model of the antecedents and consequences of satisfaction decisions. *Journal of Marketing Research*, 17, 460-69.

Oliver, R. L. (1993). Cognitive, affective, and attribute bases of the satisfaction response. *Journal of Consumer Research*, 20, 418-430.

Patterson, P. (1993). Expectations and product performance as determinants of satisfaction for a high-involvement purchase. *Psychology & Marketing*, 10(5), 449-465.

Pearce, P. L. (1980). A favorability-satisfaction model of tourist evaluations. *Journal of Travel Research*, 19 (Summer): 13-17.

Pizam, A., Neumann, Y. & Reichel (1978). Dimensions of tourist satisfaction with a destination. *Annals of Tourism Research*, 18: 226-37.

Pizam, A. & Milman, A. (1993). Predicting satisfaction among first time visitors to a destination by using the expectancy disconfirmation theory. *International Journal Hospitality Management*,12(2), 197-209.

Ryan, C. (1995). *Researching tourist satisfaction: Issues, Concepts, Problems*. London: Routledge.

Singh, J. & Sirdeshmukh, D. (2000). Agency and trust mechanisms in consumer satisfaction and loyalty judgements. *Journal of the Academy of Marketing Science*, 28(1), 150-167.

Szymanski, D. M. & Henard, D. H. (2001). Customer satisfaction: A Meta analysis of the empirical evidence. *Journal of the Academy of Marketing Science*, 29(1), 16-35.

Tse, D. & Wilton, P. (1988, May). Models of consumer satisfaction formation: An extension. *Journal of Marketing Research*, 25, 204-212.

Uysal, M. & Hagan, L.A.R. (1993), "Motivation of Pleasure Travel and Tourism," In *VNR's Encyclopedia of Hospitality and Tourism*, M. Khan, M. Olsen, and T. Var (Eds.), New York: Van Nostrand Reinhold, pp. 798-810.

Uysal, M. & Williams, J. (2003). The role of expressive and instrumental factors in measuring visitor satisfaction. The paper presented at *The Third Symposium of the Consumer Psychology of Tourism, Hospitality and Leisure (CPTHL) Conference*, January 5-8, Melbourne, Australia.

Woodside, A. G. & Jacobs, L. W. (1985). Step two in benefit segmentation: Learning the benefits realized by major travel markets. *Journal of Travel Research*, 24(1), 7-13.

Yi, Y. (1990). A critical review of consumer satisfaction. In V. A. Zeithaml(Ed.), *Review of Marketing* (pp. 68-123). Chicago: American Marketing Association.

Yuksel, A. & Rimmington, Y. (1998). Tourist satisfaction and food service experience: Results and implications of an empirical investigation. *Anatolia: An International Journal of Tourism and Hospitality Research*, 9(1), 37-57.

Yuksel, A. & Yuksel F. (2001). Measurement and management issues in customer satisfaction research: Review, critique and research agenda: Part two. *Journal of Travel & Tourism Marketing*, 10(4), 81-111.

The Effect of Length of Stay on Travelers' Perceived Satisfaction with Service Quality

Janet D. Neal

SUMMARY. Consumer satisfaction related to service quality during the vacation experience is of paramount importance to the travel and tourism industry. This study tests empirically the effects the number of nights spent on a vacation have on the levels of satisfaction recent travelers report for three service aspects of the travel destination: perceived satisfaction with tourism service providers; perceived "freedom from defects" of tourism services; and perceived reasonableness of the cost of tourism services. Differentiation in satisfaction scores between "short-term visitors" (i.e., those who stayed from one to six nights) and "long-term visitors" (i.e., those who stayed seven or more nights) were examined. Significant differences between the two groups of visitors were present for (1) perceived satisfaction with industry professionals delivering the service experience at the travel destination, (2) perceived satisfaction with "freedom from defects" of the actual services at the destination, and (3) perceived reasonableness of the cost of services at

Janet D. Neal is Assistant Professor, The Hospitality Management Program, The University of North Carolina at Greensboro, P.O. Box 27170, Greensboro, NC 27402-7170 (E-mail: jdneal@uncg.edu).

[Haworth co-indexing entry note]: "The Effect of Length of Stay on Travelers' Perceived Satisfaction with Service Quality." Neal, Janet D. Co-published simultaneously in *Journal of Quality Assurance in Hospitality & Tourism* (The Haworth Hospitality Press, an imprint of The Haworth Press, Inc.) Vol. 4, No. 3/4, 2003, pp. 167-176; and: *Current Issues and Development in Hospitality and Tourism Satisfaction* (ed: John A. Williams and Muzaffer Uysal) The Haworth Hospitality Press, an imprint of The Haworth Press, Inc., 2003, pp. 167-176. Single or multiple copies of this article are available for a fee from The Haworth Document Delivery Service [1-800-HAWORTH, 9:00 a.m. - 5:00 p.m. (EST). E-mail address: docdelivery@haworthpress.com].

the travel destination. Suggestions for how tourism industry professionals can make use of this information are presented. *[Article copies available for a fee from The Haworth Document Delivery Service: 1-800-HAWORTH.
E-mail address: <docdelivery@haworthpress.com> Website: <http://www.HaworthPress.
com> © 2003 by The Haworth Press, Inc. All rights reserved.]*

KEYWORDS. Consumer satisfaction, length of stay, service quality, travel and tourism

INTRODUCTION

The concept of length of stay is vital to the careful examination of many travel/tourism issues (Butler 1974; Masberg 1998). The importance of length of stay when studying many aspects of travel has been clearly established in prior research (see for example Uysal, Fesenmaier, and O'Leary 1994). This paper seeks to explore how the length of stay can and does affect the satisfaction of travelers.

Understanding and enhancing consumer satisfaction has, understandably, become a major goal in contemporary businesses (Yi 1990). The success of any business is contingent upon attracting and retaining satisfied customers. The profitability and ultimate survival of hospitality and tourism businesses is to deliver high-quality products in an effort to generate continued demand for their services from both new and returning customers. Previous research stud-ies have examined the importance of consumer satisfaction in lodging (Barsky 1992; Barsky and Labagh 1992; Saleh and Ryan 1991), restaurant (Dube, Ren-aghan and Miller 1994) and tourism (Pizam and Milman 1993) industries. Many of these studies established that consumer satisfaction with various as-pects of the purchase experience, including the service aspects, brings about desired consumer behavior, such as repeat business and positive word-of-mouth communications with others (see, for example, Anderson, Fornell and Lehmann 1994; Boulding, Kalra, Staelin and Zeithaml 1993; and Cronin and Taylor 1992). Further, increased satisfaction with the service aspects of travel/tourism experiences can lead to enhancing the overall life satisfaction (i.e., quality of life) of vacationers (Neal, Sirgy, and Uysal 1999).

LITERATURE REVIEW

The importance and seasonal variation of length of vacation stay in forty-eight states in the United States has been clearly established in previous research (Uysal et al. 1994). This was accomplished by developing a trip index for each state that was used to calculate the length of stay and seasonal variation of length of stay in each state in addition to information related to length of stay in all states visited. Uysal and his colleagues clustered states into five groups that show high to low concentration in pleasure travel. The findings indicated that not only do different states tend to attract tourists that are "destination-oriented" (traveling specifically to that destination, thus having a greater length of stay), but also that the attractiveness of these states tends to be seasonal.

While length of stay is often used to define the supply side of tourism (e.g., to help determine the number and types of visitors in order to develop the proper facilities; to ascertain how information centers affect the visitors' length of stay to specific states) (Getz 1986; Gunn 1988; Tierney 1993), it can be argued that the length of stay can be a useful measure in examining the demand side of tourism as well (e.g., visitor satisfaction). For instance, Uysal (1998) indicated that the length of stay (tourist nights spent on vacation) is one of the most commonly-used methods of measuring tourism demand. The length of stay is usually defined as the amount of time travelers spend at a destination and is frequently measured in the number of days or nights tourists spend at the site (Pearce and Elliott 1983; Uysal, McDonald, and O'Leary 1988).

Length of stay has been shown in prior research to be an effective tool in measuring demand. The duration of time (i.e., number of nights) a traveler spends on his or her vacation has been used as an indicator of tourism demand. One study conducted at national parks used length of stay (the number of "ski-touring" days at the destination site) as a measure of demand by regressing variables such as direct cost of skiing, distance traveled, number of previous skiing trips, and a myriad of site characteristics on it (Uysal et al. 1988). Another study used length of stay to examine tourism demand at resort destinations (Crouch 1994), based on the rationale that the most basic product being purchased by tourists is a "night's stay." Therefore, length of stay is an appropriate measure for tourism demand.

It is logical to conclude that this increase in demand for particular tourism services is likely a function of the tourists' satisfaction among other factors at the destination site. That is, the more satisfied tourists are with the destination services, the more they will demand that service, and the greater the length of stay is likely to be at that particular destination site. This is consistent with the finding of many researchers who have discovered that an increase in quality leisure time enhances leisure satisfaction (e.g., Driver 1976; Buchanan 1983).

The general hypothesis of the study is that satisfaction with the perceived quality of travel and tourism services at the travel destination is a positive function of the length of stay of the overnight traveler. Based on the review of the literature, the following three specific hypotheses were generated:

H1: Satisfaction with the perceived quality of travel and tourism service providers at the travel destination is a positive function of the length of stay of the traveler. Visitors that spend little time on a vacation experience have less time to enjoy the amenities of the trip. Putting forth the effort to correct mistakes made by service providers tends to consume a much larger ratio of the overall time spent on the vacation. With so little time to enjoy the experience, every minute counts for short-term visitors. Additionally, there is less time for service industry providers to become familiar with the guests in a personal way such that individual needs and tastes can be addressed to the fullest.

H2: Satisfaction with the perceived efficiency (i.e., "freedom from defects") of services at the travel destination is a positive function of the length of stay of the traveler. If a service system failure occurs during a vacation taken by short-term visitors, a larger portion of the vacation time is consumed by the mistake, thus making the magnitude seem greater. For instance, if a visitor is staying for a month at the beach and one day a service system failure occurs (e.g., water pipes break), only one day of many (i.e., 1/30th) of the vacation time is ruined. However, if the vacation lasts only 4 days and the same problem occurs, a large proportion of the overall vacation is destroyed (i.e., 1/4th), thus making a much larger impact on the guest's overall perception of satisfaction with the vacation. Moreover, guests are less likely to bring service system failures to the attention of the service provider during short visits, so there is less opportunity for service recovery. Additionally, in those instances in which guests do report system defects, the service providers have much less time to implement service recovery procedures for short-term visitors than for long-term visitors.

H3: Satisfaction with the perceived cost of travel and tourism services at the travel destination is a positive function of the length of stay of the traveler. Since short-term visitors have less time to fully enjoy a vacation experience, it is believed that the perception of value-related costs will be less favorable than for those that have added time to "get more out of" the vacation experience. For example, if two guests travel the same distance to a vacation destination and one has the opportunity to relax, enjoy the vacation experience, and accomplish the purpose of the trip (e.g., resting and relaxing); whereas the other vacationer that has traveled the same distance has to rush to try to squeeze in as many adventures into a short time as possible and perhaps not have the time to accomplish the purpose of the trip (e.g., unwinding and rejuvenating), it is likely that the perceived monetary value will be much more favorable for the long-term visitor than for the short-term one.

METHODS

A self-reported survey was mailed to individuals who had recently traveled. The sample population consisted of individuals who (1) reside in Southwest Virginia and who (2) have participated in leisure travel (or leisure travel combined with business travel) within the last year. The names and addresses of the random sample were obtained via a reputable mailing list provider. Several techniques were employed to enhance the response rate. Self-addressed, stamped envelopes were included in the package being mailed to the respondents to ensure ease of return. Each of the cover letters was signed individually in blue ink in an attempt to show personalization and increase the response rate. Additionally, each envelope was stamped individually with a regular postage stamp to prevent the surveys from looking like a mass mailing, again, to try to increase the response rate. Three weeks after the survey was mailed, a reminder postcard was sent to those who had not returned their surveys.

The survey addressed travelers' perceptions of satisfaction with several aspects of service quality in relation to their most recent trip. A five-point Likert-type scale was used to capture responses to the questions, with "5" recording the highest level of satisfaction and "1" the lowest. A total of 826 useable surveys were returned from the 2,000 travelers who received the cover letter and survey questionnaire, thus making the response rate 47.69%.

RESULTS

Travelers were split into two groups: short-term overnight visitors (those who stayed from one to six nights on their trip) and long-term overnight visitors (those who stayed seven or more nights on their trip). Both groups of survey respondents tended to be satisfied in general with three very important aspects of service quality at the travel destination: perceived quality of services provided by travel and tourism professionals related to the travel destination; perceived "freedom from defects" of services at the travel destination; perceived reasonableness of the cost of travel and tourism services at the travel destination (see Table 1).

Independent samples t-tests were conducted to determine if differences between the means of the groups were statistically significant. Levine's Test for Equality of Variances showed that no significant differences existed between the two population variances for any of the factors being analyzed (satisfaction with quality of service providers, $F = 1.689$, $p = 0.194$; satisfaction with freedom from defects, $F = 0.558$, $p = 0.455$; satisfaction with cost, $F = 0.184$, $p = 0.668$). Therefore, the equal variances assumed test was used in each instance.

TABLE 1. Group Statistics for Length of Stay of Short-Term versus Long-Term Visitors*

Satisfaction with perceived quality of tourism service providers at the travel destination				
Length of Stay	N	Mean	SD	SEM
Short term visitors	167	3.982	0.861	0.067
Long term visitors	289	4.256	0.719	0.042
Satisfaction with "freedom from defects" of services at the travel destination				
Length of Stay	N	Mean	SD	SEM
Short-term visitors	176	4.028	0.935	0.070
Long-term visitors	290	4.228	0.800	0.047
Satisfaction with reasonableness of the cost of services at the travel destination				
Length of Stay	N	Mean	SD	SEM
Short-term visitors	165	3.847	0.908	0.071
Long-term visitors	277	4.072	0.865	0.052

*NOTE: "Short-term visitors" are defined as those who stayed from one to six nights at their vacation destination, whereas "long-term visitors" are defined as those who stayed seven or more nights at their vacation destination (1 = low satisfaction; 5 =high satisfaction). N = number of respondents; SD = standard deviation; SEM = Standard Error Mean.

TABLE 2. Results from Independent Samples t-Test for Length of Stay of Short-Term versus Long-Term Visitors

Measurement item	t	df	Sig. (2-tailed)	Mean Difference	SE Difference	95% Confidence Interval of the Difference	
						Lower	Upper
Perceived satisfaction w/service providers	3.642	454	p < 0.001**	0.2740	0.07524	.12616	.42187
Perceived satisfaction w/freedom from defects	2.443	464	p = 0.015**	0.1992	0.08153	.03896	.35940
Perceived satisfaction w/cost	2.581	440	p = 0.010**	0.2237	0.08667	.05338	.39406

Sig = Significance; SE = Standard Error
Significant "p" values are shown in bold
* indicates significance at the 0.05 level
**indicates significance at the 0.01 level
Equal Variances Assumed

The results for evaluating H1 indicated that long-term visitors were more satisfied with the quality of tourism service providers at the travel destination (M = 4.256; SD = 0.719) than were short-term visitors (M = 3.982; SD = 0.861). The results of the independent samples t-test indicated that the long-term visitors experienced significantly more satisfaction with the quality of tourism services during their vacation than did short-term visitors (t = 3.642; df = 454; p < 0.001).

The results for evaluating H2 indicated that long-term visitors reported greater satisfaction with the perceived efficiency (i.e., "freedom from defects") during their vacation experience (M = 4.228; SD = 0.800) than did short-term visitors (M = 4.028; SD = 0.935). The results of an independent samples t-test indicated that the levels of satisfaction for long-term visitors were significantly higher than for short-term visitors (t = 2.443; df = 464; p = 0.015).

The results for evaluating H3 indicated that long-term visitors reported greater levels of satisfaction (M = 4.072; SD = 0.865) with the cost of the trip than did short-term visitors (M = 3.847; SD = 0.908). The results of the independent samples t-test determined that long-term visitors were more satisfied with the perceived reasonableness of the cost of services at the destination than were short-term visitors (t = 2.581; df = 440; p = 0.010) (Table 2).

In order to further understand the relationship between Length of Stay and the travelers' perceived satisfaction with service quality and how the relationship may show variation for demographic and travel behavior variables, the study also used Analysis of Co-Variance to determine if the relationship would still hold while controlling for various demographic and travel behavior characteristics of the study. These "control variables" included age, income, marital status, gender, and the "type of trip" ("type of trip" categories included beach, resort, theme park, festival/special events, recreation, outdoor, combined business and pleasure, visiting friends and relatives, and touring).

The results revealed that none of the control variables tested influenced the relationship between the overall satisfaction of tourists' and the Length of Stay of travelers. Although previous research studies have indicated that, by definition, long-term travelers tend to be older than short-term travelers, age does not significantly affect satisfaction within length of stay categories (Wilks' Lambda, F = 2.283, p = 0.079). The same was true for income (Wilks' Lambda, F = 1.031, p = 0.379), marital status (Wilks' Lambda, F = 0.822, p = 0.482), gender (Wilks' Lambda, F = 21.221, p = 0.302), and type of trip (p = 0.822, p = 0.482). When controlling for each of these factors, satisfaction with length of stay remained significant across all categories being tested.

All three hypotheses were supported by the analyses of the data. This indicates that the length of stay of travelers at the tourism destination has an effect on their levels of satisfaction with service professionals, with the perceived efficiency of the service systems, and with the perceived cost of services.

CONCLUSION

The results from this study show that perceived levels of satisfaction with various service-related aspects of vacations are influenced by the amount of time visitors stay on the trip. Although both groups of travelers (e.g., short-term and long-term) experienced satisfaction with the service-related aspects of travel that were measured, significant differences for levels of satisfaction were determined based on the number of nights the travelers stayed on their vacations. Short-term visitors (i.e., those who stayed from one to six nights) tended to experience lower levels of satisfaction with perceived quality of service providers, perceived freedom from defects, and the perceived reasonableness of the cost at their travel destinations than did long-term visitors.

IMPLICATIONS

The results show that, indeed, the length of stay impacts the consumer perception of satisfaction with several aspects of service quality. From a theoretical perspective, this study empirically established: (1) the effects of length of stay on the perceived quality of travel and tourism service providers at the travel destination, (2) the effects of length of stay on the perceived satisfaction with the efficiency (i.e., "freedom from defects") of travel and tourism services at the tourism destination, and (3) the effects of length of stay on the perceived cost of travel and tourism services at the travel destination. In all three instances, the satisfaction levels were significantly higher for "long-term visitors" than for "short-term visitors."

Practical implications might include providing incentives to short-term visitors that would likely help them extend their stay (e.g., discounts provided to those that stay seven or more nights; added amenities and opportunities for those that stay at least seven nights at a single destination) in an effort to enhance their overall satisfaction. Other suggestions include product development designed to cater to the special on-site experience needs of guests with differing lengths of stay and activity development activities for both types of visitors while vacationing. Additionally, on the supplier side, developing a mechanism by which the industry can also monitor levels of satisfaction during the course of the vacation is suggested.

Future research in this area might include performing an analysis designed to break down the travel experience into different phases to ascertain if the findings fluctuate during various stages of the trip. For example, if no significant differences are detected with service aspects of the en route and return trip phases of the trip, but significant differences are detected for satisfaction with service aspects at the destination site, this would be useful to industry professionals as they create plans to enhance the overall vacation satisfaction of short-term visitors.

REFERENCES

Anderson, Eugene W., Claes Fornell, and Donald R. Lehmann (1994). "Customer Satisfaction, Market Share, and Profitability." *Journal of Marketing*, 58 (3) (July): 53-66.

Barsky, J.D..and Labagh (1992). "A Strategy for Customer Satisfaction." *The Cornell H.R.A. Quarterly*. October: 32-40.

Barsky, J.D. (1992). "Customer Satisfaction in the Hotel Industry: Meaning and Measurement." *Hospitality Research Journal* 16 (1), 51-73.

Boulding, W., A. Kalra, R. Staelin, and V. A. Zeithaml (1993). "A Dynamic Process Model of Service Quality: From Expectations to Behavioral Intentions." *Journal of Marketing Research*, 30 (February): 7-27.

Buchanan, T. (1983). "Toward an Understanding of Variability in Satisfaction within Activities." *Journal of Leisure Research* 15: 39-51.

Butler, R. W. (1974). "Social Implications of Tourism Development." *Annals of Tourism Research* 2 (2): 100-11.

Cronin, J. J. and Taylor, S. A. (1992). "Measuring Service Quality: A Reexamination and Extension." *Journal of Marketing* 56(3): 55-68.

Crouch, Geoffrey (1994). "Demand Elasticities for Short-haul Versus Long-haul Tourism." *Journal of Travel Research* 33 (2): 2-7.

Driver, B. L. (1976). *Toward a Better Understanding of the Social Benefits of Outdoor Recreation Participation*. Asheville, North Carolina: Southwestern Forest Experiment Station, U.S. Department of Agriculture, Forest Service.

Dube, L., Renaghan, L.M., and Miller, J.M. (1994). "Measuring Customer Satisfaction for Strategic Management." *The Cornell H.R.A. Quarterly*, February, 30-47.

Getz, Donald (1986). "Models in Tourism Planning." *Tourism Management* (March): 21-32.

Gunn, Clare A. (1988). *Tourism Planning*, 2d. ed. New York: Taylor and Francis.

Masberg, Barbara A. (1998). "Defining the Tourist: Is It Possible? A View From the Convention and Visitors Bureau." *Journal of Travel Research* 37 (1): 67-70.

Neal, Janet D., M. Joseph Sirgy, and Muzaffer Uysal (1999). "The Role of Satisfaction with Leisure Travel/Tourism Services and Experiences in Satisfaction with Leisure Life and Overall Life." *Journal of Business Research* 44 (3): 153-164.

Pearce, D. G. and J. M. C. Elliott (1983). "The Trip Index." *Journal of Travel Research* 22: 6-9.

Pizam, A. & Milman, A. (1993). "Social Impacts of Tourism: Host Perceptions." *Annals of Tourism Research* 20 (4): 650-665.

Saleh, F., and Ryan, C. (1991). "Analyzing Service Quality in the Hospitality Industry using the SERVQUAL Model." *Service Industries Journal*, 11(3), 324-45.

Tierney, Patrick T. (1993). "The Influence of State Traveler Information Centers on Tourist Length of Stay and Expenditures." *Journal of Travel Research* 31 (3): 28-32.

Uysal, Muzaffer (1998) "The Determinants of Tourism Demand: A Theoretical Perspective." In *The Economic Geography of the Tourist Industry: A Supply-Side Analysis*, Dimitri Ioannides and Keith G. Debbage (eds.). London, England and New York: Routledge.

Uysal, Muzaffer, Daniel R. Fesenmaier, and Joseph T. O'Leary (1994) "Geographic and Seasonal Variation in the Concentration of Travel in the United States." *Journal of Travel Research* 32 (3): 61-64.

Uysal, Muzaffer, C. D. McDonald, and J. T. O'Leary (1988). "Length of Stay: A Macro Analysis for Cross-Country Skiing Trips." *Journal of Travel Research* 26 (3): 29-31.

Yi, Y.K. (1990). "A Critical Review of Consumer Satisfaction." In V. Zeithaml (Ed.), *Review of Marketing*. Chicago: American Marketing Association, 68-123.

Satisfaction with Cultural/Heritage Sites: Virginia Historic Triangle

Jin Huh

Muzaffer Uysal

SUMMARY. This study attempted to investigate the relationship between cultural/heritage destination attributes and overall satisfaction, and to identify the difference in the overall satisfaction of tourists in terms of selected demographic and travel behavior characteristics. The expectancy-disconfirmation theory provided a conceptual framework for this study. This theory holds that consumers first form expectations of products or service performance prior to purchasing or use. The study area for this study was Virginia Historic Triangle (Williamsburg, Jamestown, and Yorktown). The survey was conducted at five different sites in the Virginia Historic Triangle. The findings indicate that there is a relationship between destination attributes and overall satisfaction with cultural/heritage experience. The study also reveals that overall satisfaction may show variation by gender, length of stay, and decision horizon. The study concludes with appropriate marketing and management implications. *[Article copies available for a fee from The Haworth Document Delivery Service: 1-800-HAWORTH. E-mail address: <docdelivery@haworthpress.com> Website:*

Jin Huh (E-mail: jhuh@vt.edu) and Muzaffer Uysal (E-mail: samil@vt.edu) are affiliated with the Department of Hospitality and Tourism Management, Virginia Polytechnic Institute and State University, 362 Wallace Hall, Blacksburg, VA 24061-0429.

[Haworth co-indexing entry note]: "Satisfaction with Cultural/Heritage Sites: Virginia Historic Triangle." Huh, Jin, and Muzaffer Uysal. Co-published simultaneously in *Journal of Quality Assurance in Hospitality & Tourism* (The Haworth Hospitality Press, an imprint of The Haworth Press, Inc.) Vol. 4, No. 3/4, 2003, pp. 177-194; and: *Current Issues and Development in Hospitality and Tourism Satisfaction* (ed: John A. Williams and Muzaffer Uysal) The Haworth Hospitality Press, an imprint of The Haworth Press, Inc., 2003, pp. 177-194. Single or multiple copies of this article are available for a fee from The Haworth Document Delivery Service [1-800-HAWORTH, 9:00 a.m. - 5:00 p.m. (EST). E-mail address: docdelivery@haworthpress.com].

KEYWORDS. Cultural/heritage tourism, Virginia historic triangle, expectancy-satisfaction theory, expectation and satisfaction

INTRODUCTION

Because of people's inclination to seek out novelty, including that of traditional cultures, heritage tourism has become a major "new" area of tourism demand, which almost all policy-makers are now aware of and anxious to develop. Heritage tourism, as a part of the broader category of "cultural tourism," is now a major pillar of the nascent tourism strategy of many countries. Cultural/heritage tourism strategies in various countries have in common that they are a major growth area, that they can be used to boost local culture, and that they can aid the seasonal and geographic spread of tourism (Richards, 1996).

In recent decades, there is a trend toward an increased specialization among travelers, and cultural/heritage tourism is the fastest growing segment of the industry. Americans' interest in traveling to cultural/heritage destinations has increased recently and is expected to continue.

Recent studies about cultural/heritage tourism have focused on identifying the characteristics, development, and management of cultural/heritage tourism, as well as on investigating demographic and travel behavior characteristics of tourists who visit cultural/heritage destinations. Pearce and Balcar (1996) analyzed destination characteristics, development, management, and patterns of demand through an element-by-element comparison of eight heritage sites on the West Coast of New Zealand. Silberberg (1995) provided a common pattern of cultural/heritage tourists by analyzing age, gender, income, and educational level. Formica and Uysal (1998) explored the existing markets of a unique annual event that blends internationally well-known cultural exhibitions with historical settings. Behavioral, motivational, and demographic characteristics of festival visitors were examined by using a posteriori market segmentation.

The study also researched cultural/heritage tourists' demographic and travel behavior characteristics in order to help tourism marketers better understand their customers. In addition, because there have been few studies that identify the relationship between cultural/heritage destination attributes and satisfaction, this study investigates which attributes satisfy tourists who visit

cultural/heritage destinations in order to help tourism planners develop strategies to increase their market share and attract new customers.

Therefore, two specific objectives of the study are (1) to identify the relationship between cultural/heritage destination attributes and the overall satisfaction of tourists who visit cultural/heritage destination and (2) to analyze the
relationship between cultural/heritage destination attributes and tourists' overall satisfaction, controlling for their demographic and travel behavior characteristics.

THEORETICAL BASIS

The study is based on a consumer behavior model, which postulates that
consumer satisfaction is a function of both expectations related to certain attributes, and judgments of a performance regarding these attributes (Clemons
and Woodruff, 1992).

One of the most commonly-adopted approaches used to examine the satisfaction of consumers is expectancy-disconfirmation theory. This theory with
its enhanced conceptualizations and variations currently dominates the study
of consumer satisfaction and provides a fundamental framework for satisfaction studies (Oliver, 1980; Parasuraman, Zeithaml, and Berry, 1985). Expectancy-disconfirmation theory holds that consumers first form expectations of
products' or services' performance prior to purchase or use. The gap between
the two is of a major concern to service providers and decision makers.

CULTURAL/HERITAGE DESTINATION ATTRIBUTES

The study attempts to identify cultural/heritage destination attributes which
satisfied tourists when they visited these destinations. Therefore, after investigating previous research related to this topic, the researchers decided to select
several attributes of cultural/heritage tourism.

Andersen, Prentice and Guerin (1997) researched the cultural tourism of
Denmark. They chose several attributes, such as historical buildings, museums, galleries, theaters, festivals and events, shopping, food, palaces, famous
people (writer . . .), castles, sports, and old towns. They identified the important attributes as being castles, gardens, museums, and historical buildings,
when tourists made a decision to visit Denmark. Richards (1996) focused on
the marketing and development of European cultural tourism. He chose several attributes related to cultural/heritage destinations in order to analyze European cultural tourism. Especially, through analyzing these attributes, this article

indicated a rapid increase in both the production and consumption of heritage attractions. Peleggi (1996) also examined the relevance of Thailand's heritage attractions to both international and domestic tourism, including an analysis of the state tourism agency's promotion of heritage and the ideological implications of heritage sightseeing in relation to the official historical narrative. This research provided several attributes, such as traditional villages, monuments, museums, and temples. In addition to the research discussed above, many other researchers have studied cultural/heritage destination attributes. For example, Sofield and Li (1998) studied the cultural tourism of China by selecting history, culture, traditional festivals, historical events, beautiful scenic heritage, historical sites, architecture, folk arts (music, dancing, craft work) and folk culture villages as the attributes of significance. Janiskee (1996) emphasized the importance of events through several attributes such as festivals, historic houses, traditional ceremonies, music, dancing, craftwork, food, and the direct experience of traditional life.

The current study generated a list of 25 attributes based on previous studies. These attributes include cultural/heritage attributes as well as infrastructure attributes, such as, food, shopping places, accommodations, etc.

TOURIST CHARACTERISTICS

The characteristics of tourists are important factors when the researcher analyzes satisfaction with cultural/heritage destinations. Therefore, socioeconomic, demographic, and behavioral indicators are commonly used in tourism research to profile tourists by age, gender, income, marital status, occupations, and education or ethnic background. These indicators are easy to identify and use in marketing decisions (Yavuz, 1994).

Silberberg (1995) provided a common pattern of cultural/heritage tourists. This study identified the cultural/heritage tourist as one who: earns more money and spends more money while on vacation; spends more time in an area while on vacation; is more highly educated than the general public; is more likely to be female than male, and tends to be in older age categories.

Master and Prideaux (2000) analyzed the variance by age, gender, occupation and previous overseas travel of Taiwanese cultural/heritage tourists to determine if demographic and travel characteristics influenced responses on importance of attributes and satisfaction levels.

Lee (1998) examined demographic variables of tourists in his tourism research. In particular, he investigated individuals' trip characteristics (trip group types) and past experience with a destination. Past experience was measured by asking tourists to indicate the number of trips they have taken to the chosen destination. His study analyzed the relationship between past experience and place attachment.

Fomica and Uysal (1998) explored the existing markets of a unique annual event, the Spoleto Festival in Italy that blends internationally well-known cultural exhibitions with historical settings. The behavioral, motivational, and demographic characteristics of festival visitors were examined by using a posteriori market segmentation. The results of the study showed statistically significant differences between the groups in terms of age, income, and marital status.

Kerstetter, Confer, and Graefe (2001) also investigated whether types of heritage tourists exist and, if so, whether they differ based on socio-demographic characteristics. This study found that tourists with an interest in visiting heritage or cultural sites (i.e., "heritage tourists") tend to stay longer, spend more per trip, are more highly educated, and have a higher average annual income than the general tourists.

This study provides tourists' demographic and travel behavior characteristics in order to explain the differences in attributes and satisfaction. Tourists' demographic characteristics in the study included age, gender, total household incomes, and educational level. On the other hand, tourists' travel behavior characteristics included party in a group, past experience, length of stay, decision time taken to select a destination, and sources of information about the destination.

TOURIST SATISFACTION

Tourist satisfaction is important to successful destination marketing because it influences the choice of destination, the consumption of products and services, and the decision to return (Kozak and Rimmington, 2000). Several researchers have studied customer satisfaction and provided theories about tourism. For example, Parasuraman, Zeithaml, and Berry's (1985) expectation-perception gap model, Oliver's expectancy-disconfirmation theory (Pizam and Milman, 1993), Sirgy's congruity model (Chon and Olsen, 1991), and the performance-only model (Pizam, Neumann, and Reichel, 1978) have been used to measure tourist satisfaction with specific tourism destinations. Some researchers have also looked at comparison of standards used in service quality and satisfaction and provided excellent discussion points on different measures of service quality and satisfaction (Ekinci, Riley, and Chen 2001; Liljander 1994). However, regardless of the nature of satisfaction measures, the theory of expectancy-disconfirmation has received the widest acceptance among satisfaction-based theories because it is broadly applicable.

Pizam and Milman (1993) utilized Oliver's (1980) expectancy-disconfirmation model to improve the predictive power of travelers' satisfaction. They introduced the basic dynamic nature of the disconfirmation model into hospitality research, while testing part of the original model in a modified form. In order to assess the causal relationship between two different disconfirmation methods, they employed a regression model with a single "expectation-met" measure as the dependent variable, and 21 differences-score measures as the independent variable. Some studies on customer satisfaction are also notable in tourism behavior research. For example, Pizam, Neumann and Reichel (1978) investigated the factor structure of tourists' satisfaction with their destination areas. The authors showed eight distinguishable dimensions of tourist satisfaction.

Barsky (1992) and Barsky and Labagh (1992) introduced the expectancy-disconfirmation paradigm into lodging research. Basically, the proposed model in these studies was that customer satisfaction was the function of disconfirmation, measured by nine "expectations met" factors that were weighted by attribute-specific importance. The model was tested with data collected from 100 random subjects via guest comment card. As a result, customer satisfaction was found to correlate with a customer's willingness to return.

Kozak and Rimington (2000) reported the findings of a study to determine destination attributes critical to the overall satisfaction levels of tourists. Pizam, Neumann, and Reichel (1978) stated that it is important to measure consumer satisfaction with each attribute of the destination, because consumer dis/satisfaction with one of the attributes leads to dis/satisfaction with the overall destination. Furthermore, Rust, Zahorik, and Keininghan (1996) explained that the relative importance of each attribute to the overall impression should be investigated because dis/satisfaction can be the result of evaluating various positive and negative experiences.

STUDY AREA

The study area for this study was Virginia Historic Triangle (Williamsburg, Jamestown, and Yorktown). Virginia Historic Triangle has been called the 'largest living museum in the world.' Furthermore, it is one of America's most popular vacation destinations. Jamestown is where America began when in 1607 a few hardy souls carved out of the wilderness the first permanent English settlement in the New World. Williamsburg is the world's premier living history site, an entire town that has been restored to the days when it was the political and economic center of the American colonies. Yorktown is where

General George Washington defeated England's troops in 1781 in the final battle of the American Revolution.

Although famous throughout the world, Virginia Historic Triangle is still a 'small town.' However, every year more than 4,000,000 tourists come to visit. Due to its varied, year-round attractions, it is one of the most popular visit destinations in the United States.

SAMPLE

The sample population for the study was composed of tourists who visited Virginia Historic Triangle (Williamsburg, Jamestown, and Yorktown) in June and August, in 2001. The survey was conducted at five different places that are frequently visited in Virginia Historic Triangle over a 2-week period. Distribution of questionnaires was carried out only during the daytime. Respondents were approached and informed about the purpose of the survey in advance before they were given the questionnaire. They then were asked whether they would participate in the survey. Self-completion questionnaires were provided at five different places in the Virginia Historic Triangle. Respondents younger than age 18 were automatically excluded. Personal observations revealed that tourists who were age 18 or older visit cultural/heritage destinations either individually or with their friends or families as groups. No particular attempt was made to apply a random sample or to select particular segments. However, tourists were selected at different times of the day. A total sample size of 300 was completed.

VARIABLES

The study analyzed which cultural/heritage destination attributes were important in satisfying tourists who visited cultural/heritage destinations, and identified the differences in terms of tourists' characteristics. To develop an instrument for this study, previous literature was examined to identify instruments used with studies having similar objectives. A preliminary questionnaire was developed based upon previous instrumentation used by Kozak and Rimmington (2000). Kozak and Rimmington's study reported findings about destination attributes critical to the overall satisfaction levels of tourists visiting Mallorca, Spain during the winter season.

The questionnaire used in this study consisted of two sections. The first section explored destination attributes affecting tourists' expectations, perceptions, and satisfaction levels in relation to a cultural/heritage destination. Respondents were requested to give a score to each of the 25 attributes on the levels of expectations and satisfactions separately using a 5-point Likert-type scale ranging from very low expectation (1) to very high expectation (5) and from very dissatisfied (1) to very satisfied (5). A final question in this section was asked about respondents' overall level of satisfaction with the Virginia Historic Triangle (1 = extremely dissatisfied, 7 = extremely satisfied).

A section of the questionnaire gathered the respondents' demographic and travel behavior characteristics. Total household incomes were operationalized as a categorical variable. The categories ranged from "less than $19,999" to "$100,000 or more." Educational level also was operationalized as a categorical variable. The categories ranged from "no high school degree" to "graduate school/professional degree." Party in a group was investigated by asking respondents to select one response among the choices of alone, family, friends, and organized groups. Past experience was measured by asking respondents to indicate the number of visits to cultural/heritage destinations in the past 3 years, from 1999 to 2001 (not including the present trip).

DATA ANALYSIS

The data analysis of the study was done using Statistical Package for Social Sciences (SPSS). Statistical analyses such as Factor Analysis, Multiple Regression, Analysis of Variance (ANOVA) and Multivariate Analysis of Covariance (MANCOVA) were used according to the respective objectives of the study.

Factor analysis was conducted to create correlated variable composites from the original 25 attributes and to identify a smaller set of dimensions, or factors, that explain most of the variance between the attributes and the derived factor scores. The delineated factor scores were then applied in subsequent regression analysis. In this study, factors were retained only if they had values greater than or equal to 1.0 of eigenvalue and a factor loading greater than 0.4. Multiple regression analysis was used to examine tourists' overall levels of satisfaction with the cultural/heritage destination. The dependent variable (tourists' overall satisfaction levels with the cultural/heritage destination) was regressed against each of the factor scores of the independent variables (cultural/heritage dimensions) derived from the factor analysis. Analysis of variance (ANOVA) was used to identify the difference in overall satisfaction with respect to demographic and travel behavior variables. Multivariate Analysis of Variance (MANCOVA) was performed to reveal the control variables, which influenced the relationship between the overall satisfaction of tourists' and cultural/heritage destination attributes.

CHARACTERISTICS OF RESPONDENTS

The demographic characteristics of the respondents are shown in Table 1. The gender distribution of the respondents was quite even, with 51.4% female respondents and 48.6% male respondents. The dominant age group of the respondents was 38 to 47 years (37.5%), followed by 48 to 57 years (22.3%), 28 to 37 years (19.5%), and 58 years and older (10.8%), whereas 18 to 27 years (10%) made up the smallest group, representing 10% of the respondents. Most of the respondents (68.9%) reported that they live in other states of the United States and 25.5 % of the respondents live in Virginia, whereas 5.6% of the respondents were international travelers. In terms of level of education, almost 52% of the respondents had the university education level, 32.3% of the respondents had the post graduate education and 15.9% of the respondents had the secondary school education. No respondent in the research study was at primary level or below. This shows the relatively high educational attainment of the respondents. With regard to respondents' annual household income, the largest group included those with an annual household income of US $80,000 or above (45.4%), followed by US $40,000 to US $59,999 (20.3%), US $ 60,000 to US $79,999 (18.3%), and US$20,000 to US $ 39,999. Only 4.8% of the respondents had an annual household income of US $19,999 or below.

The travel behavior characteristics of the respondents are also shown in Table 1. In the category of the number of previous visits to the Virginia Historic Triangle, 25.1% of the respondents did not have previous experience with the Virginia Historic Triangle. Almost 44% of the respondents visited 1 to 2 times. Furthermore, 16.4% of the respondents visited 3 to 4 times, whereas 14.7% of the respondents visited 5 times or more. With regard of the plan of the travel, the distribution of the respondents was quite even. Around 40% of the respondents planned in advance 4 to 6 months of the travel and 39.5% of the respondents planned in advance 3 months or below of the travel. The smallest group of the respondents (20.4%) planned in advance 6 months or above. In the category of the length of stay, 58.2% of the respondents stayed for 2 to 4 days, followed by for 5 to 7 days (24.3%), and for 1 day (13.5%). Only 4% of the respondents stayed 8 days or above. With regard of party in the group, most respondents (97.2%) traveled with a partner, friends, and family members, whereas only 2.8% of respondents traveled alone or organized group members. Lastly, in the category of travel miles one way, the largest group of the respondents (50.2%) traveled 301 miles or above, the middle group of the respondents (33%) traveled 101 to 300 miles, and the smallest group of the respondents traveled 100 miles or below.

TABLE 1. Characteristics of Respondents

Variable	N	(%)
Gender		
Male	122	48.6
Female	129	51.4
Age (years)		
18-27	25	10
28-37	49	19.5
38-47	94	37.5
48-57	56	22.3
58-67	18	7.2
67+	9	3.6
States		
Virginia	64	25.5
Other States	173	68.9
Abroad	14	5.6
Education levels		
Primary & Second school	40	15.9
College	130	51.8
Graduate school	81	32.3
Total house incomes (USD)		
19,999 or less	12	4.8
20,000-39,999	28	11.2
40,000-59,999	51	20.3
60,000-79,999	46	18.3
80,000 or above	114	45.4
Past experience in cultural/heritage sites		
Yes	188	74.9
No	63	25.1
How long in advance planed to visit Virginia Historic Triangle		
3 month or below	99	39.5
4-6 months	101	40.2
6 months or above	51	20.4
Length of stay		
1 day	34	13.5
2-4 days	146	58.2
5-7 days	61	24.3
8 or above	10	4.0
Party in the group		
Alone	3	1.2
A couple	50	19.9
Family members	154	61.4
Friends/relatives	40	15.9
Organized groups	4	1.6
Distance of travel (miles)		
50 or less	22	8.8
51-100	20	8.0
101-200	39	15.5
201-300	44	17.5
300 or much	126	50.2

Note: The useable questionnaire consisted of 251 respondents out of 300 sampled respondents.

OVERALL SATISFACTION VIRGINIA HISTORIC TRIANGLE

Respondents were also questioned about their overall satisfaction with Virginia Historic Triangle. The results indicated that 72.5% of the respondents were satisfied, very satisfied, or extremely satisfied with Virginia Historic Triangle, 13.9% were neutral in their opinions, and 21.6% of the respondents were dissatisfied, very dissatisfied, or extremely dissatisfied. The mean value of respondents' overall perceived level of satisfaction was 5.45, which tended toward the high end of satisfaction scale. This suggests that Virginia Historic Triangle provide tourists with a satisfactory experience.

FACTOR ANALYSIS OF CULTURAL/HERITAGE ATTRIBUTES

The principal components factor method was used to generate the initial solution. The eigenvalues suggested that four-factor solution explained 57.65% of the overall variance in destination attributes. The factors with eigenvalues greater than or equal to 1.0 and attributes with factor loadings greater than 0.4 were reported. Table 2 illustrated the results of the factor analysis. Two attributes were dropped due to the failure of loading on any factor at the level of 0.40 (or higher). These were "religious people" and "expensiveness." The communality of communality of each variable ranged from 0.416 to 0.743. The four factors were named as: General Tour Attraction, Heritage Attraction, Maintenance Factors, and Cultural Attraction.

The overall significance of the correlation matrix was 0.00, with a Bartlett test of sphericity value of 1541.42. The statistical probability and the test indicated that there was significant correlation between the variable, and the use of factor analysis was appropriate. The Kaiser-Meyer-Olkin overall measure of sampling adequacy was 0.882, which was meritorious (Hair, Anderson, and Black 1999).

To test the reliability and internal consistency of each factor, Cronbach's alpha of each was determined. The results showed that the alpha coefficients ranged from 0.702 to 0.879 for the four factors. The results were considered more than reliable, since 0.50 is the minimum value for accepting the reliability test (Nunnally, 1967).

The four factors underlying tourists' perceptions of cultural/heritage attributes in Virginia Historic Triangle were as follows. General Tour Attraction (Factor 1) contained nine attributes and explained 40.45% of the variance in the data, with an eigenvalue of 9.708 and, a reliability of 87.88%. The attributes associated with this factor dealt with the general tour items, including "religious places," "souvenir," "theaters," "theme parks," "tour package," "festivals/events," "food,"

TABLE 2. Factor Analysis Results of Perception of Attributes in Virginia Historic Triangle

Attributes	Factor Loading				Communality
	Factor 1	Factor 2	Factor 3	Factor 4	
Factor 1: General Tour Attraction					
Religious places	0.817				0.737
Souvenirs	0.700				0.643
Theaters	0.670				0.628
Theme parks	0.617				0.600
Tour packages	0.580				0.582
Festivals/events	0.565				0.587
Food	0.565				0.416
Shopping places	0.548				0.502
Guides	0.511				0.593
Factor 2: Heritage Attraction					
Handcrafts		0.705			0.588
Architecture		0.685			0.541
Traditional scenery		0.664			0.616
Arts (Music/dance)		0.599			0.499
Factor 3: Maintenance Factors					
Accessibility			0.722		0.624
Indoor facilities			0.681		0.743
Atmosphere/people			0.623		0.574
Information centers			0.580		0.529
Accommodations			0.557		0.577
Factor 4: Culture Attraction					
Museums				0.787	0.683
Galleries				0.602	0.465
Culture villages				0.581	0.577
Historic building				0.499	0.522
Monuments				0.470	0.541
Eigenvalue	9,708	1,616	1,339	1,173	
Variance (%)	40.449	6.735	5.577	4.888	
Cumulative variance (%)	40.449	47.184	52.761	57.649	
Reliability Alpha (%)	87.88	70.2	72.85	80.00	
Number of items (total = 23)	9	4	5	5	

Note: Extraction Method–Principal Component Analysis
Rotation Method–Varimax with Kaiser Normalization
KMO (Kaiser-Meyer-Olkim Measure of Sampling Adequacy) = 0.882
Bartlett's Test of Sphericity: $p = 0.000$ ($x2 = 1541.422$, $df = 276$)

"shopping place," and "guides." Heritage attraction (Factor 2) accounted for 6.74% of the variance, with an eigenvalue of 1.616, and a reliability of 70.20%. This factor was loaded with four attributes that referred to heritage attraction. The four attributes were "handcrafts," "architectures," "traditional scenery," and "arts (music/dance)." Maintenance factors (Factor 3) loaded with five attributes. This factor accounted for 5.58% of the variance, with an eigenvalue of 1.339, and a reliability of 72.85%. These attribute were "accessibility," "indoor facilities," "atmosphere/people," "information centers," and "accommodations." Cultural attraction (Factor 4) contained five attributes that referred to cultural dimension. This factor explained 4.88% of the variance, with an eigenvalue of 1.173, and a reliability of 80%. These attributes were "museums," "galleries," "culture villages," "historic buildings," and "monuments."

MULTIPLE REGRESSION ANALYSIS

In order to further reveal the factors that influenced overall satisfaction, the four orthogonal factors were used in a multiple regression analysis. The multiple regression procedure was employed because it provided the most accurate interpretation of the independent variables. The four independent variables were expressed in terms of the standardized factor scores (beta coefficients). The significant factors that remained in the regression equation were shown in order of importance based on the beta coefficients. The dependent variable, tourists' overall level of satisfaction, was measured on a 7-point Likert-type scale and was used as a surrogate indicator of tourists' evaluation of the perception in Virginia Historic Triangle.

Table 3 shows the results of the regression analysis. The model was significant and explained almost 30% of the variance in overall satisfaction (F = 14.02, p = 0.00).

The beta coefficients also revealed that Factor 2 (Heritage Attraction, β_2 = 0.300, p = 0.00) carried the heaviest weight for overall satisfaction, followed by Factor 4 (Culture Attraction, β_4 = 0.282, p = 0.00), Factor 1 (General Tour Attraction, β_1 = 0.277, p = 0.00), and Factor 3 (Maintenance Factors, β_3 = 0.279, p = 0.001). The results also indicated that a one-unit increase in satisfac-

TABLE 3. Regression Results of Tourists' Overall Satisfaction Level Based on the Dimensions

Dependent variable: Tourist's overall satisfaction with Virginia Historic Triangle

Independent variable: Four factors

Regression Analysis

Independent variables	B	SE	Beta	t	p
(constant)	5.365	0.780		68.419	0.000
Factor 2	0.314	0.079	0.300	3.988	0.000*
Factor 4	0.296	0.079	0.282	3.755	0.000*
Factor 1	0.290	0.079	0.277	3.684	0.000*
Factor 3	0.279	0.079	0.266	3.539	0.001*

Note: adjusted R^2 = .294, F ratio = 14.02 (* p = .00)

tion with the Heritage Attraction factor would lead to a 0.300 unit increase in tourists' overall level of satisfaction with Virginia Historic Triangle, other variables being held constant.

In conclusion, all underlying dimensions are significant. Thus, the results of multiple regression analysis reveal that there is a significant relationship between the selected cultural/heritage destination attributes and the overall satisfaction of tourists.

OVERALL SATISFACTION AND DEMOGRAPHIC AND TRAVEL VARIABLES

Table 4 presents the results of t-test and one-way ANOVA statistics. The results indicated that no significant difference of the overall satisfaction of the respondents was found by age, origin of visitors, education level, and total household incomes. Significant difference of the overall satisfaction of the respondents was found only by gender (t = 54.491, p < 0.05). The results revealed that female respondents had a higher overall satisfaction score (M = 5.59) than did the male respondents (M = 5.30). The results found no significant difference in the overall satisfaction of respondents in relation to the travel behavior variables of length of stay, party in a group, and the distance of travel (one-way). However, the results illustrated that significant differences were found by past experience (t = 54.140, p < 0.05) and decision time to travel (F = 3.213, p = 0.05). The study also revealed that the respondents who had a previous experience of visiting a heritage/cultural site reported a higher satisfaction score than did the respondents who did note have a previous travel experience to similar sites. Furthermore, the study showed that the respondents who took their time to plan the trip to Virginia Historic Triangle seemed to report a statistically significant higher satisfaction with their overall experience.

MULTIVARIATE ANALYSIS OF COVARIANCE

In order to further understand the relationship between cultural/heritage destination attributes and overall satisfaction with such attributes and how the relationship may show variation controlling for demographic and travel behavior variables, the study also used Multivariate Analysis of Covariance (MANCOVA) to see if the relationship would still exist while controlling for the significant variables, including gender, past experience, and the decision time to travel as part of the demographic and travel behavior characteristics in the study (Table 5). The results of MANCOVA revealed that only one of the control variables (past experience) influenced the relationship between the

TABLE 4. T-Test and One-Way ANOVA

Variable	Frequency	Mean
Gender (t = 54.491*)		
Male	122	5.303
Female	129	5.597
Age (years) (F = 1.436)		
18-27	25	5.240
28-37	49	5.449
38-47	94	5.394
48-57	56	5.500
58-67	18	6.056
67+	9	5.222
Origin (F = 0.060)		
Virginia	64	5.469
Other States	173	5.457
Abroad	14	5.357
Education levels (F = 0.394)		
Primary & Second school	40	5.425
College	130	5.408
Graduate school	81	5.543
Total house incomes (USD) (F = 0.300)		
19,999 or less	12	5.250
20,000-39,999	28	5.321
40,000-59,999	51	5.549
60,000-79,999	46	5.457
80,000 or above	114	5.465
Past experience in cultural/heritage sites (t = 54.140*)		
Yes	188	5.532
No	63	5.222
How long in advance planned to visit Virginia Historic Triangle (f = 3.213*)		
3 month or below	99	5.556
4-6 months	101	5.248
6 months or above	51	5.667
Length of stay (F = 0.670)		
1 day	34	5.529
2-4 days	146	5.397
5-7 days	61	5.590
8 or above	10	5.200
Distance of travel (miles) (F = 2.264)		
50 or less	22	5.955
51-100	20	5.050
101-200	39	5.513
201-300	44	5.591
300 or more	126	5.365

Note: Overall satisfaction mean ranges from 1 (extremely dissatisfied) to 7 (extremely satisfied)
*p < 0.05

overall satisfaction of tourists' and the delineated factor grouping of Maintenance Factors (Wilks' Lambda, F = 3.209, p = 0.014). On the other hand, gender (Wilks' Lambda, F = 0.964, p = 0.087) and decision time to travel (Wilks' Lambda, F = 0.985, p = 0.485) did not control the relationship between the derived factors and the overall satisfaction of tourists. Controlling for past experience, the relationship between overall satisfaction and factor 2 (Heritage Attraction) still remained significant.

IMPLICATIONS

Based upon the results of this study, several recommendations can be made to increase tourist satisfaction with Virginia Historic Triangle. The results of the study revealed that even if four factors (General Tour attraction, Heritage Attraction, Maintenance Factors, and Culture Attraction) had significant relationships with the overall satisfaction, Heritage Attraction and Cultural Attraction appear to be more important factors that influence overall satisfaction than General Tour Attraction and Maintenance Factors do. This finding can be of use to the planners and marketers of cultural/heritage tourism in formulating strategies to maintain or enhance their competitiveness. In the other words, destination promoters would be able to know which destination attribute they should highlight and/or downplay in allocating resources. Thus, the study helps to identify the importance of cultural/heritage destination factors as perceived by tourists to Virginia Historic Triangle.

It is hoped that the results of the study would provide some insights that may be of help to tourism marketers in their attempt to develop specific promotional strategies. Since the study revealed that overall satisfaction show variation by gender, past experience, and decision time to travel, services and destination attributes could be reoriented and adjusted depending upon respon-

TABLE 5. Multivariate Analysis of Covariance

	Factor 1 (F, p)	Factor 2 (F, p)	Factor 3 (F, p)	Factor 4 (F, p)	Wilks' Lambda
Gender	0.164 (0.686)	3.858 (0.05)*	0.022 (0.883)	0.078 (0.781)	2.062 (0.087)
Past experience	0.003 (0.955)	1.972 (0.162)	8.141 (0.005)*	0.491 (0.219)	3.209 (0.014)
Decision Time	0.002 (0.966)	0.260 (0.611)	0.970 (0.326)	1.130 (0.289)	0.867 (0.485)

Note: Significance levels are indicated in parentheses ($^*p < 0.05$)

dents' gender, past experience, and decision making behavior. For example, such maintenance factors as accessibility, indoor facilities, ambiance, and accommodation types would be an important source of satisfaction or dissatisfaction for tourists who are repeat visitors. Female visitors tend to value the elements of handicraft, architecture, scenery, and art (music and dance) as part of their experience more than male visitors. Destination promoters should be able to have such information at their disposal to be able to provide more satisfying experience for visitors. Furthermore, an empirical study such as this could allow decision makers to classify and place attributes on a dis/satisfaction continuum by knowing the degree to which destination attributes have confirmed or disconfirmed visitor expectations. This classification could help tourism marketers and planners to maintain or enhance their strengths and improve their weaknesses.

Implications drawn here also were subject to several limitations. First, the attributes chosen, as independent variables, could be a limitation because other attributes, which were not used in this study, could impact tourist satisfaction. Second, the population sample obtained by the survey instrument presented some challenge due to insufficient information. This limitation resulted from a one-time measurement for data collection, a limited questionnaire, and a timing of survey. Third, Virginia Historic Triangle may not be representative of all cultural/heritage destinations. Nevertheless, it is hoped that such limitations could suggest and encourage additional directions and guidelines for future study.

REFERENCES

Anderson, V., Prentice, R., and Guerin, S. (1997). Imagery of Denmark among visitors to Danish time arts exhibitions in Scotland. *Tourism Management, 18*(7), 453-464.

Balcar, M. & Pearce, D. G. (1996). Heritage tourism on the West Coast of New Zealand. *Tourism Management, 17*(3), 203-212.

Chon, K.S. & Olsen, M.D. (1991). Functional and Symbolic Approaches to Consumer Satisfaction/Dissatisfaction. *Journal of the International Academy of Hospitality Research, 28*(1), 1-20.

Clemons, Sott D. & Woodruff, Robert B. (1992). Broadening the view of Consumer (Dis)satisfaction: A proposed Means-end Disconfirmation model of CS/D. *American Marketing Association, (Winter)*, 413-421.

Ekinci, Y., Riley, M., and Chen. J. (2001). A review of comparisons used in service quality and customer satisfaction studies: emerging issues for hospitality and tourism research. *Tourism Analysis, 5*(2/4): 197-202.

Formica, S. & Uysal, M. (1998). Market Segmentation of an International Cultural-Historical Event in Italy. *Journal of Travel Research, 36*(4): 16-24.

Glasson, J. (1994). Oxford: A Heritage City under Pressure. *Tourism Management, 15*(2), 137-144.

Janiskee, R.L. (1996). Historic Houses and Special Events. *Annals of Tourism Research, 23*(2), 398-414.

Kaufman, T.J. (1999). *A study of the motivations behind heritage site selection in the United States.* Virginia Polytechnic Institute and State University.

Kerstetter, D.L., Confer, J.J., & Graefe, A.R. (2001). An Exploration of the Specialization Concept within the Context of Heritage Tourism. *Journal of Travel Research, 39*(3): 267-274.

Kozark, M. & Rimmington, M. (2000). Tourist Satisfaction with Mallorca, Spain, as an Off-season Holiday Destination. *Journal of Travel Research, 38*(3): 260-269.

Liljander, V. (1994). Modeling perceived service quality using different comparison standard. *Journal of Costumer Satisfaction and Dissatisfaction,* 7: 126-142.

Lee, C. (1999). *Investigating tourist attachment to selected coastal destinations: An application of place attachment.* Clemson University.

Light, D. & Prentice, R. (1994). Market-based Product Development in Heritage Tourism. *Tourism Management, 15*(1), 27-36.

Light, D. (1996). Characteristics of the audience for events' at a heritage site. *Tourism Management, 17*(3), 183-190.

Master, H. & Prideaux, B. (2000). Culture and Vacation Satisfaction: A Study of Taiwanese Tourists in South East Queensland. *Tourism Management, 21*(5): 445-449.

Oliver, Richard L. (1980). A Cognitive Model for the Antecedents and Consequences of Satisfaction Decisions. *Journal of Marketing Research, 27*(4): 460-69.

Parasuraman, A., Zeithaml, V.A. & Berry, L. (1985). A Conceptual Model of Service Quality and Its Implications for Future Research. *Journal of Marketing, 49*(Fall), 41-50.

Peleggi, Maurizio (1996). National Heritage and Global Tourism in Thailand. *Annals of Tourism Research, 23*(2), 340-364.

Philipp, Steven F. (1993). Racial Differences in the Perceived Attractiveness of Tourism Destinations, Interests, and Cultural Resources. *Journal of Leisure Research, 25*(3), 290-304.

Pizam, A., Neumann, Y. & Reichel, A. (1978). Dimensions of Tourist Satisfaction with a Destination. *Annals of Tourism Research, 5*(2): 314-322.

Pizam, A. & Millman, A. (1993). Predicting Satisfaction among First-time Visitors to a Destination by Using the Expectancy-disconfirmation Theory. *International Journals of Hospitality Management, 12*(2), 197-209.

Richards, G. (1995). Production and Consumption of European Cultural Tourism. *Annals of Tourism Research, 22*(2) 261-283.

Rust, R.T., Zahorik, A.J., & Keininghan, T.L. (1993). *Return on Quality,* Chicago, IL: Probus Publishing.

Silbkerberg, T. (1995). Cultural Tourism and Business Opportunities for Museums and Heritage Sites. *Tourism Management, 16*(5): 361-365.

Sofield, Trevor H.B. (1998). Tourism Development and Cultural Policies in China. *Annals of Tourism Research, 25*(2), 362-392.

Yavuz, N.F (1994). *A market segmentation study of visitors to North Cyprus through importance-performance analysis of destination attributes.* Virginia Polytechnic Institute and State University.

Index

http://www.haworthpress.com/web/JQAHT
© 2003 by The Haworth Press, Inc. All rights reserved.
Digital Object Identifier: 10.1300/J162v04n03_13

SPECIAL 25%-OFF DISCOUNT!

Order a copy of this book with this form or online at:
http://www.haworthpress.com/store/product.asp?sku=5160
Use Sale Code BOF25 in the online bookshop to receive 25% off!

Current Issues and Development in Hospitality and Tourism Satisfaction

_____ in softbound at $22.46 (regularly $29.95) (ISBN: 0-7890-2434-9)
_____ in hardbound at $37.46 (regularly $49.95) (ISBN: 0-7890-2433-0)

COST OF BOOKS _____
Outside USA/ Canada/
Mexico: Add 20%. _____

POSTAGE & HANDLING _____
US: $4.00 for first book & $1.50
for each additional book
Outside US: $5.00 for first book
& $2.00 for each additional book.

SUBTOTAL _____

In Canada: add 7% GST. _____

STATE TAX _____
CA, IL, IN, MIN, NY, OH, & SD residents
please add appropriate local sales tax.

FINAL TOTAL _____
If paying in Canadian funds, convert
using the current exchange rate,
UNESCO coupons welcome.

❑ **BILL ME LATER:**
Bill-me option is good on US/Canada/
Mexico orders only; not good to jobbers,
wholesalers, or subscription agencies.

❑ **Signature** _____

❑ **Payment Enclosed: $** _____

❑ **PLEASE CHARGE TO MY CREDIT CARD:**

❑ Visa ❑ MasterCard ❑ AmEx ❑ Discover
❑ Diner's Club ❑ Eurocard ❑ JCB

Account # _____

Exp Date _____

Signature _____
(Prices in US dollars and subject to change without notice.)

PLEASE PRINT ALL INFORMATION OR ATTACH YOUR BUSINESS CARD		
Name		
Address		
City	State/Province	Zip/Postal Code
Country		
Tel	Fax	
E-Mail		

May we use your e-mail address for confirmations and other types of information? ❑Yes ❑ No
We appreciate receiving your e-mail address. Haworth would like to e-mail special discount
offers to you, as a preferred customer. **We will never share, rent, or exchange your e-mail
address.** We regard such actions as an invasion of your privacy.

Order From Your Local Bookstore or Directly From
The Haworth Press, Inc.
10 Alice Street, Binghamton, New York 13904-1580 • USA
Call Our toll-free number (1-800-429-6784) / Outside US/Canada: (607) 722-5857
Fax: 1-800-895-0582 / Outside US/Canada: (607) 771-0012
E-Mail your order to us: Orders@haworthpress.com

Please Photocopy this form for your personal use.
www.HaworthPress.com

BOF04